SECOND EDITION

Kylene Beers

When Kids Can't Read

What Teachers Can Do

A GUIDE FOR TEACHERS • GRADES 4–12

HEINEMANN Portsmouth, NH

Heinemann
145 Maplewood Avenue, Suite 300
Portsmouth, NH 03801
www.heinemann.com

Offices and agents throughout the world

Acknowledgments for borrowed material begin on page 418, which constitutes an extension of the copyright page.

Library of Congress Cataloging-in-Publication Data
is on file with the Library of Congress.
ISBN 978-0-325-14459-7

Editor: Anita Gildea
Production: Patty Adams, Melissa L. Inglis
Cover and interior designs: Suzanne Heiser
Composition: Gina Poirier Design
Manufacturing: Val Cooper

Printed in the United States of America on acid-free paper
1 2 3 4 5   MP   27 26 25 24 23
PO 4500866927

"Be an opener of doors," wrote poet and abolitionist
Ralph Waldo Emerson.
That's what books are—openers of doors.
And that's what teachers are.
This book, therefore, is for teachers everywhere
who open doors for their students.
Fling them wide open!
Secure them wide against the censors!
Then know you have done your job and done it well.

—KB

CONTENTS

Figures

PROLOGUE
Twenty Years Later

BEGINNING TO WRITE A BOOK THAT I'VE ALREADY WRITTEN has been an odd experience. I had to return to where I was in 2002, to where the world was in 2002, before I could move on. I had to be there, so I could later be here.

Twenty years ago, I watched as *When Kids Can't Read—What Teachers Can Do* made its way into teachers' hands. I wrote that first edition in the shadow of the 9/11 attack. Nearly three thousand people were killed that day. The horror of that day was felt by all. Race, gender, age, political affiliation—all were cast aside as people mourned all those who had been lost.

Within months, our American military was soon involved in two wars: more immediate was the war against the Taliban in Afghanistan; later, the US invaded Iraq.

While these events dominated thoughts on an international level, other events caused changes at the national level. The National Reading Panel released its report on teaching reading in 2001. This report caused a new flurry of direct and systematic phonics instruction in primary grades. No Child Left Behind legislation was passed. That legislation demanded stronger accountability of schools, which meant state-mandated tests became high-stakes tests.

The Department of Homeland Security was created, and some wondered how effective this department would be; two snipers in Washington, DC, killed ten people, and we all wondered when the gun killings would stop. The Nokia cell phone entered lives, offering a calculator, a stopwatch, and four games. Colin Powell became secretary of state. Tom Brady quarterbacked his first Super Bowl. Janet Jackson was honored with the first ever MTV Icon award. Less than 3 percent of books published for children featured characters of color (Cooperative Children's Book Center 2022), and I did not notice or wonder about that.

And Now

I'm writing this new edition in the shadow of the COVID-19 pandemic, a pandemic we suspected would someday arrive and yet were surprised when it did. As of November 4, 2022, more than one million US lives (1,068,667) have been lost to this virus (CDC 2022). For a while, this nation pulled together, reminding me of the spirit, determination, and love for one another I saw after 9/11.

As the world battles this new virus, there's another war that has moved to center stage. In early 2022, Russia invaded Ukraine. Our nation, along with the rest of the world, watches to see what will happen next.

Between February and August of 2021, American troops were finally withdrawn from Afghanistan.

A movement advocating the "science of reading" has recently emerged on the educational—and political—landscape. It encourages teaching early-grade reading with a phonics-forward philosophy, and I feel as if I have returned to 2001 and the National Reading Panel's report. The No Child Left Behind Act is now called the Every Student Succeeds Act, and high-stakes tests are still directing far too much of what we teach.

In 2021, our nation elected Kamala Harris, the first Black vice president and the first female vice president, and Congress recently affirmed our nation's first Black female associate justice of the Supreme Court. We still applaud the election of our first Black president, Barack Obama.

Twenty years later, Homeland Security is still here; gun killings have not diminished; the iPhone replaced the Nokia with 2.2 million apps to consider downloading. Android users can choose from among 3.48 million apps. Former secretary of state Colin Powell died in 2021. Tom Brady is still quarterbacking the Super Bowl. The Foo Fighters won the MTV Global Icon award, but I have no idea who they are. Now, approximately 23 percent of children's fiction features characters of color, 50 percent features white characters, and 27 percent features talking animals (CCBC 2022; Stechyson 2019), and, unlike my earlier ignorance of who was represented in literature and who was not, I now analyze this carefully. Furthermore, I study my own interactions with literature and academic texts. Whom am I reading? Whom else should I be reading? What do my selections say about me? What else do I need to learn? Those questions were barely forming in me twenty years ago.

In 2001 and 2002, we were in two wars; in 2022, we stand at the precipice of another war. In 2002, schools faced public criticism and new demands regarding phonics instruction with the publication of the National Reading Panel's report; today they face similar criticisms and demands as a result of reports, blog posts, news articles, and social media campaigns from science-of-reading advocates.

Twenty years later, I turn to writing this book, again.

Why I Wrote a New Edition

"After twenty years, why revisit this text?" I asked myself. In part, it was because I had learned so much and that learning had changed my understanding of many issues. To let the original edition sit, undisturbed, suggested my thinking had sat, undisturbed. But that was not right. In fact, this is more a new edition than a second edition. Timely second editions update titles, share some newer research, perhaps change cultural references. This edition needed to do far more than update the overhead projector to an interactive whiteboard or the book on tape to an audio file (though those 2002 references did need to be updated). This revision reflects more definitive thoughts about the teaching of reading and why reading is necessary to the preservation of our democracy.

Throughout this edition, you'll find references to Dr. Robert E. Probst, my colleague and coauthor of several texts. Bob and I have worked together for over twenty years. He has challenged my thinking, and, at times, I'm sure he would say I have challenged if not his thinking, then certainly his patience. Bob is coauthor with me of four books: *Notice and Note, Reading*

Nonfiction, Disrupting Thinking, and *Forged by Reading*. I refer to him throughout this book as Bob. In large measure, Bob has pushed me to consider what it means to be a responsible and responsive reader.

My thinking has also been changed by other educators who have encouraged me to consider how I, as a white educator, can become a more inclusive educator. Early on it was Dr. Beverly Tatum's *Why Are All the Black Kids Sitting Together in the School Cafeteria?* that directed my thinking. Later, Lisa Delpit's *Other People's Children* influenced my thinking. When I had the opportunity to work with the James Comer School Development Program at Yale University School of Medicine, I read *Maggie's American Dream: The Life and Times of a Black Family*, by Dr. Comer. I still have the copy he gave me. After meeting Melba Pattillo Beals, one of the nine students who integrated Central High School in Little Rock, Arkansas, I rushed to read her autobiography, *Warriors Don't Cry*. This book caused me to reach out to my parents asking them what they did as they watched nightly news stories from Walter Cronkite about the events surrounding this horrific time.

> "We can have a single goal in mind—helping students become skilled, engaged, and curious readers—and recognize the unique path each student might travel in getting there."

Other books have help shape who I am now: *The Fire Next Time* (James Baldwin), *Ain't I a Woman* (bell hooks), *The Warmth of Other Suns* (Isabel Wilkerson), *The New Jim Crow* (Michelle Alexander), and more recently, *Between the World and Me* (Ta-Nehisi Coates), *White Fragility* (Robin DiAngelo), *Stamped from the Beginning* (Ibram X. Kendi), *How to Be an Antiracist* (Ibram X. Kendi), *Moving to Higher Ground* (Wynton Marsalis), *The Word: Black Writers Talk About the Transformative Power of Reading and Writing* (edited by Marita Golden), and *Black Ink: Literary Legends on the Peril, Power* (edited by Stephanie Stokes Oliver).

To those I now add very recent books that help us all think about classroom practices: *Cultivating Genius* (Gholdy Muhammad), *Textured Teaching* (Lorena Escoto Germán), *We Want to Do More Than Survive* (Bettina L. Love), *Open Windows, Open Minds* (Afrika Afeni Mills), *Coaching for Equity* (Elena Aguilar), *We Got This.* (Cornelius Minor), and *Teaching for Racial Equity* (Tonya Perry and Steven Zemelman with Katy Smith). These authors and their books have helped me grow as an educator and an individual.

Though revising this book offered me a chance to revisit earlier thinking, what it mostly did was allow me to continue to share my ongoing commitment to help those of you who teach students who struggle with reading.

There is no one answer to understanding why an adolescent has difficulties with reading. For there to be only one answer, there would have to be only one cause, and for there to be one cause, all students would have to be alike, learn alike, and have had the same experiences. Indeed, there is no single template for the struggling reader; therefore, there is no single answer. But there *are* answers, and I wrote this book to help you with those answers. If we want classes grounded in equity, then it is critical that we understand that different students will require different types of help. We can have a single goal in mind—helping students become skilled, engaged, and curious readers—and recognize the unique path each student might travel in getting there.

When our nation shut down during the COVID-19 pandemic, one of the first things teachers did was figure out how to get books into kids' hands. You arranged times where students could come by their school and leave with armloads of books. School buses drove into neighborhoods, becoming mobile libraries. Schools and businesses provided needed laptops and tablets, and online groups made digital books free to all. You wanted kids to be able to read. As much as you worried about where some would get food—and schools helped provide that, too—you were also concerned about children and teens having books to read. You understood that as food nourishes the body, books nourish the mind.

In the aftermath of George Floyd's murder, the racial ouroboros of this nation was recognized, finally, by more, though still not enough, white people. As a result, thousands of (mostly) white people reached for books to better understand what we should have already realized, books such as *Stamped from the Beginning* or *White Fragility*. And while reading and discussing is not enough, it is a beginning.

Reading offers us that chance to revise our lives. Such change often begins with a book. A simple thing called a book. I am excited, now, to hand this one over to you.

> *"There is no one answer to understanding why an adolescent has difficulties with reading. For there to be only one answer, there would have to be only one cause, and for there to be one cause, all students would have to be alike, learn alike, and have had the same experiences."*

Part 1

Reading Matters

Dear George,

It was 1979 and we were both in seventh grade. You were a wide-eyed student; I was a nervous, first-year teacher.

You were not excited to read, never wanted to write, and often avoided all group discussions. You were years behind your classmates in reading abilities. "It's too hard," you would say of almost any text I offered you. "I don't get it," you would announce after skimming through pages. I had little to offer. I was a twenty-one-year-old novice teacher, an English major who had never taken one class to help me teach kids to read.

If you were not excited to learn to read, George, I can promise I was not excited to teach you to learn this skill. I was a secondary teacher. I wanted to teach literature, not reading. Furthermore, I had not taken any courses that could have guided me. I fear I did not teach you much that first year.

But you taught me. And so did your parents. Did they ever tell you about the meeting I had with them? In October, they asked to meet with Anne Black, the assistant principal, and me. They wanted me to explain why you had such a difficult time with reading. In that early-morning conference, as we all sat in that small conference room, me stumbling through comments that were not helpful, it was evident that I had been hired to do a job—teach their son—and I did not know what to do.

That meeting with your parents and all my interactions with you, George, changed the direction of my teaching career, sending me on a journey to discover what to do when kids can't read. Because of you, I decided I was less interested in the teacher I had dreamed of being—a twelfth-grade, Advanced Placement literature teacher—and more interested in the teacher you needed me to be. You were with me my first year of teaching and memories of you have been with me ever since.

CHAPTER 1

Why We Read

THIS NEW EDITION, LIKE THE ORIGINAL EDITION, is based on my bedrock belief that reading, though not an innate ability for anyone, is a critical skill for all.

Reading changes us. It changes the way we think, the way we see the world, the way we process information and dream new thoughts. It allows us to discover more about ourselves and the world around us so that we might become better versions of ourselves, fully participating in our communities and our nation, and flourishing intellectually, emotionally, creatively, and socially as passionate and compassionate beings.

Some argue that great turning points in Western civilization—the Renaissance, the Reformation, the Age of Enlightenment—were dependent upon the printed word (Dewar 1998; Eisenstein 1980; Lyon 2009). Those printed words—first hammered into clay tablets, then copied onto scrolls, then printed on pages—opened the door to knowledge. And that knowledge equaled power. In 1867, an article in *Harper's Weekly* proclaimed that "the alphabet is an abolitionist" (*Harper's Weekly* staff 2006). The act of turning those pesky squiggly letters on the page into thoughts in your mind is the the path to empowerment.

"This new edition, like the original edition, is based on my bedrock belief that reading, though not an innate ability for anyone, is a critical skill for all."

And to keep some groups from that power, they were—and often still are—denied those letters.

In the United States, by the 1830s, all slave states except Maryland, Kentucky, and Tennessee enacted laws making it illegal to teach a Black person—free or enslaved—to read or write. White people who broke those laws were fined and occasionally imprisoned. The Black people who broke the laws by acting as teachers were flogged, imprisoned, or both; the enslaved people who were caught learning to read or write or practicing those skills were punished with savage beatings or the amputation of fingers or toes.

In California, in the early 1880s, Chinese children were banned from attending any public schools. In 1921, California law prohibited Native American children from attending public schools. In 1944, still in California, Gonzalo Mendez was told his young children could not attend the nearby elementary school because it was for "whites only." Instead, they needed to attend a distant school, run down and with far fewer supplies, for "Mexican children" (Tonatiuh 2014).

In 1957, nine Black students agreed to integrate Central High School in Little Rock, Arkansas. White parents, white students, and local white citizens and lawmakers staged violent protests. The governor, Orval Faubus, announced he would bring in the Arkansas National Guard to prevent the Black students' entrance to the school. On the first day of school, these students were spat upon, yelled at, pushed, and ultimately kept out of the school. Eventually, a federal judge ordered the National Guard to be removed, and federal troops were called in to protect these young teens. When some, such as Faubus, realize the power of a literate mind, they are threatened, and racist suppression of literacy is the result.

Light in the Darkness by Lesa Cline-Ransome, *Landed* by Milly Lee, *Separate Is Never Equal* by Duncan Tonatiuh, and *We Are Still Here!* by Traci Sorell are picture story books that tell powerful stories of people fighting for the right to read.

More currently, in 2011 young school-age girls in Pakistan had battery acid thrown in their faces as they walked to school, breaking the Taliban law that prohibited girls from an education; in 2012, then twelve-year-old Malala Yousafzai was shot in the face for speaking out about what was happening in Pakistan regarding the education of girls. In March 2022, the Taliban announced that no girls in Afghanistan would be allowed to attend school after fifth grade (Ahmadi and Ebadi 2022).

Censoring Thinking

Beginning in 2022, the ongoing censorship of books and authors reared its ugly head at an unprecedented pace in the United States. The American Library Association reported 330 official book challenges in 2021, an increase from previous years (Beauchamp 2022); the Intellectual Freedom Center of the National Council of Teachers of English helped more teachers with challenges than ever before and explained that increased book challenges and "infringements on intellectual freedom [were] a result of polarizations across the country" (NCTE 2022). Conservative groups now spread titles they want removed from schools with ease via social media (Harris and Alter 2022). Censorship advocates are not encouraging parents to work with teachers to determine what is appropriate for an individual child to read—something every parent has always had the right to do. They are, instead, demanding the removal of books from classrooms, school libraries, and curriculum to deny access to all students. Such a wide sweep, under the genteel smile of the concerned parent, oversteps their rights while undermining the rights of others.

This resurgence of censorship is happening beyond the classroom and school level. In October 2021, in Cheyenne, Wyoming, a county prosecutor was asked to prosecute the county librarian for including books about sex education and information about the queer community, something a special prosecutor later refused to do (Gruver 2021). In December 2021, Wake County North Carolina Public Libraries removed *Gender Queer* from their public libraries shelves, declaring it did not "align with selection policies"— yet this same system continues to provide the entire Fifty Shades of Grey series (Duncan 2021). In January 2022, the mayor of Ridgeland, Mississippi, decided to withhold $110,000 of the funds earmarked for the *city* library until books by or about members of the queer community were removed (Associated Press 2022).

> Friends in the queer community told me they prefer "queer community" over "LGBTQIA+" as a descriptor.

Throughout late 2020 and continuing until the writing of this book in spring 2022, numerous award-winning books have been challenged in schools, school districts, and states. These books include *New Kid* (Jerry Craft), *George* (Alex Gino), *All American Boys* (Jason Reynolds and Brendan Kiely), *The Hate U Give* (Angie Thomas), *Maus* (Art Spiegelman), *Stamped: Racisim, Antiracism, and You* (Jason Reynolds and Ibram X. Kendi), *Animal Farm* (George Orwell), and *Fahrenheit 451* (Ray Bradbury). Yes, some parents and law makers in some districts want to ban *Fahrenheit 451*, a book about the consequences of banning books.

The ideological and political desires of those wanting more power for some and less for others or wanting to impose their values and beliefs on others can fan the flames of censorship at almost any time. We would be wise to remember what Franz Kafka wrote as he encourged us to read books that challenge our beliefs, that shake current understanding:

"The ideological and political desires of those wanting more power for some and less for others or wanting to impose their values and beliefs on others can fan the flames of censorship at almost any time."

I think we ought to read only the kind of books that wound and stab us. If the book we're reading doesn't wake us up with a blow on the head, what are we reading it for? So that it will make us happy, as you write? Good Lord, we would be happy precisely if we had no books, and the kind of books that make us happy are the kind we could write ourselves if we had to. But we need the books that affect us like a disaster, that grieve us deeply, like the death of someone we loved more than ourselves, like being banished into forests far from everyone, like a suicide. A book must be the axe for the frozen sea inside us. That is my belief. (1958/1977, 16)

"A book must be the axe for the frozen sea inside us." When we ban books, we do harm to individuals and ultimately to communities and society.

Heal, Reflect, Create

Modern neuroscience research shows us that reading changes the way our brains work (Kweldju 2015).

In *Proust and the Squid: The Story and Science of the Reading Brain*, neuroscientist and literacy advocate Maryanne Wolf explained,

We were never born to read. Human beings invented reading only a few thousand years ago. And with this invention, we rearranged the very organization of our brain, which in turn expanded the ways we were able to think, which altered the intellectual evolution of our species. (2008, 4)

But more than heightening the language centers in the left temporal cortex of the brain (Berns et al. 2013), reading is uniquely situated to carry us into the mind of the writer while simultaneously allowing us to create our own thoughts.

When I am reading deeply, lost in the author's world or words, I am also keenly aware of myself, my questions, my current knowledge, my awe, and sometimes my horror. I recognize my limitations and I speculate on my possibilities. I am wholly in the pages, and I am wholly in my mind. And somehow, during that time when those words and my world meet, if I am open to growth, I can discover something about myself that offers me the chance to emerge from those pages with the confidence or the commitment to change.

To those who would encourage us to focus only on the thoughts of the writer, to read "within the four corners of the text" (Coleman and Pimentel 2012, 4), I would suggest if that is the way we read, then we have done only one half of the reading. What you read on a page, on *this* page or any other, acts as a catalyst for what *you* think. Thoughts that might come from what we read give us the chance not only to have new thoughts but to revise our past thoughts. Imagine this: reading, the act of picking up a single text, provides the opportunity to examine our past ideas, our past perceptions, and our past prejudices, and in examining those pasts we give ourselves the opportunity to change our futures. All that from reading a text. We read in the present, examine our past, and then, if called to, alter our future. That is when we become independent, become that person with a mind that creates as it learns, that forges its own understandings.

"We read in the present, examine our past, and then, if called to, alter our future. That is when we become independent, become that person with a mind that creates as it learns, that forges its own understandings."

In ancient Greece, "A Healing Place for the Soul" was engraved above the doorway to a library in Thebes. In modern times, scholar Rudine Sims Bishop explained that books become "mirrors, windows, and sliding glass doors" for readers (1990, ix–xi). And most recently, Wolf (2016, 135) explained that reading allows us to have that "new, never-before-encountered-thought."

As we read, as we think alongside the author or the character, we decide to agree or disagree; we become curious or satisfied; we discover more about . . . everything: ourselves, others, the world, ideas, what was, and what might someday be, who we might someday be. When we read fiction, we step into that world the author has created and when we read nonfiction, we allow that author with her ideas, her understandings, her vision of reality to step into our world (Beers and Probst 2016).

The Independent Mind

And when we don't read, when kids *can't* read, all that is gone. We lose that ability to learn in this transformative way. We run the risk of being manipulated by others. We are diminished. And in that moment of being less, all around us might suffer, too. Our understanding of complex issues—race, the environment, foreign policy, health care, taxes, women's reproductive rights, the elderly, childcare, poverty—then becomes dependent on what someone else tells us. Our democracy becomes shaped by the fewest with the loudest voices. And perhaps some would like it that way. James Baldwin (1960) explained it this way: "It is very nearly impossible, after all, to become an educated person in a country so distrustful of the independent mind."

"To create an independent mind, we must embrace change as we stand against mediocrity and for honesty."

But all children should become independent thinkers. Such a goal means we stop teaching to a single high-stakes test. We stop evaluating a school, a faculty, a student by a single test score. We stop getting lost in the arguments of whether or not texts should be decodable or leveled or whether or not students should ever have some choice in what they read. Such arguments feel like distractions to me, loud voices that want to keep us away from what matters most: giving all students the chance to thrive, the chance to develop as independent readers—that reader with independent thoughts.

We cannot be distracted by those who claim that teachers who offer inclusive books and a complete narrative of our country's history are teaching critical race theory. Until recently (2020), that was an obscure term used in law schools to explain a particular approach—or lens—for studying US policies. It has been co-opted by those who fear changes in education, or perhaps, more accurately, want to instill fear in others. This distraction is to keep us from seeing what is happening: as some schools offer students more and more books that do indeed act as mirrors, windows, and sliding glass doors, some white people feel threatened. When we see past the distraction to the real issue, then the power of a literate life is evident.

To create an independent mind, we must embrace change as we stand against mediocrity and for honesty. If we continue to teach toward irrelevance, if we offer our students mindless lessons that might raise test scores but could lower learning, if we let ourselves define skilled reading as nothing more than careful extraction from a text, then we will again have failed to teach kids to become independent readers.

And when that happens, when we avoid the discomfort of change, when we refuse to disrupt the comfort of established habits and long-held beliefs, when we offer our students a limited understanding of what it means to read, we are failing our students. And in doing that, we are failing our nation.

Dear George,

I know so much more than I knew that year you sat in my classroom. There is a prayer in the Episcopal church in which the penitents ask forgiveness for the things they have done and the things they have left undone. I have always liked that line, its reminder that leaving things undone is as much a problem as doing some things. I left much undone with you, George.

✧ ✧ ✧

Dear George,

One day you asked me why reading was so important. I asked you to tell me more. You asked what would happen if as an adult, you never read anything. You explained you could listen to news and that lots of books are turned into movies, so you could enjoy the stories as movies. Your question was sincere, and you waited patiently for my answer. I don't remember what I said, but I know you walked away saying, "I think I'll be just fine without reading."

What Happens When Kids Can't Read

NONE OF US WHO READ WOULD BE THE PEOPLE WE
are if we never read.

In part, that's because reading lets us consider complex ideas. I try to
imagine understanding Einstein's theory, medical insights about breast
cancer, research about world hunger, a contract to purchase a home,
or information about new vaccines only through oral lectures and oral
directions and discover I can't envision how to accomplish those tasks. But
reading does more than help us understand complex ideas;
reading helps us become better—better versions of ourselves. If we never entered the world of books, we would
be diminished, be less. Books let us experience other times
and other places and, at least for a moment, stand alongside others. Those vicarious experiences become a part of
who we are and offer us the chance to become empathetic
and compassionate people.

> *"Those vicarious experiences become a part of who we are and offer us the chance to become empathetic and compassionate people."*

Perhaps most important, reading helps us resist manipulation and
control by others. When we can't read, then someone other than us—
a deceitful car salesperson, a duplicitous politician—has the opportunity to step in and tell us what that person has decided we need to
know. If reading empowers, then the inability or the unwillingness to
read disempowers.

See *Disrupting Thinking* (Beers and Probst 2018) for our most thorough examination of responsible and responsive readers.

But reading that empowers is a particular type of reading. It is responsible and responsive reading. Between 2002 and 2022, Bob Probst and I wrote extensively about the importance of creating responsible and responsive readers.

Responsible Reading

Bob and I have previously defined *responsible readers* as those who attend to the text, those who do not attribute to the text what the text does not say. They know how to use evidence in the text to help them reach justifiable conclusions. When emotions are awakened—curiosity, compassion, delight, doubt—responsible readers know how to examine the text to see what evoked such reactions; they question the author's biases and motives to determine if their response to the text is warranted. Responsible readers know how to use stated and implied evidence that is *in the text* to help them justify positions. Responsible readers, therefore, know how to set aside their own beliefs and dispositions to consider what a text has to offer.

This is hard, as most of us read with our worldview shaping our understanding of the text. For instance, people who think sex education has no place in a curriculum dismiss research that shows kids who take a sex-education class delay sexual activity (Doheny 2007; Mueller et al. 2008; Pound et al. 2017). They might claim the research is not real or, worse, decide that even though there is research, it doesn't matter because that's not what they believe. The language arts teacher who continues to teach grammar in isolation even after decades of research consistently reveal that such a practice does not improve writing (Braddock, Lloyd-Jones, and Schoer 1963; Hillocks 1986; Weaver 1996; Graham and Perrin 2007; Applebee and Langer 2009) might be the same person who wonders why students are such poor writers.

Content area teachers often want their students to read better but are reluctant to change their instruction to include teaching any reading strategies, even after reading research that shows them that changing their instruction can make a difference (Hall 2005; Neufield 2005/2006). People who smoke dismiss research about the harms of smoking; people who distrust science question the value of the COVID-19 vaccine. Our belief systems often trump science (Baekgaard and Serritzlew 2015). Dismissing evidence because that evidence contradicts what we *want* to believe is irresponsible reading that can lead to harm—to individuals, to communities, and ultimately to our nation and world.

Responsive Reading

Responsive readers know that careful reading does more than allow them to answer multiple-choice questions. Responsive readers expect that what they read will result in thoughts, wonderings, curiosities. We read to have a response, and if we aren't reading to have some sort of thought, some reaction to the text, then I would wonder why we are reading at all. I suspect this is a reason that many students turn away from reading: as reading has become a tested skill rather than an experience to enjoy, students have lost that ability to respond to a text. They have lost that ability to let a text awaken their imagination, their curiosity, their desire to know more.

> "We read to have a response, and if we aren't reading to have some sort of thought, some reaction to the text, then I would wonder why we are reading at all."

Responsive readers understand that reading can help them develop intellectually and emotionally. Students who merely pass their eyes over words looking for the details that will help them pass the multiple-choice test, will be, at best, surface-level readers. They will not be readers who examine what the information means to them, who consider what the text might mean to others, who understand what a text might mean in the shaping of our democracy. That said, a response *from* a text is without merit if responsibility *to* the text is overlooked. Response and responsibility are connected.

So, reading causes a response and then, as responsible readers, we look back to the text to determine if that response is justified. Turning to evidence, however, has become increasingly difficult to do when accepting evidence means losing stature within an affinity group—something that people do now with public shaming via social media. The first two decades of the twenty-first century have shown us that with increasing frequency, we contemplate complex decisions and make them align with political affiliations (Gerber, Huber, and Washington 2010). Complex decisions that affect our nation and our world cannot be guided by red facts and blue facts and most certainly not by alternative facts.

"When kids can't read, they run the risk of failing more than tests; they run the risk of losing the ability to be independent, critical readers who know when to stand alongside a text and when to stand in opposition to it."

If reading is the gateway to education, then responsive reading and responsible reading are mandatory if education is to be meaningful, transformative, and empowering. To ignore either is to put students in danger of falling prey to manipulation by those who will be pleased to tell them what a text means. When kids can't read, they run the risk of failing more than tests; they run the risk of losing the ability to be independent, critical readers who know when to stand alongside a text and when to stand in opposition to it. Without this ability, our nation faces a growing problem, which Kavanagh and Rich (2018) have identified as "truth decay."

Truth Decay

Truth decay is the outcome of the following interrelated trends:

1. Increasing disagreement about facts

2. A blurring of the line between opinion and facts

3. The increasingly relative volume, and resulting influence, of opinion and personal experience over fact

4. Declining trust in formerly respected sources of factual information (Kavanagh and Rich 2018, x–xi)

Truth decay, therefore, is a multifaceted phenomenon that occurs when people no longer agree on facts; don't distinguish between fact and opinion; value personal experience over fact; and no longer trust sources they previously respected. Whether called "fake news" or "'truth decay" the outcome is the same as we all suffer when verifiable facts are discounted.

Kavanagh and Rich explain that this is happening because, in part, we live in a time with increasing political and social polarization and this too encourages a growing disregard of the truth:

> *Creating groups on each side [of the political spectrum that] can become insular in their thinking and communication creating a closed environment in which false communication*

*proliferates. Data suggests that political, social, and
demographic polarization are not only severe and worsening
in the contemporary United States but also overlapping and
reinforcing one another. (Kavanagh and Rich 2018, xv)*

I wrote about the problems of insular thinking in 2006 in an editor's
message for *Voices from the Middle*, a national literacy journal:

> *While globalization is about stretching boundaries, if
> not completely eliminating them, retribalization is about
> reestablishing boundaries. As religious fundamentalists provide
> a rhetoric of intolerance; when disagreeing with a political
> position means one is un-American; when our national leaders
> choose inflammatory language over thoughtful response; then
> we find boundaries constructed, walls built, and a search for
> others that talk like us, look like us, think like us, share exact
> same beliefs, values, and position. We turn against all that is
> different—for different becomes wrong or bad. (Beers 2006, 4–5)*

Perhaps my greatest fear when kids can't read is that they will default to
insular thinking and insular lives and find themselves living as far more than
dependent readers; they will be dependent. Period. And with that, we lose
sight of truth.

What Teachers Can Do

To fight against such an outcome, we must encourage responsive and responsible reading. Such an endeavor might begin by helping some students with
word recognition skills. It might mean helping some improve their reading
rate, their fluency, and their automaticity. It might mean improving their will
to read. And, it most certainly means improving comprehension.

Throughout this text, you'll see that I use the terms *strategies, scaffolds,
comprehension processes,* and *skills.* I'm defining them here so that you understand my use of these terms. More and more, I am less and less sure that
any of these terms really matter, but they do help in writing.

Skills, Thinking Processes, and Strategies

From the 1950s until the 1970s, much of comprehension instruction focused on teaching skills: identifying the main idea, sequencing, or seeing causes and effects, for instance. This was, in part, because reading basals were gaining in popularity and at the end of selections, students were asked questions that supposedly measured mastery of those skills. The logic was apparent: if students could, for example, identify the main idea of a passage, then they must be able to understand the passage.

If you are of the age that you remember the tune and lyrics to *Cat's in the Cradle* when it was first released, then you might remember worksheets that told students to "Read the following passage. After each passage, read options A, B, C, and D. Circle the option that is the main idea." We offered instructions (directions) and not instruction (explanations of how to think a particular way). Such instructions were easy to follow if you understood the main idea, but it was hard if you didn't. As one student asked me once, "How does you telling me to circle the main idea help me understand the main idea if I don't already know what the main idea is?" Hmmm. "How do I know if I don't already know?" I tried repeating those instructions to him louder and slower, but that merely bothered the rest of the class and frustrated that student. In actuality, those drills on skills lacked research supporting the idea that teaching any skill in one text helped students understand any subsequent text. But it was in the basal, so we did it.

By the 1970s, research on comprehension strategies began to emerge. Comprehension strategy instruction focused on helping students think metacognitively through a text. For instance, questioning a text is a strategy that helps students think about *any* text. As they question the text, they might then notice cause and effect relationships or the order in which events occur (comprehension skills). In the mid- to late 1980s, teachers began to teach comprehension strategies to students. Some defined a comprehension strategy as "predicting" or "visualizing" while others said "study the title" was the strategy. Confusion over what is and is not a comprehension strategy was emerging.

In the classroom, I realized that though I could say "Don't forget to question the text" to my students as they began to read, the only question they would offer is "Do we have to finish this at home?" I realized I needed to model what that meant, and began using Think-Alouds. A Think-Aloud (see page 118) was the strategy I used to help the thinking process of questioning emerge. Eventually, I began using a variety of what I called strategies to help encourage those invisible thinking processes. This helped students hone reading skills (see Figure 2.1 on the following page). To help students monitor their understanding, I might teach them Syntax Surgery (page 122) or Genre Reformulation (page 141). To encourage paraphrasing, I might teach Sketch to Stretch (page 120) or Somebody Wanted But So (page 137); to help students make an inference, I would turn to It Says, I Say, And So (page 157).

By the 2000s, the term *comprehension strategy instruction* was used by many, including me in the first edition of *When Kids Can't Read*. By the second decade of this millennium, the term had become so widely used that it had lost its original meaning. For many, strategy instruction was less about thinking and more about doing: give yourself a high-five for good work, guess at the word, keep your pencil handy, study the pictures.

Because different people define the term *strategy* in different ways, I'm going to try to avoid that term in this edition. I'm now using the term *scaffold* when I can. If you want to call Syntax Surgery a strategy, do; if it makes more sense to call it a scaffold, that's fine, too. I suggest, though, that you think about language collaboratively with colleagues and together define this term.

The Simple View of Reading

The Simple View of Reading (Hoover and Gough 1990) says that reading comprehension is the product of two skills: decoding and oral language comprehension. Put another way: decoding × oral language comprehension = reading comprehension. The numeral 1 can be assigned to each of the terms thus creating the algorithm $1 \times 1 = 1$. If decoding is lacking (and therefore is seen as 0) or oral language comprehension is lacking (0), then the algorithm changes to $0 \times 1 = 0$ or $1 \times 0 = 0$. Put simply, when either of those two skills is lacking, then reading comprehension suffers.

Word recognition, which is discussed in Chapter 13, is a critical and necessary skill for reading comprehension. It is, however, not sufficient. Word recognition must be taught. By contrast, oral language comprehension skills start developing naturally from birth. All that we learn through interactions with others and the world help us make sense of the words that we eventually learn to sound out.

Teaching Specific Scaffolds	Brings Invisible Thinking Processes to the Visible Level	and Sharpens These Reading Skills	to Foster
ABC Boxes		Automaticity and fluency	COMPREHENSION
Anticipation Guide		Clarifying	
Book Head Heart		Comparing and contrasting	
Genre Reformulation		Connecting cause to effect	
It Says, I Say, And So		Decoding	
Knowledge Rating Chart		Decoding single- and multisyllable words	
KWL 2.0			
Linear Arrays		Distinguishing between implicit and explicit information and fact and opinion	
Most Important Word	Connecting		
Notice & Note Signposts		Distinguishing details from main ideas	
Onset-Rime	Inferring		
Possible Sentences		Generalizing and drawing conclusions	
Poster	Monitoring		
Probable Passage	Paraphrasing	Identifying main ideas and events	
Retelling			
Semantic Scale	Predicting	Putting events in correct sequence	
Semantic Maps			
Sketch to Stretch	Questioning	Reading with expression	
Somebody Wanted But So	Summarizing	Recognizing areas of confusion	
Syllabification		Recognizing common roots, prefixes, and suffixes	
Syntax Surgery	Visualizing		
Tea Party		Recognizing sight words; signal words	
Think-Aloud			
Three Big Questions		Separating main events/idea from details	
Vocabulary Trees			
Word Across Contexts		Using background knowledge	
Word Axis		Using fix-up strategies	
Word Clusters		Using text clues and prior knowledge to make inferences	
Word Splash			

Figure 2.1 This chart shows the interdependent relationship of scaffolds, thinking processes, and reading skills. It is not meant to be a complete list. For instance, I've not included skimming and scanning—two scaffolds/strategies to teach students. Why not? Those are probably already a part of your teaching repertoire. Please add your own scaffolds/strategies you use or skills that must be taught in your district.

In this age of divisiveness, it might be comforting to reduce reading comprehension to a multiplication fact: $1 \times 1 = 1$. But this view, this simple view of reading, might be too simplistic. The Simple View of Reading could lead some to conclude that reading comprehension is a unidimensional cognitive task when it is more completely understood through a multidimensional lens. When we consider what it takes to comprehend a text, decoding and oral listening skills do not provide a complete picture of what happens. We must also consider the background knowledge of the reader; the task the reader is expected to complete; the sociocultural experiences of the reader; the home language of the reader; the complexity of the text; the interest the reader has in the text and the task; metacognitive fix-up strategies the reader knows to use; even the size of the print or how long the reader has to complete the reading or who assigned the reading or if the reader is hungry or angry or excited to read the selection affect reading comprehension.

Scarborough's (2001) Reading Rope model offers a more complete view of reading comprehension. Imagine two ropes intertwined. Each rope is made of different strands of fiber. One rope has three braided strands that represent three aspects of word recognition: phonological awareness, decoding, and sight word recognition. The other rope is made up of five strands: background knowledge, vocabulary, language structure, verbal reasoning, and literacy knowledge. Those two ropes then twist into one rope—the rope called reading comprehension.

This model offers us that multidimensional view and yet it is still not complete. The story of reading is complex and requires that we know research, instructional practices, and our students' needs. When we take all into account, we have created best practices (see Figure 15.9 on page 262).

Science of Reading

The science of reading is a term long-used to represent the collected body of empirical research that offers insights into how the brain learns to read. I offer a more detailed discussion of the science of reading in Chapter 15. Here, in definitions, I want only to mention that the science of reading relies on the large body of experimental studies showing that young children should receive instruction in the following six areas:

Phonological awareness

Phonics and word recognition

Fluency

Vocabulary

Oral language comprehension

Text comprehension

It is frustrating that now, in 2022, we have returned to the "reading wars" of the previous decades. Once again, some urge early reading programs to focus only on teaching phonics while others encourage a more balanced approach to literacy instruction. This "balance" urges students to consider the question of "does this make sense" while sounding out a word. Students are better served when we understand the research concerning phonological awareness and phonics instruction for early readers as well as understand the research regarding comprehension instruction. Again, see Chapter 15 for more on this topic.

· · · · ·

When Kids Can't Read offers you scaffolds that help change your *instruction* so that your students approach a text as responsible and responsive readers. When students read responsibly and responsively, then they are independent readers. They may still struggle through a text from time to time, but they will know how to struggle and they will understand the value in that struggle. When we fail to nurture that independence, then we will have another generation of kids who can't read. They might call words; they might extract information; but they will not, in the fullest sense of the word, be readers.

Dear George,

You were the one who first said to me, "I can't read." It took a long time for you to say those words. You were the one who started my journey to understand what to do when kids can't read.

Early on, I think my concern was what it meant to you in our class; then as the year progressed, I saw the problems you had in your other classes. As years passed and I saw you in other students, I was told that diminished reading skills would affect test scores and that would affect the school's standing. Eventually, those low scores would affect not only a school's rating but a teacher's rating. The focus shifted from you to the school to the teacher.

But that was wrong; the focus should always be *you* and what happens when you can't read. When kids can't read, so much is lost—for the nation, for the community, for a school, but mostly, George, for you, for all the kids who are you.

Dear George,

Much too late in the year, I asked you what you needed me to do to help you be a better reader.

"You could just do it all for me," you said, hiding behind what I was coming to recognize as truth hidden behind flip responses.

"I'm afraid I can't do that. What's your next choice?" I said.

You stared for a moment and said, "What makes you think there's anything you could do? I can't read. That's it."

CHAPTER 3

How We Know What to Do

Helping kids become skilled readers begins by understanding what kids can do and what they need help doing better. Take a look at the list of reading behaviors in Figure 3.1 (see pages 24–27). The left column describes what skilled readers might do as they read. The right column describes what less skilled readers are more likely to do. As you read through this purposefully long list, think of yourself as a reader and then think of a couple of your skilled readers and a couple more of your less-skilled readers. Put check marks by the behaviors that describe what you notice in your own reading and that of your students' reading.

I will warn you now that the list is long! I made it long because, in part, I think it is easy to reduce reading behaviors to value-laden terms: "good readers" or "bad readers." It is also easy to reduce all we should be doing to create independent readers to two mandates: teach decoding and teach comprehension. Those two terms encompass much and simultaneously leave much out. And though this chart presents many reading behaviors, I'm sure I've omitted something. Add whatever you see as an omission now. This is a work in progress, not an authoritative, definitive list.

Skilled and Less Skilled Readers

Skilled Readers	Less Skilled Readers
Enjoy reading and read for pleasure	Do not enjoy reading and do not read for pleasure
May or may not enjoy hearing books read aloud to them	Prefer being read to over reading on their own
Generally prefer to read a book before seeing the movie about it	Generally prefer seeing a movie about a text before reading it
Can name favorite authors and books	Cannot name favorite authors and books
Can explain differences between genres, for example, realistic fiction and historical fiction	Cannot explain differences between genres, for example, realistic fiction and historical fiction
Can name types of nonfiction that are fun to read	Cannot name types of nonfiction that are fun to read
Have an opinion about listening to audiobooks or listening to someone read aloud	Have no opinion about being read to or listening to audiobooks
Are willing to read and rarely forget to bring a book to class	Avoid reading and often "forget" to bring reading material to class
Like to go to the library and look through books to choose one to read	Do not enjoy choosing a book to read or cannot choose a book to read
Are interested in doing well in classes	Appear uninterested in doing well in classes
Start a text with curiosity by remarking on the title, looking through the table of contents, reading the cover flap of the book, looking at any graphics, or skimming through the text	Do not start a text with curiosity by remarking on the title, looking through the table of contents, reading the cover flap of the book, looking at any graphics, or skimming through the text
Can describe fix-up strategies to use when confused	Cannot describe any fix-up strategies to use when confused
Can easily and quickly decode single-syllable words	Cannot easily and quickly decode single-syllable words
Can easily and quickly decode multisyllable words	Cannot easily and quickly decode multisyllable words

Figure 3.1 Skilled and Less Skilled Readers *continues*

Skilled and Less Skilled Readers

Skilled Readers	Less Skilled Readers
Can easily and quickly recognize sight words	Cannot easily and quickly recognize sight words
Can use the context as a clue to help with word recognition or word meaning	Do not know how to use the context as a clue to help with word recognition or word meaning
Use knowledge of word parts to help with word recognition or word meaning	Have limited or no knowledge of word parts to help with word recognition or word meaning
Have a grade-appropriate academic vocabulary	Have a limited academic vocabulary
Understand various definitions of certain words (such as *skate, run, will*)	Do not understand various definitions of certain words
Read smoothly	Read haltingly, one word at a time
Read silently when appropriate and choose to read aloud quietly when that could help with understanding	Read aloud or whisper-read when silent reading would be more appropriate
Read fluently and pay attention to punctuation	Read very slowly, paying no attention to punctuation
Read aloud with fluency and prosody	Read aloud with little or no expression
Read aloud at appropriate rate	Read aloud too fast, blurring words, rushing through punctuation
Can visualize the text	Have trouble visualizing the text
"Hear" the words when reading silently	Do not "hear" the words when reading silently
Vary reading rate based on needs and purpose of text	Fail to vary reading rate based on needs and purpose of text
Reread to clarify meaning	Do not reread to clarify meaning
Understand that reading is about creating meaning	Think finishing is the goal
Sequence events in a text easily	Cannot keep events of text in correct order
Can identify and discuss cause-and-effect relationships	Do not recognize cause-and-effect relationships

Figure 3.1 Skilled and Less Skilled Readers

continues

Skilled and Less Skilled Readers

Skilled Readers	Less Skilled Readers
Can compare and contrast events, settings, and characters	Have trouble comparing and contrasting events, settings, and characters
Predict easily and connect predictions to events in the text	Do not predict without prompting and then guess more than rely on what is happening in the text
Easily answer literal-level questions about the text	Have difficulty answering literal-level questions about the text
Easily make inferences, draw conclusions, or make generalizations from texts	Do not easily make inferences, draw conclusions, or make generalizations from texts
Easily explain the main idea of texts and offer details that support that main idea	Have trouble explaining the main idea of texts and offering details that support that main idea
Easily offer a summary of the text	Have difficulty summarizing the text
Can explain how point of view affects a text	Cannot explain how point of view affects a text
Can set own purpose for reading a text	Do not set a purpose for reading other than to complete the assignment
Can identify literary elements in a text or discuss how those elements affect the text	Cannot identify literary elements in a text or discuss how those elements affect the text
Connect events in the text to other texts or to events in personal experiences	Do not connect events in the text to other texts or to events in personal experiences
Try to connect new knowledge gained from reading a text to existing knowledge already held	Do not try to connect new knowledge gained from reading a text to existing knowledge already held
Can recall information from a text	Have trouble recalling information from a text
Recognize when comprehension breaks down and can identify where confusion occurs	Do not recognize when comprehension is not taking place or explain what parts are confusing

Figure 3.1 Skilled and Less Skilled Readers   *continues*

Skilled and Less Skilled Readers

Skilled Readers	Less Skilled Readers
Can express thoughts or ideas about a text when talking with others	Have a difficult time expressing thoughts or ideas about a text when talking with others
Can write about a text	Have a difficult time organizing thoughts about a text in writing
Spell words appropriate for grade level	Have difficulty with spelling
Use text features to aid in comprehension (for instance, charts, graphs, index, italicized words, boldfaced words, headings and subheadings, chapter titles, and cover information)	Do not know how to use or do not use features of a text to aid in comprehension
Are willing to struggle through a text when a text is tough	Stop reading at first sign of difficulty
Know when to pause and work on comprehending a section or passage	Continue reading through the text even when confusion has occurred and pausing to clarify would be important
Try to understand a text without immediately turning to the teacher	Expect the teacher to explain what the text means instead of working to explain the text to themselves
Recognize that comprehension takes effort, effort often not seen because thinking is invisible	Think "good" readers comprehend a text by merely decoding it
Exhibit stamina when reading a complex text	Are frustrated easily by a text
Say that reading is enjoyable and respect others who like to read	Say that reading is boring and dumb and might make fun of others who like to read
Look for opportunities to read	Avoid reading at all costs
Identify as readers	Would not describe themselves as readers
See themselves as skilled or "good" readers	See themselves as "bad" readers

Figure 3.1 Skilled and Less Skilled Readers, *continued*

Now that you have read through all these behaviors, what did you notice that surprised you? What skills do you think your students—your own Georges—lack? What other behaviors would you add to this list?

Instructional Plans

I wish someone had shared such a reading behavior list with me before I had met with George's parents. I could have looked through it, and, as you just did, marked the behaviors I had noticed when George was reading. That list would have sparked ideas, given me language, and helped me understand what I needed to do.

If I were to have that meeting now, I would begin by telling them what George can do. I would tell them their son enjoys listening to stories and even has some favorite types of texts he likes to hear. He gravitates toward funny stories more than scary stories, likes stories with a lot of action, and will interrupt me when I am reading aloud to remind me to "add more excitement to my voice."

I would share that after listening to George read, I've recognized that he has trouble decoding some single-syllable words, is overwhelmed by most multisyllable words, and confuses sight words such as *of* and *off* or *were* and *where*. When he has skipped words or decoded them inaccurately, he rarely catches his mistake to fix it. I would tell them that some of his comprehension problems are related to a slow reading rate. He is spending so much cognitive energy on getting through the words, that he doesn't have energy left to spend on meaning making.

This reading behaviors list would have provided me with the language to tell them that he can make inferences that are obvious, but he doesn't recognize more subtle implications. He rarely generalizes and doesn't relate what he's reading to other texts or to his own life. Then I could have offered an instructional plan like the one in Figure 3.2 (see Appendix A for a blank template) which would have used his strengths to help me create a plan for growth. Such a plan would have directed me and encouraged his parents to trust me.

Once you have identified your students' strengths and areas for growth, use this book as a handbook. Read the parts you most need to read in the order that best addresses your students' needs. The Instructional Assessment Chart (see Figure 3.3 on page 30) can guide your reading.

Student Name _____ Date _____

	Can accurately recognize sight words	S-	Continue to assess with sight word lists.
	Reads with appropriate expression	R	Work on reading rate; look at punctuation; use choral reading + readers theater
	Reads at an appropriate rate	R	Repeated timed readings
	Spells words using knowledge of letters and sounds	R	Use spelling assessment! Teach patterns within appropriate levels
Comprehension	Recalls information, makes connections, and summarizes text easily	R	SWBS Retelling rubric Probable Passage/ Possible Sd. ABC Boxes Genre Reformulation
	Uses prior knowledge	S-	Probable Passage Possible Sentence KWL 2.0
	Makes appropriate inferences	R	Begin w/ Syntax Surgery
	Uses close reading to understand theme	R	N+N fiction signposts
	Uses close reading to understand author's purpose or bias	R	N+N nonfiction signposts
	Uses fix-up strategies to solve confusions	R	Build a fix-up chart with George

Student Name *George*   Date _____

	Reading Behaviors	Rarely Sometimes Often	Instructional Practices
Engagement	Enjoys listening to stories	O	Read aloud more; esp. high value NF. Provide books he can/listens to while following along.
	Has a favorite genre/author	No	Might prefer funny books. Introduce range of authors
	Has stamina to stick with a text	R	Use short pieces. Increase reading rate.
Vocabulary	Understands and uses a range of Tier 1 words	O	George has a solid Tier 1 vocabulary. Use linear arrays to connect to Tier 2
	Understands and uses a range of Tier 2 words	R	Continue long. development with read alouds; use Word Axis and Word Clusters
	Can use the context to understand Tier 3 words	R	Teach signal/transition words; to help w/ contextual understanding
	Can use roots and affixes to help determine meaning of unknown words	R	Use vocabulary trees. Directly teach high value roots + affixes
	Can identify which words in a text are problematic	O	George is willing and able to identify problematic words
Decoding/Fluency/ Spelling	Decodes accurately single syllable words	S+	
	Decodes accurately multiple syllable words	S-	Some multisyllable words are in his automatic decoding ability. Others, not. Work on syllabification.

Figure 3.2 Instructional Plan for George. See Appendix A for a blank template.

INSTRUCTIONAL ASSESSMENT CHART

If a student can

- recognize sight words
- decode single-syllable words
- decode words with fluency and automaticity

But has difficulty

- answering literal-level questions about a text
- making inferences
- discussing the text
- visualizing the text
- comparing ideas or themes across texts
- using the text to predict what happens next
- seeing reading as an exciting or important activity
- making connections between texts or text and life
- using fix-up strategies

Then this student needs help with

- making inferences
- making predictions
- questioning the text
- monitoring their own understanding
- using fix-up strategies
- visualizing

See Chapters

2, 3, 5, 6, 7, 8, and 9.

If a student does

- enjoy hearing texts read aloud
- answer questions about texts that were read aloud

But has difficulty

- recognizing sight words
- decoding single-syllable and multisyllable words automatically
- reading with fluency and prosody
- reading silently
- spelling words correctly
- using roots and affixes to understand unknown words
- using signal words to navigate a text

Then this student needs help with

- word recognition
- spelling
- fluency
- signal words
- improving vocabulary

See Chapters

10, 11, 12, 13, 14, and 15.

If a student can

- decode words with fluency and automaticity
- answer questions about a text if asked

But has difficulty

- participating in small- or large-group discussions
- offering opinions about what was read
- listening respectfully to others in group conversations
- seeing self as a reader
- staying engaged with reading
- naming favorite genres or authors

Then this student needs help with

- seeing self as an avid reader
- learning how to participate in discussions
- learning to listen to diverse thoughts
- selecting authors and texts

See Chapters

16, 17, 18, 19, and 20.

Figure 3.3 Instructional Assessment Chart

Dear George,

Looking back, I'd have to say that the only things that guided my instructional decisions that first year were our textbooks. My biggest regret: I didn't have a plan for you. I didn't know how to think systematically about what you could do and needed more help to do. And when I did figure out a few things, I didn't know what I could do to help you. I didn't know how to connect the fact that you were a slow reader to the fact that you lacked decoding skills and that meant you lost track of sequences or cause-and-effect relationships. And once I realized that you had a hard time making an inference, that did not mean I knew what to do. I fear the "say it louder and slower" pedagogy became my go-to strategy.

I could have focused on your strengths. From there, we could have worked on your reading rate, built your academic vocabulary, focused on making inferences. You could have moved from being a struggling reader to a being a reader who knew how to struggle successfully. I should have told you we are all struggling readers, depending on the text. To paraphrase Maya Angelou, if I had known more, I could have done more. Thank goodness, George, you taught me to want to know more.

✧   ✦   ✧

Part 2

Comprehension

Dear George,

On yet another day, you put your book on my desk and said, "I don't get it." I had heard this line from you before and, frankly, was frustrated to be hearing it again. I tried to be patient.

"Did you read it?" I asked. You nodded. "Are you sure, George?" You nodded again. "Well, go read it again. You can get it."

What It Means to Comprehend

I THINK BACK TO ANY ONE OF MANY DAYS THAT I
promised George that if he would read the text (or reread it) then he
would get it. I fear my understanding of comprehension was guided
primarily by the motivating line in the movie *Field of Dreams*. "If you build
it, [they] will come," a guiding voice said of the baseball field the main
character envisioned. "If you read it, meaning will come," I said of the
book I'd given George.

George's complaint, "I don't get it," and my assurance that he could
get it makes it obvious that both of us saw meaning as a thing that existed
somewhere in the text. The reader's job was to find it and grab it.

Learning from Leah

That same year I taught George, I often spent Saturday afternoons with
my friend's five-year-old daughter, Leah. I would watch her so that her
mom—who eventually was my son's first-grade teacher—had time to tutor
students. One Saturday, I took Leah to the Houston Rodeo to see livestock
and enjoy the excitement of the adjacent carnival. Leah was precocious,
inquisitive, and generally willing to try any new adventure. At the livestock
show, we marveled at many types of cows, laughed at pigs rooting around
sawdust-filled pens, watched sheep stand still as they were sheered. At the
carnival, we rode on an elephant, tossed rings over bowling pins, won a cake
at the cakewalk, and then, for a final moment of fun, jumped on the carou-
sel, a beautiful reproduction with ornately painted wooden horses and the

quintessential brass ring. Leah chose a blue horse near the outside edge, and I stood next to her, ready to catch her if this ride proved too much.

The first time we went by the brass ring, she asked what that was. "It's the brass ring," I explained.

We circled again. Again, she asked, "What is that?"

Again, I replied, "It's a ring made out of brass; it's called a brass ring. You're supposed to lean over and grab it."

On the third pass, as Leah's hands clutched the pole rising out of her wooden horse, she released one hand to quickly point at the brass ring and yelled over the calliope music, "So what is it?"

"It's a thing; you're supposed to get it," I said. The ride slowed, then stopped. As we got off, she walked up to the brass ring and stood there, hands on nonexistent hips, a look of complete confusion on her face.

"So, *what is it?*" she tried a fourth time.

I tried, too: "It's like a prize. See, you're on your horse and as the horse goes past it, you grab it. It's made out of a metal called brass, so it's called a brass ring." She shook her head slowly as her frustration began to erupt.

"Are you listening to me at *all? How* do you grab it? And what do you grab it *for* and what do you do with it once you have it, and do you have to give it back? And why is it made out of brass? And is that like what our candlestick holders are made out of because they both are that shiny yellow? Is it heavy and if you drop it, then how do you get it without getting off your horse because the man said don't get off your horse until we come to a complete standstill and if you get it but don't drop it, then what do the other kids on their horses get to get?" Then, thankfully, she spotted the cotton candy and headed for that.

Look carefully at our exchange, and you'll see what was and wasn't being said in that conversation. The biggest problem was that four times her question remained the same: "What is it?" I, not understanding any of the subtext of her question—or perhaps not even recognizing there was a subtext—kept answering the question essentially the same way, though I believe I did move from not very helpful to not helpful at all.

Analyzing My Talk

My first response: "It's the brass ring." Here, I offer her a straightforward definition.

Second response: "It's a ring made out of brass; it's called a brass ring. You're supposed to lean over and grab it." Now, I elaborate the definition a bit and add an explanation of what she's supposed to do.

Third response: "It's a thing; you're supposed to get it." Here, I'm as confused as she is, so I offer a simpler definition by substituting *thing* for *brass ring*.

Fourth response: "It's like a prize." I hope comparing the ring to a prize will give her the definition she needs. Plus, I obviously think that if she understands what brass is, she will understand the point of the brass ring: "It's made out of a metal called brass, so it's called a brass ring."

Finally, Leah asks if I'm listening at all. This is an interesting comment, revealing for the first time all that she thought her simple question conveyed. Look at what she thought she was asking as she repeatedly asked, "What is it?"

1. How do you grab it?

2. What do you grab it for?

3. What do you do with it once you have it?

4. Do you have to give it back?

5. Why is it made out of brass?

6. Is that like what our candlestick holders are made out of because they both are that shiny yellow?

7. Is it heavy?

8. If you drop it, then how do you get it without getting off your horse because the man said don't get off your horse until we come to a complete standstill?

9. If you get it but don't drop it, then what do the other kids on their horses get to get?

Teaching George

I thought about Leah's litany of questions anytime George would approach my desk to say, "I don't get it." He must, I decided, have had many more questions he was expecting me to answer. I began encouraging him to ask more questions. Our conversations now went like this:

George:	I don't get it.
Me:	Don't get what?
George:	It.
Me:	It what?
George:	*It.* I don't get *it.*

I was confused. Why could a five-year-old identify all the things she wanted to know about a brass ring when a twelve-year-old couldn't explain what he needed to know about a book?

Me:	But, George, *it* has to stand for something. What is it that you don't understand?
George:	The story.
Me:	Great, George. This is good. What about the story?
George:	I don't get it, the story. I don't get the story.
Me:	What about it don't you get?
George:	It. All of it.

"Slowly, I began to understand that George—and I—saw comprehension as a thing that existed in the text. Comprehension, I mistakenly thought, was a brass ring that the reader grabbed as his eyes moved across the sentences."

Unlike Leah, who could fluently rattle off all her questions, George lacked the ability to verbalize his. For him, the complexities of comprehension had been reduced to a single phrase: *getting it.* Slowly, I began to understand that George—and I—saw comprehension as a thing that existed in the text. Comprehension, I mistakenly thought, was a brass ring that the reader grabbed as his eyes moved across the sentences.

Comprehension Isn't a Thing to Get

Researchers have long been studying the question *What does it mean to comprehend?* The problem I was facing as an early-career teacher was that I began my teaching career without ever studying, or considering, that question. Remember, my certification was for grades 6–12; in those grades when I began teaching in 1979, few teachers were discussing comprehension issues, though reading researchers had long been discussing this.

The first compendium of research on this topic appeared in 1908: *The Psychology and Pedagogy of Reading*, by Edmund Huey. Huey's own work in this field was predictive of work today as he discussed the role of eye movements, how best to teach children the relationship between sounds and letters, how we make an inference, and the difference in what our brains and our minds do regarding comprehension. A cognitive psychologist, he believed that the singular goal of reading was to create meaning, that our prior knowledge affected new knowledge, and that the best reading instruction was connected to students reading texts of interest to them.

"Meaning is situational, and the more experiences we have with varied situations, the easier it is to predict what will happen next in any given text."

Huey recognized that some basic meaning occurs at the letter and sound levels, that some occurs at the word and sentence levels, but that the most important meaning making occurs at a deep level as we bring our prior knowledge of words, of situations, of texts, and of ideas to the text. Meaning is situational, and the more experiences we have with varied situations, the easier it is to predict what will happen next in any given text. This is one reason why reading aloud to young children is so important. They not only learn about words and the world as we read to them but also learn how texts work. This knowledge of story grammar and text structure is a critical scaffold to understanding, and Huey's early work in this area guided the later work of many.

High school teachers recognize the importance of understanding the structure of a text the first time they introduce sonnets to students. Most students don't encounter sonnets until high school and once they understand the pattern of a sonnet, they move more fluently through it. When middle school teachers give students plays to read, that first one is hard as students figure out how to orally read the play—what part of the text is read aloud and what part is directions regarding actors' feelings and movements and should not be read aloud. Again, we see that practice creates fluency. When we think about the importance of understanding story grammar and text structure, we see why reading series books (Frog and Toad, Bluford High, or the Robert Langdon books, for example) is valuable. Huey recognized that the ability to predict character actions and feelings, to recognize text structures, and to use our prior knowledge changed how easily one comprehended a text.

Louise Rosenblatt wrote her landmark text about comprehension in 1938. In *Literature as Exploration*, she expanded Huey's understanding of the role of background knowledge as she explained the critical role of the individual reader in the creation of meaning. Meaning, as Rosenblatt explained, did not reside in the text; it was not, as I inaccurately understood, something to grasp. Meaning was created in the interaction—what she called the *transaction*—between the words in the text and the thoughts in the mind of the reader. Meaning is created.

In 1990 scholar Rudine Sims Bishop explained that books act as our "mirrors, windows, and sliding glass doors." Those texts give us the opportunity to see ourselves, to see beyond ourselves, and to vicariously experience other places, times, and events. Dr. Bishop explained that "literature transforms human experience and reflects it back to us" (ix). It is in that reflection—when we see ourselves—that reading can become an affirming experience. Imagine, then, what it would mean to never see yourself, or consider what it would mean to see yourself portrayed in only one way. And then think of the power of seeing yourself far stronger or wiser or happier than you ever could have imagined yourself.

> *"The author who writes so compellingly that I am transported into another's world has, if I am willing, helped me be more than my own circumstances have allowed me to be."*

Books give us that moment when we can find ourselves and, hopefully, they give us the opportunity to step outside our own worlds and into another's world. The author who writes so compellingly that I am transported into another's world has, if I am willing, helped me be more than my own circumstances have allowed me to be.

Imagine the thinking that must happen for us to stop being ourselves and allow someone else's experiences and thoughts to become ours while we are between the covers of a book. Consider all that happens when our reading lives never offer us mirrors, or offer distorted mirrors, as has been the situation of so many students of color in this nation. Imagine never seeing yourself or never seeing beyond yourself—and some of you reading this won't need to work hard to do that imagining. You are a person of color who perhaps grew up in a time with few books for you as a child or teen that were written by authors of color or contained characters of color. If you did see books with characters of color, perhaps they were always stories about struggle. Or perhaps you are member of the queer community who rarely read a book with queer characters, or if you did, bad things happened to those characters. Perhaps you know people who live with physical or neurological challenges who rarely see characters who reflect their lives. Some of us always had books with mirrors; others rarely did.

Out of My Mind by Sharon M. Draper and the sequel *Out of My Heart* are musts for any collection of books.

When I was an undergraduate, I began purposefully seeking books that expanded my worldview. I can thank Dr. Mike King in the English department at the University for Texas for that. He offered a class called Black Literature and I took that course. That sophomore course changed my reading life so that I no longer sought books that offered me mirrors—my childhood was filled with those. I instead reached for books that offered me windows and sliding glass doors. I remember reading *Roll of Thunder, Hear My Cry* for the first time in 1979 (it was published in 1976) with my first class of seventh graders. That book remains on my list of books that changed me. I would say the same for *I Know Why the Caged Bird Sings; The Color Purple; Thomas and Beulah; Parable of the Sower; Heart of Aztlán; Leaving Home; The House on Mango Street; Living Up the Street* . . . the list is long. Thank goodness it is long. These books did not offer me a mirror of my life; they offered me doors that opened my world. I would be so much less if I had never walked through those doors. These books changed me. Far more than windows, they offered me sliding glass doors I could step through, allowing me to experience a different life and return with keener a vision of myself and others. These books helped me change myself, become a better version of myself.

"Comprehension is so much more than a thing to test and score. Comprehension of a text is an experience that, if we read well enough, can change us."

Bishop's understanding of what diverse collections of books can offer all students should guide anyone who creates libraries—for themselves, for homes, for classrooms, for schools, for cities. Bishop's work underscores that comprehension isn't a brass ring to be grabbed; comprehension is so much more than a thing to test and score. Comprehension of a text is an experience that, if we read well enough, allows us to change ourselves.

All I Left Unsaid

Huey understood that "to completely analyze what we do when we read would almost be the acme of a psychologist's achievements, for it would be to describe very many of the most intricate workings of the human mind, as well as to unravel the tangled story of the most remarkable specific performance that civilization has learned in all its history" (1908, 6). All who work with struggling readers work to unravel each student's tangled story.

When I sat in that conference room with George's parents, when George stood before me and said he didn't get it, I should have said, "Understanding *is* hard. Understanding how we understand is harder. There is so much to consider: decoding, fluency, vocabulary, making an inference, connecting texts to our lives, understanding the structure of a story, realizing that some words mean some things in one context and another in another context, figuring out what prior knowledge is most important, reconciling new information that might conflict with existing information, monitoring our own understanding, knowing how to fix up confusions . . ." I should have said that George and I would untangle his story, discover what he needed.

But no. I told him to try again and he could get it.

Dear George,

I was almost on the right track the day I asked you to define what *it* was when you told me, once again, "I don't get it." I knew *it* stood for something. But I should have been focused on your word *get*. What would have happened if I had helped you change your comment from "I don't get it" to "I'm not sure how to figure this out"? Then, you would have more quickly focused on what *this* was and we both would have been working from the assumption that readers do far more than hunt for a meaning. Readers create meaning and that creation requires many tools.

Teachers never forget some missteps, cringing each time they come to mind. George, who finally gave you the tools you needed?

Dear George,

Sometimes I'd give in and tell you what something meant. "Look, George, this part, it means . . ." You would nod your head in agreement and later return, asking me about another passage. One time, I did say that you had to try to make it make sense.

"Like what?" you asked.

"You have to ask yourself what something means," I explained.

"But that's the problem. I don't know what it means," you said patiently.

We were on our own merry-go-round, both of us wondering how to reach that brass ring.

Struggling Through a Text

I HAVE LONG THOUGHT THAT IF WE ARE GOING TO
successfully teach students who struggle with reading, then we need to
sometimes feel what those students feel. What follows is an essay that I
hope challenges you: "She Unnames Them" by Ursula Le Guin (1985).
While I've occasionally used this text with twelfth-grade AP English classes,
I more often use it with teachers. It's hard to find a text that challenges
teachers, but this one sometimes does. In the margins, you'll see notes
I made the first time I read this story. As you read, cover my notes with
paper while making your own notes. Then, when you've finished reading,
compare my notes with your own. What do you notice?

"She Unnames Them" by Ursula Le Guin

*Most of them accepted namelessness with the perfect indifference
with which they had so long accepted and ignored their names.
Whales and dolphins, seals and sea otters consented with particular
grace and alacrity, sliding into anonymity as into their element. A
faction of yaks, however, protested. They said that "yak" sounded
right, and that almost everyone who knew they existed called them
that. Unlike the ubiquitous creatures such as rats and fleas, who
had been called by hundreds or thousands of different names since
Babel, the yaks could truly say, they said, that they had a name.
They discussed the matter all summer. The councils of the elderly
females finally agreed that though the name might be useful to
others it was so redundant from the yak point of view that they*

So the animals are the
"them" in first sentence?

They like being anonymous?
They who? I need to reread.
Oh, some of the yaks said
"yak" sounded right. Maybe
because they make a sound
that sounds like "yak"?
Do yaks make a sound?

Tower of Babel? So is
this going to have a lot
of biblical references?

Yaks didn't ever talk about their own name, but they wanted to keep it? That seems like a contradiction.

Who is the donor? Need to reread this section.

Dean Swift? Same as Jonathon Swift?

Cats?

Actually funny; are cats thinking about their name or the perfect mouse? Is a platonic mouse one a cat would not eat?

The animals don't care if they give up a generic name—dog, cat, bird—but they want to keep their personal name, like Froufrou or Polly. This might be about how labels are bad. Makes me think of labeling kids "gifted" or "struggling" or "athletic" or "band kid." I recall the principal who called kids close to passing the state test as "pushables"—kids who with a little push can score the coveted 3. I think this essay is about problems of labels.

Linnaean qualifiers? Linnaeus = classification system.

Ephemeral syllables—what is an ephemeral syllable?

never spoke it themselves and hence might as well dispense with it. After they presented the argument in this light to their bulls, a full consensus was delayed only by the onset of severe early blizzards. Soon after the beginning of the thaw, their agreement was reached and designation "yak" was returned to the donor.

Among the domestic animals, few horses had cared what anybody called them since the failure of Dean Swift's attempt to name them from their own vocabulary. Cattle, sheep, swine, asses, mules, and goats, along with chickens, geese, and turkeys, all agreed enthusiastically to give their names back to the people to whom—as they put it—they belonged.

A couple of problems did come up with the pets. The cats, of course, steadfastly denied ever having had any name other than those self-given, unspoken, ineffably personal names which, as the poet Eliot said, they spend long hours daily contemplating— though none of the contemplators has ever admitted that what they contemplate is their names and some onlookers have wondered if the object of that meditative gaze might not in fact be the Perfect, or Platonic, Mouse. In any case, it is a moot point now. It was with the dogs, and with some parrots, lovebirds, ravens, and mynahs, that the trouble arose. These verbally talented individuals insisted that their names were important to them, and flatly refused to part with them. But as soon as they understood that the issue was precisely one of individual choice, and that anybody who wanted to be called Rover, or Froufrou, or Polly, or even Birdie in the personal sense, was perfectly free to do so, not one of them had the least objection to parting with the lowercase (or as regards German creatures, uppercase) generic appellations "poodle," "parrot," "dog," or "bird," and all the Linnaean qualifiers that had trailed along behind them for two hundred years like tin cans tied to a tail.

The insects parted with their names in vast clouds and swarms of ephemeral syllables buzzing and stinging and humming and flitting and crawling and tunneling away.

As for the fish of the sea, their names dispersed from them in silence throughout the oceans like faint, dark blurs of cuttlefish ink, and drifted off on the currents without a trace.

None were left now to unname, and yet how close I felt to them when I saw one of them swim or fly or trot or crawl across my way or over my skin, or stalk me in the night, or go along beside me for a while in the day. They seemed far closer than when their names had stood between myself and them like a clear barrier: so close that my fear of them and their fear of me became one same fear. And the attraction that many of us felt, the desire to smell one another's smells, feel or rub or caress one another's scales or skin or feathers or fur, taste one another's blood or flesh, keep one another warm—that attraction was now all one with the fear, and the hunter could not be told from the hunted, nor the eater from the food.

This was more or less the effect I had been after. It was somewhat more powerful than I had anticipated, but I could not now, in all conscience, make an exception for myself. I resolutely put anxiety away, went to Adam, and said, "You and your father lent me this—gave it to me, actually. It's been really useful, but it doesn't exactly seem to fit very well lately. But thanks very much! It's really been very useful."

It is hard to give back a gift without sounding peevish or ungrateful, and I did not want to leave him with that impression of me. He was not paying much attention, as it happened, and said only, "Put it down over there, O.K.?" and went on with what he was doing.

One of my reasons for doing what I did was that talk was getting us nowhere, but all the same I felt a little let down. I had been prepared to defend my decision. And I thought that perhaps when he did notice he might be upset and want to talk. I put some things away and fiddled around a little, but he continued to do what he was doing and to take no notice of anything else. At last I said, "Well, goodbye, dear. I hope the garden key turns up."

He was fitting parts together, and said, without looking around, "O.K., fine, dear. When's dinner?"

"I'm not sure," I said. "I'm going now. With the—" I hesitated, and finally said, "With them, you know," and went on out. In fact, I had only just then realized how hard it would

---

Who is this?

Labels separate us. Rich kids. Poor kids.

Hunter from hunted. Depends on where you are in food chain. Are we all both the hunter and the hunted?

Am I supposed to infer this was her idea to unname animals?

Husband? Is she supposed to be Eve?

Infer father = God?

What is "it"? Not her name because you can keep personal names. Maybe I'm supposed to infer that she is giving back her label—wife?

Is this about how labels confine us or define us and she is tired of being defined as a wife? "Talk was getting us nowhere" sounds like she wants a divorce. Did not liking her label make her want to get rid of all the animals' categories?

Garden of Eden?

Infer: he isn't interested in her.

have been to explain myself. I could not chatter away as I used to do, taking it all for granted. My words now must be slow, as new, as single, as tentative as the steps I took going down the path away from the house, between the dark-branched, tall dancers motionless against the winter shining.

Your Response

I hope you are still with me, dear reader.

I've shared "She Unnames Them" with enough teachers to know that some of you reread the essay repeatedly, staying with a passage until it made sense. Some of you might have decided to read my notes as you were reading, hoping that might help you understand confusing parts. And, perhaps, some of you skimmed through it once and decided that I'd probably discuss the meaning, so you'd move on to this section.

Any of us might act in a similar way with any challenging text, and you might recognize that those behaviors mimic things your students do. Some of your students have the tenacity to stick with a text no matter the challenges it presents. Others might turn to other students to hear what they have to say about a text while others stop reading and wait for you to provide guidance. Any of those responses happen when we struggle, and all of us can be struggling readers given the right text.

I hope you made your own comments and perhaps you have shared your thinking with colleagues. Possibly you, too, weren't sure who was our narrator at the beginning of the story, and you wondered if Eliot is T. S. Eliot and if Dean Swift is Jonathan Swift. Maybe the paragraph about dogs and cats keeping their proper-noun names but giving up the generic names offered insight into the story. Perhaps you also wondered why the narrator returned to Adam. Did you also conclude this had something to do with the problems labels create? Have you ever considered that labels help us with some needed tasks? It's hard when we don't know the hunter from the hunted, the eater from the food.

My notes provide some insight into the thinking I was doing:

- noting confusing parts
- making inferences
- asking questions

- creating a sequence

- questioning events

- making connections

My notes made some of my thinking visible. By contrast, a lot of my thinking was invisible. None of my notes revealed the rereading I did. You could not see that at times I kept reading on through the text, hoping that something later would solve my confusion. My notes didn't mention when I changed my reading rate, usually slowing but sometimes skimming through a part that was too confusing. There's no record that I used my finger to point to a few parts as I reread them or read a few sentences aloud very quietly. And I certainly didn't record that a couple of times I wondered if there was an online commentary that could answer my questions.

Less skilled readers don't see all that skilled readers do to struggle successfully. They might see some of the notes that others have taken, but they don't see the internal work of rereading, pausing, moving on, pondering, noticing, and rereading again. They don't know that skilled readers, too, sometimes feel overwhelmed by a text; they think skilled readers just get it, and when the struggle is overwhelming, too often, they give up. Then, too often, we become frustrated at students' dependence on us to explain everything to them. In moments of exasperation, we tell them what they need to know. I certainly did that. I encouraged dependence every time I told students what something meant.

> *"Helping kids become skilled readers requires teaching kids how to struggle successfully through a text."*

Meaning making is far more complex than simply getting it. And teaching kids how to do all the things you did while reading "She Unnames Them" means becoming aware of what you do when the text is tough. From time to time, you must read outside your comfort zone. Pick up an article from a technical journal and read it, noting what you do when the struggle feels overwhelming.

Helping kids become skilled readers requires teaching kids *how* to struggle successfully through a text. We can all be struggling readers. Your least skilled reader of a history text might be your most skilled reader with a text on baseball *if* she loves baseball. Your most skilled reader of fantasy books might be your least skilled reader of poetry. Teaching kids how to struggle through a text successfully helps create independent readers.

Teaching kids to struggle means avoiding what I would sometimes do when George would stand in front of me asking what something meant. Sometimes, in frustration or desperation, I would tell him what *I* thought the text meant. Every time I did that, I was encouraging dependent reading behavior as I denied him the opportunity to struggle through a text. I should have offered him tools; instead, I offered him answers.

Dear George,

I once won the Outstanding Student Teacher award. Discovering I had been nominated and later learning I had received the award made me proud and confident. I thought that award meant I was prepared to be a teacher. I quickly learned it meant I had been a very good student teacher, but that didn't mean I was prepared to be a teacher and certainly not an outstanding teacher.

I wasn't prepared. I wasn't prepared for deciding what needed to be taught. I wasn't prepared for there to be 150 students with 150 different needs and 150 different questions. I wasn't prepared for all the grading, for all the forms to be completed, for all the nights of not knowing what I was going to teach tomorrow. No one told me that my lesson plans would not fit neatly into the lesson plan book the district provided, or that I'd need to submit those plans weekly, or that I'd need to send home Friday progress reports for over half my students. No one told me I'd be alone so much of the day, surrounded by seventh graders and still so alone. No one told me that parents would be angry if I gave too much homework or disappointed if I did not give enough. No one told me what to do when students from Vietnam with no English language skills were placed in my class.

No one told me that some days we would all laugh so much from one silly comment that for a moment, no one would remember I did not really know what I was doing. No one told me how important laughter and joy would be.

And no one told me that in my first year I would have a student die from an asthma attack, on a Sunday, while at a family birthday party celebration. No one told me how to break that news to classmates. Anne called and told me what had happened. She said I would need to tell my class. I said no, I didn't know how. I asked her to do it. "Or Susan. Send Susan. She's the school counselor."

Anne said I had to do it. "You are their teacher."

No one told me what to do when his parents came to clear out his locker. No one told me how angry I would be when the custodian showed up to remove his desk from the front row and no one told me how later to apologize for yelling at him to "leave that desk right there." No one told me how not to cry when the next day his three best friends suggested we move his desk to one side of the room with another chair near it so they could sit there quietly whenever they wanted, perhaps looking at some pictures his mom had brought. No one told me how my heart would swell with admiration for these eleven-year-olds who were showing me that grief isn't something that is felt for a while and then disappears. It simply is.

No one told me that I would love my students.

No one told me, George, what it would mean to me when I discovered I could not help a young man, one hovering near adulthood, learn how to read.

You and your classmates taught me everything I really needed to know. Yes, I had much to learn about content, and many other teachers stepped forward to help me with that, but you—all of you—taught me about heart.

Dear George,

I read "Top Man" to your class, and you, along with your classmates, seemed to enjoy this story of two men climbing K6. I asked you who you thought the top man was. You shrugged. I asked you what the shrug meant.

"I don't know," you replied.

"You don't know the answer to the question, or you don't know why you shrugged?" I pressed.

"The question. It didn't say who was the top man."

"You're supposed to make an inference, George. That's how you answer the question. Make an inference."

You stared at me for a moment, then said, "No, I guess I don't know. Don't you think if I did know, I'd just do it and get you off my back? Jeez."

I heard anger. I should have heard embarrassment and hurt.

CHAPTER 6

Making an Inference

MAKING AN INFERENCE IS THE CORNERSTONE OF comprehension.

Inferential thinking requires that readers be able to hold in short-term memory the explicit information they read and place it alongside information not explicitly presented in the text or the information they have stored in their long-term memory. While skilled readers readily search for any information that will create coherence in what they are reading, less skilled readers won't do that. Sometimes, they don't have the cognitive energy; other times, they don't understand they are expected to bring their experiences to the text. Too many times, students lack world knowledge, and that has a direct effect on their ability to make an inference. You've experienced this, perhaps, when you have read an editorial joke and haven't understood why it was supposed to be funny.

> *"While skilled readers readily search for any information that will create coherence in what they are reading, less skilled readers won't do that."*

I remember a day about five years into my teaching career when Anne had been promoted from assistant principal to principal. I had progressed from the generalized complaint that "these kids can't read" to a more specific comment: "They can't make an inference."

One day, after repeating that complaint yet again, Anne replied, "How do you know?"

"Because I ask them questions that require them to make an inference, and they can't do it," I replied.

"Maybe you are **asking the** wrong questions," she said, peering, as always, over her half-rim glasses. I left her office.

I knew she was right. I knew it. But what were the right questions? Part of my problem (all of it?) was that I had not taken the time to notice the types of inferences I made as I read. I'm not sure I had considered if there were various types of inferences. In this chapter, we'll begin with that task: noticing some of the types of inferences we make.

When we infer, we visualize; we make connections; we predict; we monitor our understanding; we summarize. If you hear, "That short but fierce thunderstorm resulted in five inches of rain," in addition to understanding how much rain fell, you might have imagined rain slamming against windows, lightning bolts flashing across the sky, flowers bending to the pelting rain, puddles forming everywhere. You inferred all those images of the thunderstorm and saw them in your mind's eye. You might have remembered the time you were in a thunderstorm that was what your grandmother called a gully washer. That connection was an inference. You might have predicted that following the thunderstorm, there could have been flash floods and mudslides. And those were inferences. You might have reminded yourself that you needed to read some more to see where this storm occurred to check that prediction. All those comprehension processes are related to making an inference.

When someone tells you that you need to help students make an inference *and* you need to teach them to predict, or you need to help students make an inference *and* you need to focus on cause-and-effect connections, then **you know** that person doesn't understand that helping students make stronger inferences means helping them do those other things. What follows are the various types of inferences that any reader might need to make (see Figure 6.1). I do not suggest that you set about teaching these types of inferences. I do hope you'll listen to the logic your students offer (or fail to offer) and notice what types of inferences they are making (or failing to make). As you note their confusions, think about these various types of inferences and then decide what you need to teach your students.

A tenth grader came into class one day and immediately put his head on a desk. "What's wrong?" I asked.

"My inference with my girlfriend has been severed," he responded.

"Hmm?" I said.

"You know—you said an inference was a connection. She said we were done. My inference has been severed."

SUMMARY OF TYPES OF INFERENCES AND HOW TO HELP STUDENTS

If we need students to make an inference based on...	**Then** we can help by teaching students to...	Examples
Pronouns	Find what anaphoric and cataphoric pronouns refer to	The students got permission to go on the field trip. They were excited. She stood there, shocked. It was clean! His mom looked at his room and marveled at the floor!
Transition words	Understand categories of signal words and what they mean	Words that emphasize a point: *for that reason, in fact, with this in mind* Words that indicate a conclusion: *in summary, finally, in brief*
Omissions	Read aloud to "hear" what is missing, using punctuation as a clue	There were many breeds of dogs *such as* to consider: collies, labs, poodles, retrievers. So many! *breeds* *excited to make a choice*
Punctuation	Read aloud what's confusing and discuss what the punctuation helps them infer	The doctor—a young person, probably barely twenty-five—was going to do the surgery? *really?*
Substitutions	Make synonym links with terms used in texts	On March 28, Venus, Saturn, and Mars were aligned. This triplet of planets clustered in the early dawn. A similar conjunction of the trio will be visible in 2024.

Figure 6.1 Summary of Types of Inferences and How to Help Students

continues

SUMMARY OF TYPES OF INFERENCES AND HOW TO HELP STUDENTS

If we need students to make an inference based on . . .	**Then** we can help by teaching students to . . .	**Examples**
Knowing multiple meanings of words	Note and discuss common words that have multiple meanings	What word means "to not eat" and "to run quickly"? (*fast*) What word means "a place to play" and "what you do with your car when you arrive someplace"? (*park*)
Close causal connections	Combine sentences and add the needed transition words and explanations	*because* Her feet hurt. The soles of those shoes just didn't support her arches. *of her feet.*
Distant causal relationships	Look for transition words and vocabulary that signals the need to make an inference Make synonym links, even if that means going back several pages or passages	*meeting?* Her appointment was made on Friday. It would be a lot of work, but she knew she was ready for it. Everyone was very supportive and suggested they celebrate with a party. Chair of the board was a big step. *appointment not meeting; a job*
World knowledge	Read widely and ask questions about events	Use sites such as Newsela and Wonderopolis to share daily information about the world with students. Remind students to discuss how one text reminded them of something they read in another text.

Figure 6.1 Summary of Types of Inferences and How to Help Students, *continued*

Inferences Based on Pronouns

Quite often, we make inferences based on the pronouns the author uses. These are common inferences and could be classified as substitutions (discussed later). Usually, pronouns refer to a noun that has previously appeared in the text. When a pronoun has an antecedent in the text, it is called an anaphoric pronoun. Sometimes, though, the pronoun appears first and then the referent appears. Then, the pronoun is a cataphoric pronoun. Let's look at some examples:

1. The children were talking loudly when their teacher walked in the room. She told them they could continue talking with one another, but they needed to lower their voices.

2. Sandra was interested in what they were saying. Her friends were discussing where all would be heading to lunch.

3. That small group could not believe what he said. Ben explained to all that he had heard the Friday test had been postponed.

In the first example, *children* is subsequently replaced by *them* and *they*. *Teacher* is replaced by *she*. Most students do not have difficulty with these substitutions. In the second and third examples, the pronouns appear prior to the noun referents. In those two examples, readers need only to look to the next sentence to discover who *they* and *he* are. Cataphoric pronouns cause more difficulty for readers when the pronoun appears several sentences before the referent. Look at this sentence as an example:

> Dr. Smith was surprised by them. She had arrived at the hospital expecting a normal day. No one had told her that anything out of the ordinary would happen. There they were, though, all the babies she had delivered that past year, in their parents' arms, ready to celebrate her birthday.

Students must hold on to *them* in the first sentence until they get to the fourth sentence to discover whom *them* refers to. This stretches the short-term memory of some readers, especially those expending limited cognitive energy on decoding or fluency.

Only in the rarest of situations do I use the words *anaphoric* and *cataphoric* with kids. I learned that the hard way when one ninth grader told me that he was sure he was catatonic after that boring lesson. I do, however, think we need to understand the terms. It helps us understand the specific problems kids might have.

Inferences Based on Signal Words

Another common type of inference is supported by signal words such as *first, later, after, before, notwithstanding, in conclusion, by contrast,* and *likewise.* A list of many signal words is provided in Appendix B.

Signal words provide important clues that help readers when they are not sure about word meaning. Too often, though, we assume students recognize the importance of these words or phrases. Struggling readers, however, need help identifying their function. Consider the following example:

> *He is a perspicacious reader. That is to say, he is a skilled reader who makes keen connections and inferences.*

If you recognize that "that is to say" means "here's an easier way of understanding something you just read," then you know that what follows will explain something. In a similar way, if you read, "Allegedly, it is important to teach young children all the rules that govern letters and sounds," and if you know that *allegedly* means "I'm qualifying this statement," then you might infer the author does not believe that statement.

Teaching *categories* of signal words is a concrete way of helping students make inferences. As an early-career teacher, I often focused on the more common categories of signal words:

- sequence (*first, next, last*)
- comparisons (*furthermore, as well as, related to*)
- contrasts (*however, but, on the other hand*)
- causes or effects (*because, due to, consequently*)
- conclusions (*finally, therefore, in summation*)

A list of signal words arranged by categories is provided in Appendix B.

It wasn't until later in my career that I realized the importance of focusing on other categories of signal words, including these:

- emphasis (*a key idea, most of all, above all*)
- examples (*to illustrate, specifically, for example*)
- spatial proximity (*between, closest, neighboring, bordering*)
- qualification, that is, when the author is qualifying her thinking (*allegedly, purported, seems like, supposedly, was reported, some would say, it has been suggested*)

The more work you can do with categories of transition words, the more likely students will be to use them to make an inference.

Inferences Based on Omissions

Often, authors omit words, expecting readers to complete the thought:

> *When scientists first hypothesized atoms centuries ago, they despaired of ever observing anything so small, and many questioned whether the concept of atoms could even be called scientific. (Bojowald 2008)*

Did you notice the omitted word? Sometimes skilled readers are so skilled, their mind reinserts the missing word at a subconscious level. In the phrase "and many questioned" the word *scientists* has been omitted. The author, if being more helpful, would have written "and many *scientists* questioned."

I asked a seventh grader if she had her project ready to discuss. "Nope," she replied.
   "Want to tell me more about that?" I asked.
   "Nope. I'm omitting words," she explained.

I've now paraphrased a passage that occurs later in the same article about atoms. Read it slowly and see if you notice what I've omitted:

> *Material atoms are the smallest indivisible units of chemical compounds; similarly, putative space atoms are the smallest indivisible units of distance. These are generally thought to be about 10^{-35} meter in size, far too tiny to be seen by today's most powerful instruments, which probe distances as short as 10^{-18} meter. Consequently, many scientists question whether the concept of atomic space-time can even be called scientific. Undeterred, more are coming up with other ways of detection.*

Here's what I noticed:

> *Material atoms are the smallest indivisible units of chemical compounds; similarly, putative space atoms are the smallest*
> *putative space atoms*
> *indivisible units of distance. These ∧ are generally thought to be about 10^{-35} meter in size, far too tiny to be seen by today's most powerful instruments, which probe distances as short as*

10^{-18} *meter. Consequently, many scientists question whether the concept of atomic space-time can even be called scientific. Undeterred, more* ^scientists^ *are coming up with other ways of detection* ^of atomic space-time^*.*

In an eleventh-grade science class, students reading this article understood the referent for *these* and most did not even notice that *scientists* had been omitted as they automatically inferred that word. The final omission, though, caused problems. Some thought scientists were looking to detect the putative space atoms. Others inferred "detection of anything to do with atoms." To encourage the correct inference, we first looked at the word *undeterred* and discussed what that one word meant. Then students decided that the undeterred scientists were the ones who would not stop thinking about way to detect atomic space-time. Once they understood the signal word, they were able to make the correct inference. When authors omit words, they often expect signal words or punctuation to help provide meaning.

When students have trouble with making the inferences that omitted words require they make, we often have to slow our own thinking to identify those omissions. Becoming aware of the inference we made is the first step in helping students make the same inference.

Lest you think this conversation engaged the entire class, with all working to understand the passage, consider the group that sat toward the side of the room and eventually asked, "What if you omitted the questions and just told us what it meant?"

Inferences Based on Punctuation

At one point in the history of writing, no one used punctuation. It was an extra step for those monks sitting at a dimly lit table, laboriously copying one scroll at a time. Plus, almost all reading was done orally. The masses did not have access to printed texts, and if they did, they probably had not learned to read. The orators—those charged to read texts aloud— were taught how to read aloud a particular text, and once they were ready, they performed the text more than read it. It was Aristophanes who first suggested that authors could annotate the text by adding some dots to the text—a dot near the top suggested a slight pause; one in the middle meant a longer pause; one at the bottom meant a full stop.

"Becoming aware of the inference we made is the first step in helping students make the same inference."

But his idea didn't gain traction. In particular, Cicero (an important Roman orator) believed that punctuation should be dictated by the rhythm of the prose and not something a copyist put into the text. So, for hundreds of years, *wordscontinuedtobeputtoprintwithoutspacingorpunctuationthatwascon-fusingformanytosaytheleast.*

This began to change, though, with the rise of Christianity. While pagan religions had explained their rituals by word of mouth, the new group called Christians preferred to write their letters, psalms, rules to live by, origin stories, and gospels. They thought the written word would make it faster and easier to spread their beliefs. Early Christian writers, therefore, wanted to add their own punctuation before the masses could decide how phrases and sentences should be punctuated. These early Christian writers realized that a pause here or there could change the meaning they intended the Bible to have.

By about 1450, when a Bible rolled (slowly) off Gutenberg's press, almost all punctuation that we still use appeared: periods, question marks, colons, and semicolons. Not too long afterward came the comma, exclamation point, ellipsis, dash, and parenthesis. Much later, as technology advanced, we added a cousin of punctuation to the myriad of ways authors convey meaning: formatting, such as italics and boldface. Now, even newer technology has added another means for authors to imply meaning: emoticons and emojis.

> *"We hear the words we read. But we do not hear punctuation marks; we respond to them. We see a semicolon and pause; we see a question mark and our voices reveal inflection."*

Reading words includes hearing them as you decode them. Try to read this sentence without hearing the words in your mind. You probably couldn't avoid hearing the words. We hear the words we read. But we do not *hear* punctuation marks; we respond to them. We *see* a semicolon and pause; we *see* a question mark and our voices reveal inflection. We see parentheses and take on a conspiratorial whisper. We see a dash and we pause a bit before rushing on as we recognize that those words—the ones between the dashes—explain something previously written. We follow the directions of punctuation; we don't hear the punctuation itself.

Struggling readers, by contrast, often do not follow the directions punctuation tries to impose. They read past periods, never bothering to slow between two sentences. They read what's between parentheses with the same expression as what is not. They don't understand how their voice, that internal voice of silent reading or external voice of oral reading, might sound when reading a list or a statement that follows a colon. They do not know all that punctuation might help them infer.

I often think the most required trait for teaching adolescents is a sense of humor. In a ninth-grade class, I noted one student had written in the margin of his paper, "I! f---ing! hate! school!" He saw me looking at what he had written and asked, "Did the exclamation points help you make an inference?" Yup.

I like to give students a chance to tell me what the punctuation suggests and what they, consequently, infer. For instance, I ask students how "He *ate* the cake?" differs from "He ate the cake?" I want them to explain how "He wants to go!" contrasts with "He *wants* to go?" I want them to recognize that parentheses provide insight into a character such as in one of the most famous uses of parentheses in literature: "My very photogenic mother died in a freak accident (picnic, lightning) when I was three . . ." (Nabokov 1997, 10). Such a terse explanation must mean something. Has the character spent his lifetime explaining her sudden death so that now, as an adult, he has reduced this tragic story to two words? Does the tragedy continue to haunt him so much that he can utter only these two words?

I want them to see that the well-placed exclamation point can bring the reader's attention to something important. In *No Name in the Street*, James Baldwin wrote, "If one really wishes to know how justice is administered in a country, one does not question the policemen, the lawyers, the judges, or the protected members of the middle class. One goes to the unprotected—those, precisely, who need the law's protection most!—and listens to their testimony" (2007, 149). That exclamation point underscores the point Baldwin is making, and without it, the lesson is not as powerful.

"Punctuation, as silent as it is, proclaims loudly how we are to read the text."

Punctuation, as silent as it is, proclaims loudly how we are to read the text.

Inferences Based on Substitutions

The most basic substitution is a pronoun for a noun. We've already looked at that. Now let's focus on a different type of substitution, nouns for other nouns. Authors use synonyms to eliminate redundancy, and usually, these substitutions cause little trouble. But, if readers are learning new content that uses content-specific words, recognizing synonyms is critical. Take a look at this passage:

> The Americans who remained loyal to the British Crown were
> often called Tories. These loyalists stood in opposition to those

who wanted independence from England. Seen as "royalists,"
the King's Men fought again the Patriots, even though they lived
alongside them. (Beers and Probst 2016, 211)

This passage requires that students recognize all the substitutions. *Loyalists, royalists,* and *King's Men* were substituted for *Tories.* If students can't follow those substitutions, this passage won't help them understand anything and if they can't remember that Tories were the Americans who were loyal to the king of England, then they will be confused. We must remember to help students link synonyms together.

Look at the synonyms that we can link in the short story "Thank You, M'am" by Langston Hughes (1958/1986). A woman, Mrs. Louella Bates Washington Jones, stops a young boy as he attempts to steal her purse. She keeps him from stealing her pocketbook and says angrily to him: "Pick up my pocketbook, boy, and give it here."

The woman doesn't take the boy to the police station, but she takes him to her home. As she drags him to her apartment, she tells him, "You ought to be my son."

Once in her apartment, she finally says, "What is your name?"

He answers, "Roger."

"Then, Roger, you go to that sink and wash your face," she says.

After feeding him, telling him about her life, and giving him ten dollars, she is ready to send him on his way. She explains: "I got to get my rest now. But from here on in, son, I hope you will behave yourself."

She walks him to the door of her apartment building and sends him on his way, saying: "Good night! Behave yourself, boy!"

If students have learned to link synonyms, they'll see that the woman begins by calling the would-be thief *boy*; then she says he ought to be her *son*; next she calls him his given name, *Roger*. A few sentences later, she directly calls him *son*. Finally, as she is sending him back into the world, she distances herself from him and returns to calling him *boy*.

Noticing this progression allows students to infer how the woman's feelings have changed throughout the story. In this case, these substitutions offer insight into character development.

Other times, the substitutions serve as a way of helping students learn a new term or concept. Here, linking the synonyms helps students understand *Grand Alliance* and *Axis powers*.

A group of countries worked together during World War II to fight against the aggressors. This bloc of nations helped each other. These three major powers included Great Britain, the United States, and the Soviet Union. This Grand Alliance had a common goal of defeating Germany, Italy, and Japan, but they had varying thoughts on how to fight against the Axis powers.

Inferences Based on Knowing Multiple Meanings of Words

Not only do some readers struggle with academic vocabulary, but often, they do not know the many meanings of common words. Think about the multiple meanings of *run*, *volume*, *fast*, *bolt*, and *down*. If you know only that *bolt* means to run suddenly and quickly, then when someone says, "Hand me that bolt of material," you might be confused. The following offers another example:

If there's a will, I want to be in it.

That sentence probably surprised you because you expected it to say, "If there's a will, there's a way." If the sentence had progressed as you had expected, you might have explained it by saying, "If you are determined, you will find a way to accomplish what you want to accomplish." In this case, *will* means "commitment to something or determination." But the sentence did not progress as expected and you revised your understanding.

"As we make an inference, often our knowledge of word meanings stored in our minds is more valuable than any clues in the text."

The context offers very little about what the word *will* means. The sentence does tell us that it is something the speaker wants to be in. If you know that a will is a legal document that designates heirs of an estate and if you understand that being *in it* means being listed an heir, then you understand why you might have smiled as you read it.

If you don't know that definition of *will*, then you are left wondering what this means. There are no explicit clues to the meaning. As we make an inference, often our knowledge of word meanings stored in our minds is more valuable than any clues in the text.

Remember, our knowledge of words is affected by our experiences. In one ninth-grade class in a small east Texas town, students saw the sentence "The jersey was left in the field." The students in that class who were active members of the Future Farmers of America club wanted to know if there were other cows in that field. The football players in the class said the coach would be angry if they left any football gear or uniforms on the field. As students talked, each realized that their own experiences shaped how they inferred the meaning. As they looked closely at the sentence, one football player said, "You leave a cow *in* a field but a shirt *on* the field." He then proudly added, "That was some good close reading I was doing."

In a fifth-grade class, the students read, "Lava will cascade down a mountain as nothing can stop it." One student asked, "Why would you put Cascade into a volcano?" In a seventh-grade class, a student read, "How could he get his work done with all that racket from outside?" An avid tennis player, he asked, "So, does this mean a lot of people are playing tennis outside?"

I gave a group of eleventh graders a sentence that stumped them all for a while: "The old man the boat." When they all announced that sentence didn't make sense, I asked them if they knew what all the words meant. They were positive they did. Finally, someone looked up *man* and discovered it could be a verb and mean "to equip or to occupy." Someone else decided to look up *old*. They discovered it could be a noun and mean a group of elderly people. Someone else finally explained, "You have to know those other meanings and you must read it with a pause between *old* and *man* for it to make sense: The *old* [*pause*] man the boat."

We must teach students the less common academic vocabulary of their textbooks, but we can solve many inference problems by making sure they know the multiple meanings of many common words. I've included a list of common words with multiple meanings I like to share in Appendix C.

And a few still said, "I don't get it." This shift of words—grammatically and semantically—was something these literal-level thinkers were not ready for. When we made synonym links (wrote the word *elderly* above *old* and *occupied* above *man*), then they could see it. Then they said, "Oh! I do get it!"

Can offers an example of a common word with multiple meanings. Let students look through a text together, discussing words that have multiple meanings.

Inferences Based on Close Causal Relationships

With some inferences, you know the meaning of all the words and easily recognize how ideas are related:

Jason's arms were covered in minor scratches. The new kitten loved to run up and down Jason's arms.

"When ideas are linked causally, but that relationship is not quickly apparent, more inferences are required to understand the author's intent."

All you have to do is infer that while the kitten was running up and down Jason's arms, the kitten's sharp nails scratched Jason. The two sentences have a close causal relationship; thus, the inference is easier to make. Passages that offer close causal relationships generally do not cause much confusion. If you see that there is a problem, ask students to combine the two sentences into one sentence and add any explanations that have been omitted.

Jason's arms were covered in minor scratches because the new kitten loved to run up and down Jason's arms, and the kitten's sharp claws scratched his arm.

Inferences Based on Distant Causal Relationships

When ideas are linked causally, but that relationship is not quickly apparent, more inferences are required to understand the author's intent. That takes more cognitive energy. This is where we begin to lose some readers, especially if they don't value the reward for staying with the task. Try this:

Jason went to his neighbor's house. He returned with his arms full of scratches.

The author intends a causal link between Jason going to his neighbor's house and his arms being filled with scratches, but what is it?

Did Jason walk through thorny bushes to get there?

Did he get mosquito bites and start scratching his arms?

Did he fall while playing?

Does Jason's neighbor have a cat and did Jason play with the cat?

By this time, do you care?

Distant causal links demand attention, and attention takes energy. They require readers know when to read on, reread, look to graphics, look to titles, and perhaps focus on unknown vocabulary. In the previous sentences about Jason's scratched-up arms, there's not enough information for the reader to do much more than make a series of predictions and then read on.

The following passage from *George Washington's Secret Six* (Kilmeade and Yeager 2013) requires several types of inferences, but I want you to focus on the move from the first paragraph to the second paragraph. It's at this point that the author omits commentary that would have made this easier to follow:

> *Even as Robert Townsend was settling into his new role,*
> *something happened that highlighted the precarious nature of*
> *the world in which he now lived. On July 2, 1779, British raiders*
> *had attacked Major Tallmadge's camp at dawn, killing ten men*
> *and capturing eight, plus a dozen horses. Those losses were*
> *devastating, but in the aftermath, Tallmadge made a discovery*
> *that proved unsettling and was potentially threatening to the*
> *Patriots' intelligence operations. One of the horses the British*
> *had stolen was his own, which still bore its saddlebags and*
> *some of Tallmadge's personal papers—including some money*
> *earmarked for Woodhull and a letter from Washington that*
> *specifically named George Higday, a resident of Manhattan*
> *"who I am told hath given signal proofs of his attachment to us,*
> *and at the same time stands well with the enemy."*
>
> *Eleven days later, Higday was arrested at his home and*
> *confessed to having met with General Washington to discuss the*
> *possibility of spying, but claimed that he never carried out any*
> *such activity because the payment had been in fake bills. (2013, 89)*

When I asked the eighth graders reading this book to discuss what *led* to Higday's arrest, many responded, "He was arrested because he had met

After I discussed this example with a group of eighth graders, one student remarked, "I think this writer needs help." While we all laughed, what often makes students' writing confusing is this very issue: the causal relationships are too distant.

There is no explicit discussion of what caused Higday's arrest. Students must make a distant causal connection.

with Washington to discuss spying." They avoided the question as I had asked it and instead answered one that had a more direct answer in the text. I then changed my question (Anne was right—it is always about the questions we ask) and said, "Be the author and write some more sentences at the end of the first paragraph that would help readers understand what *caused* him to be arrested." One group wrote:

> *The British took the information found in Tallmadge's personal papers and read them. As they were reading them, they discovered that George Higday was someone George Washington thought would be a good spy for the Patriots. So, the British arrested him.*

When the causal relationships are distant, meaning the reader must do more work to get from here to there, give students direction on where missing information might fit and let them write about what is missing.

Inferences Based on World Knowledge

The following passage requires knowledge of your world for it to make sense. As you read it, think about the scene you think is being described and identify all you already had to know to understand what is happening.

> *He put down $10.00 at the window. The woman behind the window gave him $4.00 back. The person next to him gave him $3.00, but he gave it back to her. So, when they went inside, she bought him a large bag of popcorn. (Weaver, Gillmeister-Krause, and Vento-Zogby 1996, 84)*

I liked the idea of the student who said, "I think it's a young son taking his mom to the afternoon movie. She wants to help him pay, but he is excited to do it on his own."

Another student said, "This must have happened in the olden days, like when you were a kid. Even matinee movies cost more than three dollars now."

I see a man and a woman who are going to the movies. Perhaps they are on a date, but it must be a matinee because tickets cost only three dollars per person. I know that amount because after paying with a ten-dollar bill, he got four dollars back. That means the woman "behind the window" kept six dollars. Presuming each person's ticket cost the same amount, each ticket cost three dollars.

I also know that you have to stand at the window to get tickets before you can enter. That helps confirm my thought that they are at a movie theatre. Later, I see they buy popcorn. That's something many people buy when they go see a movie. I think the woman doesn't want the man to buy her ticket. She tried to give him three dollars, the amount of her ticket. There is something she is not quite comfortable with yet and that's why she wants to pay her own way. I infer this means a lot to her because when he wouldn't accept her money, she decided to buy the large popcorn, which must cost about three dollars.

Some of the inferences I made were text-based inferences (such as connecting *person next to him* with *her*), and others were connected to knowledge that I have about the world: we buy movie tickets at a window; we stand in line at the ticket window before going in; when someone buys us things, we can feel beholden to them. I used those inferences to create what Durkin (1993) calls an "internal text"—thoughts about what is happening in the text. Readers construct internal texts as they connect the information in the external text (the printed information) with what they already know.

When students are reading texts with historical references, realize that they sometimes won't know those references—they're not in their world of knowledge—and so they may miss making some needed inferences. For instance, a fourth grader asked me why I said, "Dial the phone." In his world, phones aren't dialed. After 9/11, one news commentator said that when he saw all the flags hanging from windows in New York City, it was a "tie a yellow ribbon" moment for him. My son, a fifth grader at that time, asked what he meant.

And depending on your age, you might also be wondering what that phrase meant, or you will be humming "Tie a Yellow Ribbon Round the Old Oak Tree" for the rest of the day.

World-knowledge inferences require that students know a lot. As students begin studying any particular topic, we need to help them access their knowledge about that topic before they begin reading; I discuss this more in the next chapter.

Inferences Based on Textual and World Knowledge

Let's try one last passage, a poem by Judith Minty (1980). As you read it, make any marks or draw any pictures or take any notes you need to help you decide what this poem is about.

Letters to My Daughters

Your great-grandfather dreamed that his son
would be an engineer, the old man,
the blacksmith with square hands.
To the Finns up north in that snow country
engineer was like doctor today. In the forties
in Detroit, I learned to play the violin.
So did my father when he was a boy in Ishpeming.
He and I never spoke about becoming. Our conversation
was my bow slipping over the strings, my fingers
searching for notes to tell him, his foot tapping time.
That violin cracked ten years ago, it dried out
from loneliness in the coat closet,
Your grandfather, the engineer, sometimes plays his
at night behind a closed kitchen door.
Your grandmother sews and turns up the television.
But what of you two? The piano you practiced over
is still here, a deaf-mute in our living room.
I strike an imperfect chord now and remember
we never spoke of what was dreamed for you.

—*Judith Minty*

This is a tough poem requiring us to make many inferences across confusing syntax and loosely threaded together relationships. I certainly said to myself, "I don't get it," when I first read it. This poem, often shared in high school, will confound many readers. That won't be because they can't decode it. They can. It will be because the causal links are distant, and the amount of energy needed to predict all the ways relationships might be connected and then confirm or discard predictions might be more than they want to muster. As you look at Figure 6.2 you will see the annotations for this poem from a highly skilled seventh grader (Student A). Compare that student's thinking with what appears in Figure 6.3, which represents the thinking from a less skilled tenth grader (Student B). Figure 6.4 offers a look at how a highly skilled tenth grader (Student C) made sense of the same poem.

Let's begin by comparing Students A and B. Student A made several types of inferences. She connected pronouns to nouns, added the word *violin* where it had been omitted, noticed an Again and Again signpost

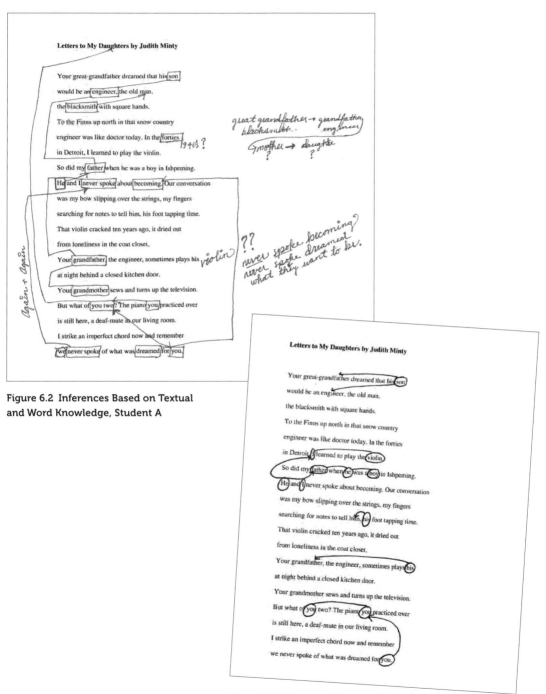

Figure 6.2 Inferences Based on Textual and Word Knowledge, Student A

Figure 6.3 Inferences Based on Textual and Word Knowledge, Student B

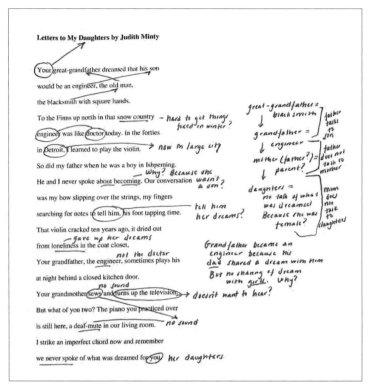

Figure 6.4 Inferences Based on Textual and Word Knowledge, Student C

(see Chapter 8 for more on signposts), recognized "forties" as a substitution for 1940s, connected "you two" to "daughters," and saw that the narrator's father and the narrator never discussed the narrator's dreams and the narrator never discussed dreams with her daughters. That's a lot of work. And still, when done, this student said, "I kind of get it, but this whole part about the 'bow slipping over the strings' is confusing. I guess it is about how the mother is sad about not asking her daughters what they wanted to be."

Compare that with Student B. This student, though older, read less, did not like to read, and did not put effort into challenging texts. Notice this student mostly connected some pronouns to nouns, though sometimes he merely connected pronouns to other pronouns. He did show an understanding that the narrator plays the violin.

In that same classroom, Student C made many inferences. The student captured some of those through underlining, arrows, and lines connecting things; others are evident in marginal notes, which offered speculations and questions. Furthermore, it is only this student that began adding world knowledge: it's hard to get things fixed in the snow country in the winter; living in Detroit means they now live in a larger city; sewing doesn't make noise.

The more distant the causal relationships are, the more they require readers to bring their background to the text; thus, the more our struggling readers retreat. They stop, declare the text is dumb, and tell us reading is boring. Our first job is to recognize that this is a defense mechanism. *They feel dumb and are tired of feeling that way.*

👥 Step Inside a Classroom

In the tenth-grade class that was reading this poem, two or three students wanted to keep reading the poem. They liked that they had to work hard for it to make sense. Four or five others read through it briefly one time and then started drawing, sleeping, or looking around the room. The majority made some attempt at the syntax surgery, with most offering connections like the ones Student B made.

Syntax Surgery is discussed on page 122 and "What Surprised You," one of the Three Big Questions, is discussed on page 149.

To encourage those inferences that require the most distant connections (not readily available in the text), I asked, "What surprised you?"

Most said, "Nothing."

I waited. Then, this conversation emerged:

Student 1: I was surprised that it said the great-grandfather dreamed his son would be an engineer instead of a doctor. Did that mean, like, *dream*? He had a dream?

Student 2: Look, *dream* is in the last line, too. Could it mean, like, he hoped his son would be an engineer? It says, "we never spoke of what was dreamed for you." Does that mean the great-grandfather did tell his son his dream, but the mother didn't tell her daughters?

That one conversation resulted in several students going back into the text. I didn't ask them to discuss inferences. I asked them to discuss what surprised them. Surprises (remember "Where there's a will, I want to be in it"?) come from inferences we make—or can't make. Start there. You just might be surprised.

To Infer, or Not to Infer

"I don't get it" is so much easier to say than "I can't infer relationships among the words, or the characters, or between the characters and myself," or "I can't use the context to help me infer the correct definitions," or "I think the causal relationships are too distant and that's causing confusion." Teaching would be easier if students would use that language. But no. "I don't get it" is the synonym for all those problems.

That elusive *it*, the beginning of understanding, originates in the text but does not fully reveal itself on the pages. *It* is in that interaction between the reader and the text, between the words on the page and the images and ideas in the mind. *It* sits in the intersection of the author's words and the reader's wonderings as the reader navigates what the author has said and has left unsaid. Bridging the two requires that readers make inferences.

Dear George,

I still like the short story "Top Man" and I enjoy discussing who was the top man. When you had shrugged, I wish we would have discussed how the phrase *top man* could refer to the person who stood atop the mountain and it could refer to the person who did something for another. We could have talked about the sacrifices both Nace and Osborne made, and you could have told me who you thought made the ultimate sacrifice. You then could have decided who you thought was the top man.

We were both so close, George. With patience on my part, you might have explained what confused you. And with more knowledge on my part, I could have helped you. But no, you shared your honest feelings, I bristled, and then I sent you out of our classroom. I sent you away from learning, though I guess you learned something about me. I am saddened to think of all that exchange must have meant to you.

Dear George,

I'm quite sure that I introduced the short stories and novels we read that year in class by telling you something about the author or something about the plot. Perhaps, for a little variation, I occasionally introduced vocabulary words. I didn't understand how important it was for *you* to be thinking about the selection before you began reading the selection. Tapping into prior knowledge meant seeing if you had read another story by that same author. Your class was about to begin reading *A Day No Pigs Would Die*. You said, "Before we get started, aren't you going to ask if any of us had bacon for breakfast?" The class laughed and for a moment, you enjoyed being the star. And that levity you provided encouraged far more engagement than my brief discussion of the author, Robert Newton Peck.

CHAPTER 7

Accessing Prior Knowledge

I STOOD IN FRONT OF THE CLASS OF SEVENTH
graders, anxious because I didn't know them and they did not know me. I
was working with a teacher across the hall for a week. She and several other
teachers had just been called into an emergency gathering with the principal
regarding an accident that the speech team had been in as they were returning from a city competition. "Our literature book is on my desk. They
should read 'Rogue Wave.' Thanks so much. I had two kids on that bus,"
she said, and she hurried down the hall.

I walked in. They *looked* like innocent twelve-year-old darlings. Then they
began speaking, simultaneously it seemed:

"Why are you here?" "Where is my teacher?" "Did you kidnap her?" "Do
you have a dog?" "Do we have to do any work today?" "Can I move my
seat? He is bothering me." "Are you a real teacher?" "Do we have to do what
you say?" "Are you going to be here a long time?" "Your name is a drink!
That is so cool!"

There I was, me and twenty-seven seventh graders who vacillated
between not caring I was there and loudly voicing their wish that I would
go away. Eventually—I think it was when they decided having a teacher
named Beers was cool—they hushed. I began. Again.

Me:	Your teacher said that today you are supposed to read a short story in your literature book. It's on page 83. Let's turn there. [*About twenty-three minutes later, they finally accomplish that task.*]
Student:	What's this about? It looks dumb.

79

Student:	It says, "Rough Wave." What's that mean?
Student:	Are you going to read this aloud? Can we put our heads down while you read to us? I'm putting my head down.
Student:	I don't think it says, "rough." It's spelled *r-o-g-u-e*. That's doesn't spell *rough*.
Student:	OK. Well, what's roe-goo-ee?
Student:	Will this be homework if we don't finish in here?
Student:	Miss, would you tell him to stop tapping his pencil? I can't stand that.

Over my years of teaching, I've gotten better at activating prior knowledge before students begin reading, but I swear, getting them to turn to the right page can still take forever.

Because time does march on, that class eventually ended. I think we got to the correct pronunciation of *rogue* and through several pages of the Theodore Taylor short story. Perhaps they took their literature books home to complete the reading. I don't remember. I do remember that my entire prereading strategy consisted of getting them to find their books, turn to the right page, and take a look at the title.

Early in my career, I often, as the above moment recounts for you, stumbled when introducing a new text. At times, getting students to the right page was hard enough. On great days, I would expand that accomplishment by telling kids about the text or the author. Eventually, I realized that I needed to do less telling and they needed to do more thinking.

While telling students something about the text might tap into prior knowledge of some students, this is not the best way to encourage students to become active meaning makers. Dependent readers are dependent in part because of their passive reading: they wait and we explain. We explain what a word means; we explain what a passage means; we explain what the book will be about. But reading is an active process, and that active thinking begins before we enter the text.

Ghost Memories, Baseball, and Cognitive Loads

In 1932, British psychologist Sir Frederic Bartlett proposed that people have mental structures—schemata—that help them make sense of the world. In his seminal study called "War of the Ghosts" (in part because he had explored what participants recalled after reading the folktale "War of the Ghosts"), he showed that memory of something affects how we recall new information (Bernecker and Michaelian 2017). Thus began our understanding of the role of prior knowledge.

About fifty years later, Recht and Leslie (1988) showed that low-skilled readers who knew a lot about baseball understood a passage about baseball better than their higher-skilled peers who had limited knowledge about the game. This study, often referred to as the baseball study, has been replicated many times, always with similar results. The kids who knew more about the topic before they began reading understood the passage better than kids who knew little about the topic. That prior knowledge affected their new learning.

Then, in 1998, Sweller, van Merrienboer, and Paas explained why prior knowledge is important. They showed that the more prior knowledge (rich schema systems) students have in their long-term memory, the more space they have in their short-term, working memory to learn more. This means the "cognitive load" of new information does not overtax short-term memory.

Put another way, the more you have already learned about a topic, the easier it is to learn even more.

In 2020, Dong, Jong, and King conducted a study that revealed that students who need the least help because they have extensive background knowledge in a topic are often the ones who seek help the most when they are confused. Students who need the most help often don't seek help. That's counterintuitive. If you know a lot, then you are willing to seek more help when confused; if you don't, then that confusion can lead to silence. To closing the book and waiting. To putting your head down to take a nap.

Students with a lot of prior knowledge about a topic are often more engaged. They think, "I've got this!" Because the cognitive load is low, they have energy to learn more. By contrast, students who enter into the new learning task with low prior knowledge are less likely to seek help because they have so much to learn that they cannot focus on formulating a question. That leads to the overused comment "I don't get it." They don't know where to begin and so, too often, they don't begin.

The folktale was well-chosen because Bartlett discovered that memories of the text as well as prior experiences haunted our recollections. These ghost memories changed our understanding of the text over time.

Scaffolds for Before Reading

What does this mean for you? First, my show-and-tell practice to introduce students to a text was the least helpful of all I could have done. Second, practices that encourage students to reflect on what they know about the topic or theme before they read are helpful. Third, talking with others about their knowledge helps everyone. This talk allows students to generate questions, raise issues, make connections, perhaps voice confusion, and use the vocabulary associated with the topic. This type of classroom talk can be most beneficial to students who lack knowledge about a topic.

Eventually, classroom talk becomes internalized. Students walk into the school library and see a book. They thumb through it, asking themselves if they've read another book similar to this one, if this book will extend their understanding of a topic, if the vocabulary looks accessible. They read the inside cover flap and predict what the book might be about. If you are someone who thinks spending time on a Saturday afternoon at your local bookstore is the perfect use of time, then you know that as you wander the book aisles, you exhibit those same behaviors. And if someone is near you, you might ask, "Have you read this? Do you know this author?" We want to talk, even before we begin to read. Even if only to ourselves.

The scaffolds presented in this chapter (see Figure 7.1 on the following page for a list) give students a chance to talk, a chance to think about what they already know, a chance to activate their prior knowledge. The scaffolds here depend on *student* talk and *student*-generated questions. The point isn't to get better at using Probable Passage or Anticipation Guides. The point is to help students become active participants in the reading process, even before the reading begins.

Anticipation Guides

An Anticipation Guide (Tierney, Readence, and Dishner 1995) presents students with a brief list of generalizations related to the theme or topic of a selection. Students decide whether they agree or disagree with each state-ment before they read and then return to those statements after reading to reconsider their earlier thoughts or to consider those same statements from another perspective, for instance, a main character's perspective. These

BEFORE-READING SCAFFOLDS

If students need help with . . .	**Then** use . . .	**See** page . . .
Understanding theme Finding evidence Recognizing point of view	Anticipation Guide	82
Questioning a topic	KWL 2.0	87
Making cause-and-effect relationships	Probable Passage	88
Comparing and contrasting	Possible Sentences	92
Sequencing events	Word Splash	95
Making predictions	Tea Party	96
Understanding vocabulary for a unit	Knowledge Rating Chart	98
	Thematic Clusters	98

Figure 7.1 Before-Reading Scaffolds

guides activate students' prior knowledge, encourage them to make a connection to the reading as they consider their thoughts about the topic, and give them a chance to corroborate their existing knowledge or reconsider their knowledge when students return to the statements after they have read. Effective Anticipation Guides present students with pertinent issues that are worth discussing but that don't have clear-cut answers.

While crafting an Anticipation Guide will take some time, remember, you need only three to five statements. You aren't writing a pretest. Don't write, "The Institute of Medicine says teens should consume three quarts of water a day." That's a true-or-false question. Try "Water is as important to your good health as is food." That's something students can discuss. Take a look at these groups of statements and decide which is the better one for an Anticipation Guide:

> NASA had a budget of twenty-three billion dollars in 2021.
>
> It is important to spend money on space exploration.

> Children cause more problems than solutions during times of war.
>
> Many children in Sweden helped adults during World War II.

👥 Step Inside a Classroom

A sixth-grade class was studying child labor around the world. One group was about to read an article about ten-year-olds in Ecuador who did not attend school so they could instead work on banana plantations; another group would be reading about Apple products (iPhones and iPads) that use a particular ore mined by children in Africa.

Because students had not previously discussed child labor, the teacher wanted students to think about bigger issues—protecting children, buying products when we know children are used to help make the products, the importance of an education in a child's life. Students worked together to discuss each statement before they read. One student's Anticipation Guide is shown in Figure 7.2 (see page 85; see Appendix D for a blank template). Before students broke into two large groups to read their appointed text, they got into smaller groups to discuss their initial reactions to the statements. Look at what two students said about the first statement:

Student 1: I said agree.

Student 2: Why? What if we don't know it's made by kids? And maybe they need the job. And is that right for someone to tell you what you can and cannot buy?

Student 1: They already do. Kids can't buy beer. And kids can't buy a house. I don't think they can buy a house.

Student 2: Yeah, well, maybe. But this is different. Like child labor is when kids are forced to work. I guess what we're reading is going to talk about this. Like maybe explain what it should be. Maybe that will change my mind.

Once they finished reading, these two students returned to their Anticipation Guides and discussed their thoughts.

Student 1: I changed my mind about the first one. I get it now. I hadn't thought about all that stuff, but if they paid parents more, then it would be OK.

Student 2: Yeah, I kept mine the same because I already said agree. I guess if stores wouldn't buy stuff made from companies that use child labor then this might make the companies rethink what they are doing. Like with Apple, look at this part of the article. It says that thousands of people wrote to Apple to complain and they were going to change their practices. That's good. But will they? How do I find out if they did, and if they didn't, should I give up my phone? I don't want to do that.

Anticipation Guide

Part 1: Before you begin reading the selection, consider each of the following statements. Do you mostly agree or mostly disagree with the statement? Write your answer in the "Before Reading" column. Then, after you finish reading the selection, reconsider each statement and write your answer in the "After Reading" column.

Before Reading	What do you think?	After Reading
Disagree	We should not be allowed to buy products from companies that use child labor to make their products.	Agree After reading "Hard at Work" I see that kids could be harmed. Companies should pay parents enough so kids don't have to work.
Disagree	Sometimes parents need their children to work. In those cases, children should not be required to attend school	Agree Parents have to feed their kids and some companies don't pay the parents enough money. This is not the parents' fault.
Disagree	No companies should be allowed to hire young children to work full-time.	Agree I learned that the banana companies won't let parents make a union to demand more money so people have to make their kids work these companies should pay parents more.
Agree	If I know that something I use exists only because children were forced to help make it, I should stop using it.	Disagree I didn't know that the bananas we eat might come from where kids have to pick them. It makes me feel bad to keep eating them but we need them and maybe if we didn't buy them then the families would have even less money. This is hard to decide.

Part 2: If any of your answers changed after you read the selection, explain what you read that encouraged you to change your mind.

A student completed this Anticipation Guide for an article about child labor.

Figure 7.2 Anticipation Guide for Text About Child Labor. See Appendix D for a blank template.

Student 1:   Me too. My article was about how kids pick the bananas, and my mom always puts a banana in my lunch. Is that a banana from what a kid in Ecuador picked? Should we stop eating them? If we do, then doesn't his family lose more money, because he wouldn't be making any money? The article didn't really say what we should do, but it did talk about what they did in Costa Rica—was it Costa Rica?—to help parents make more money. It's like we have to decide.

As these students discussed each comment, they returned to the text to help provide evidence for their points. They demonstrated they were willing to change their minds after getting more information and they generated additional questions. These students, who self-identified as "not a good reader" and "not good at figuring out what things mean," certainly proved themselves wrong. Anticipation Guides help students focus their thinking, examine what they know, and then reexamine that once they have read.

One Important Question

After reading, you should discuss whether students' prereading thinking changed. You'll want students to use the text to show you what confirmed or changed their thinking. But don't stop there. An important question needs to return students to the process: "How did thinking about these big topics help you as you were reading?" In this class, students offered comments such as the following:

"I was already thinking about my brother who works after school. This helped me see that what he does is very different because he wants to do this."

"When I started thinking about this before we were reading, it was like I had a reason to read without you saying, 'Your purpose for reading this is blah, blah, blah.'"

"It helped me start thinking about child labor before we started reading. My opinions were already, like, in my head. I liked that."

KWL 2.0

You probably know this strategy as KWL: what I *know*, what I *want* to learn, what I *learned* (Ogle 1986). KWL provides a scaffold that helps readers access their knowledge about a topic before they read, then create questions regarding what they want to learn, and finally record what they have learned. I call my revision of this scaffold KWL 2.0 because of one slight adjustment I want you to make as you move students from discussing what they know to discussing what they want to learn.

As an early-career teacher, when I tried using KWL, I would ask kids to tell me what they knew about a topic. They would, and I would list all that knowledge on the board in the first column of the KWL chart. Then we moved to the second column, and I would ask with much anticipation, "What do you want to know?" I would smile and nod my head, urging an answer.

The silence was broken only by some mumbling, "I don't know." A student once offered, "How would I know what I want to know? I just told you all I know."

I gave up on this strategy for many years. Then, I realized that my mistake was that I was failing to connect the thinking in column 1 to the questions in column 2. I tried again. This time, after students had shared all they knew about a topic, I'd choose one fact and ask, "What more do you want to know about this?" Now, they had questions. For instance, fifth graders told me all they knew about bees. One student shared, "Only one bee has babies. She's called the queen bee."

When I asked, "What do you want to know about this?" after a moment of silence several students offered questions:

"What makes a bee a queen bee?"

"What if another queen is born in that hive?"

"Why can't a hive have more than one queen bee?"

"What happens when the queen bee dies?"

"What else does the queen be do other than have more babies?"

"Do bees hatch from an egg?"

"Is there a king bee?"

The question "What else do you want to know?" is too broad. The question "What more do you want to know about this?"—about one specific fact—gives students a way to attach their current knowledge to anticipated new knowledge.

 ## Step Inside a Classroom

Students in middle school science class were beginning a unit on the volcanoes. These students had been using KWL 2.0 in several classes and understood how to use the KWL 2.0 Think Sheet (see Figure 7.3 on the following page; see Appendix E for a blank template). The teacher got students started by asking them to list what they knew about volcanoes.

As you look at Suzie's comments, you'll see she knows some basic information. She has heard about lava but doesn't mention magma. She thinks volcanoes are found only on islands. She uses the term "blows up" rather than "erupts." After listing known information, Suzie generated questions for what she wanted to know. Then, after reading about volcanoes, she answered some of her questions and listed (in column 4) new information.

? One Important Question

KWL 2.0 offers students a concrete way to connect prior knowledge to existing knowledge. That's what comprehension is: connecting new knowledge to existing knowledge. That's harder to do when existing knowledge is incorrect. That's why it is always important to ask students, "Did you discover something that contradicted what you already knew? What do you now understand?"

Probable Passage

As originally developed (Wood 1984), Probable Passage is a scaffold that works best with fiction. In the original version, the teacher presents students with a brief summary of a text, from which key words have been omitted (a cloze passage). Students then use key words provided by the teacher to complete the cloze passage.

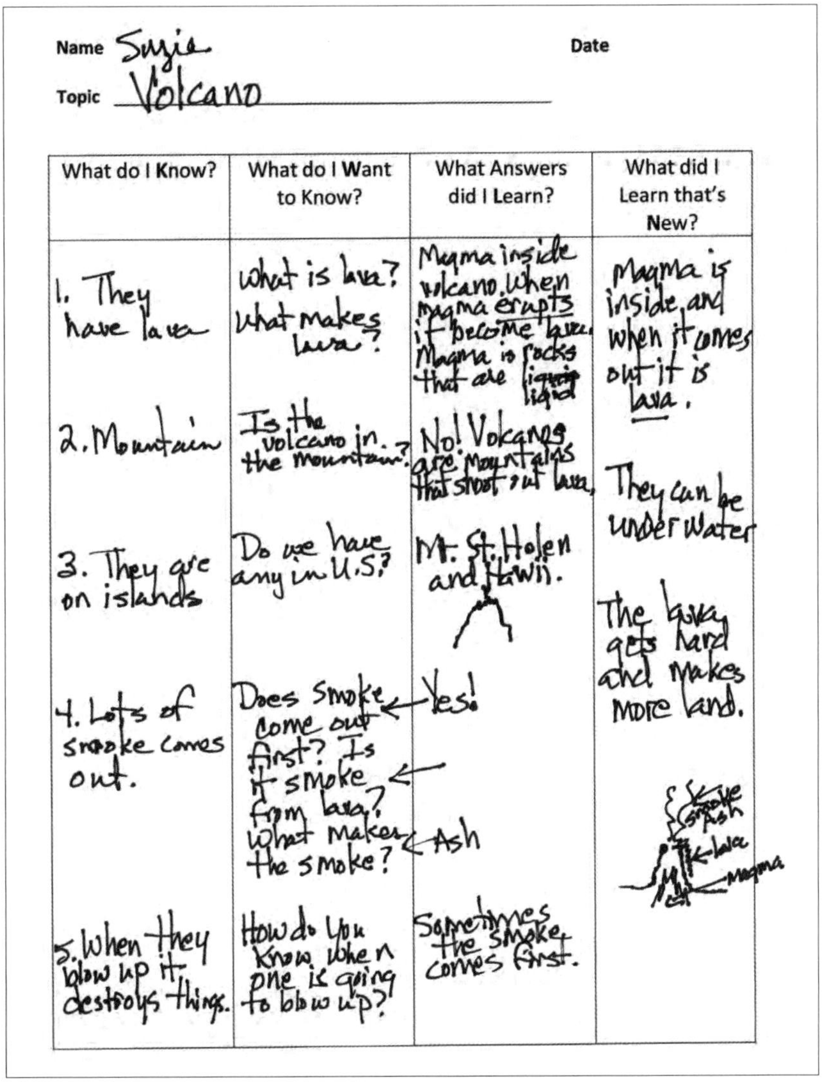

Name Suzie　　　　Date

Topic Volcano

What do I Know?	What do I Want to Know?	What Answers did I Learn?	What did I Learn that's New?
1. They have lava	What is lava? What makes lava?	Magma inside volcano. When magma erupts it become lava. Magma is rocks that are liquid	Magma is inside, and when it comes out it is lava.
2. Mountain	Is the volcano in the mountain?	No! Volcanos are mountains that shoot out lava.	They can be under water
3. They are on islands	Do we have any in U.S.?	Mt. St. Holen and Hawii.	The lava gets hard and makes more land.
4. Lots of smoke comes out.	Does smoke come out first? Is it smoke from lava? What makes the smoke?	Yes! Ash	smoke ash lava magma
5. When they blow up it destroys things.	How do you know when one is going to blow up?	Sometimes the smoke comes first.	

Figure 7.3 Suzie's KWL 2.0 Think Sheet. See Appendix E for a blank template.

I've adapted this process so that first the teacher presents students with about eight to ten key words from the text. If using with a novel, choose words from the first several chapters. Don't use characters' names; instead, use a description: "fifteen-year-old basketball player," "grandmother," "the best friend." Next, students separate the words into categories provided on the Probable Passage worksheet (see Appendix F).

After that, they write their own short gist statement that explains what the text might be about (instead of completing a cloze statement). Finally, they generate questions they hope are answered as they read the text. After reading, they return to the worksheet and see what questions they can answer. Additionally, they note where the author would have categorized the words and write a gist (summary) statement the author would have written.

Selecting key words from the first several chapters allows students to confirm or revise predictions soon after they begin reading.

👤👤👤 Step Inside a Classroom

The high school English class was about to read the poem "Sonrisas" by Pat Mora. Rather than tell students about the poet or the topic, the teacher used Probable Passage to encourage students to predict what the poem might be about. You can read this poem on page 113 in Chapter 8.

The teacher shared the key words, and students worked in groups of two or three to categorize the words and write their gist statements (see Figure 7.4; see Appendix F for a blank template). Students also used the template to describe their thinking before and after reading "Sonrisas." Let's look at a brief conversation from two students as they first contemplated where to place words:

Student 1:   I think the women in beige dresses scolded the senoras.

Student 2:   Why?

Student 1:   The senoras brought them black coffee and they wanted sweet milk coffee.

Student 2:   Maybe the women in beige dresses brought the senoras the wrong coffee

Student 1:   Yeah, maybe. I think that this word, *budgets*, goes in Problems. Like, they were going to have to cut the budget and someone would get fired.

Student 2:   OK. That's good. That's why they needed coffee.

Not only does this brief conversation show that Student 2 has an understanding of the relationship between causes and effects (cutting the budget means someone will be fired), but this student has encouraged Student 1 to see the senoras as the women in authority and the women in beige as the ones delivering coffee.

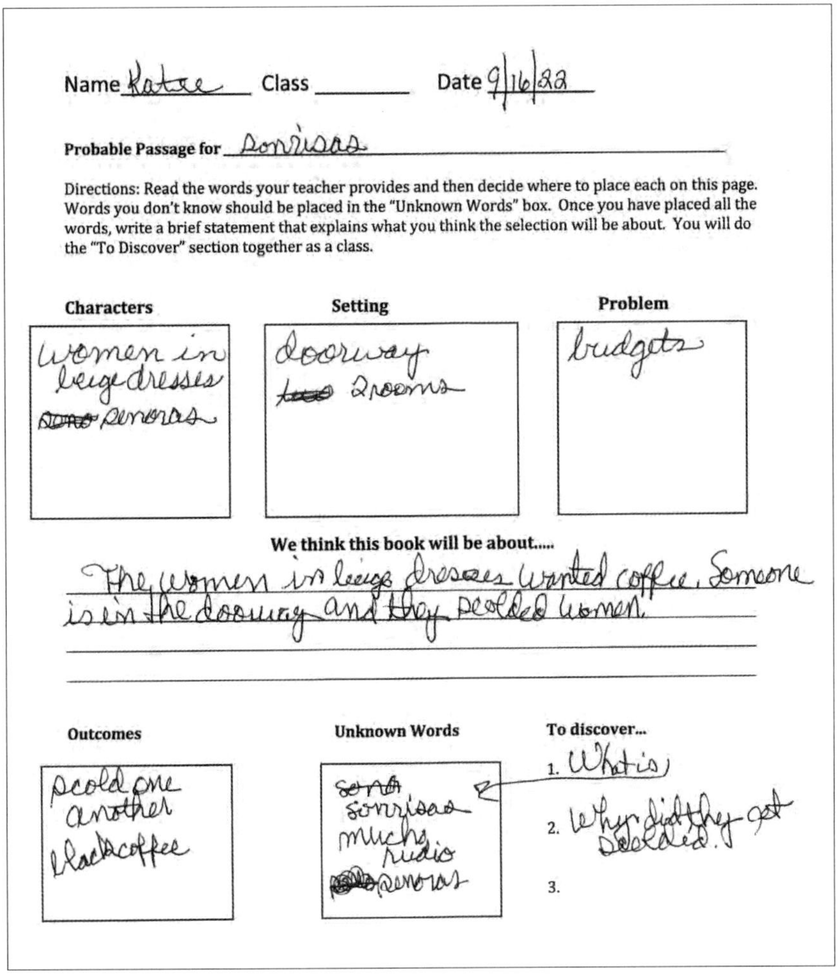

Name Katie Class ________ Date 9/16/22

Probable Passage for Sonrisas

Directions: Read the words your teacher provides and then decide where to place each on this page. Words you don't know should be placed in the "Unknown Words" box. Once you have placed all the words, write a brief statement that explains what you think the selection will be about. You will do the "To Discover" section together as a class.

Characters	Setting	Problem
women in beige dresses ~~señora~~ senoras	doorway ~~two~~ 2 rooms	budgets

We think this book will be about.....

The women in beige dresses wanted coffee. Someone is in the doorway and they scolded women.

Outcomes	Unknown Words	To discover...
scold one another black coffee	~~sonr~~ sonrisas mucha radio ~~señoras~~ senoras	1. What is 2. Why did they get scolded. 3.

Figure 7.4 Probable Passage for "Sonrisas" (page 113). You can change the labels of the categories to reflect the academic vocabulary you want your students to use. See Appendix F for a blank template.

One Important Question

After the class had read and discussed this poem, one of these two students remarked she liked her "story" (gist statement) more than she liked the poem. The teacher gently pushed her back to thinking about the poem by asking how categorizing the words helped or hindered her thinking about the text. That's always an important question to ask.

The student responded, "Because I was already thinking about the words, when I saw them in the poem, I was more interested in them. I wanted to see how the author used them and then it was cool to see that some of our thoughts were the same. Then when we had to go back and put the words where the author would put them, that was really interesting, to think about it from Pat Mora's point of view."

Possible Sentences

I used *tectonic plates* in a science classroom. Most students wrote the unhelpful sentence, "What is a tectonic plate?" though one did offer "During the earthquake, grandmother's tectonic plates broke. She had to go to the dentist."

Possible Sentences (Moore and Moore 1986) focuses students' attention on key words from a text so they can use their knowledge about those words to write possible sentences that might appear in the text. This is a prereading scaffold for nonfiction. As with Probable Passage, in Possible Sentences (see Figure 7.5; see Appendix G for a blank template) you provide students with a list of key words that are in the text. Don't select words that students won't know. For instance, if reading about earthquakes, don't choose *tectonic plates*. Or if reading about Harry S. Truman, don't use his name if this is students' first introduction to him. Instead, use "thirty-third president of the United States." Students should use three to five words from the keyword list in each sentence. After students write sentences and share them, they read the text. After completing the text, they return to their possible sentences and make any needed corrections.

For some students, seeing all the words at one time could be overwhelming. For those students, tell them what the text is about and then share only three or four of your key words at one time. Let students write one sentence that uses those words and then move on to the next set of words. Present the words in the order they will see them in the text.

Step Inside a Classroom

In one eighth-grade classroom where Bob and I worked for several months, the teacher decided to give Possible Sentences a try. She provided students with twelve key words and told them to write sentences using these words. That wasn't enough direction, so students wrote twelve sentences, one for each word. Furthermore, the sentences were not related to one another. For instance, one student wrote, "I like bananas," followed by "If you get sick,

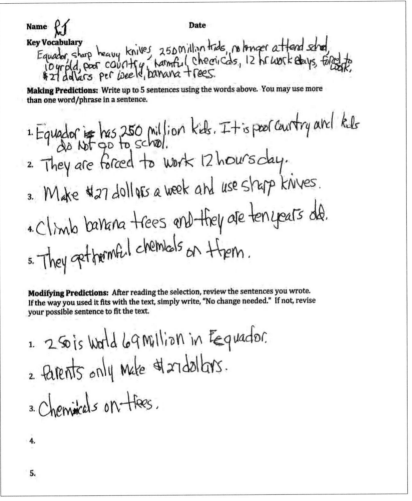

Name RJ **Date**

Key Vocabulary

Equador, sharp heavy knives, 250 million kids, no longer attend school, 10 yr old, poor country, harmful chemicals, 12 hr work days, forced to work, $27 dollars per week, banana trees.

Making Predictions: Write up to 5 sentences using the words above. You may use more than one word/phrase in a sentence.

1. Equador is has 250 million kids. It is poor country and kids do not go to school.

2. They are forced to work 12 hours day.

3. Make $27 dollars a week and use sharp knives.

4. Climb banana trees and they are ten years old.

5. They get harmful chemicals on them.

Modifying Predictions: After reading the selection, review the sentences you wrote. If the way you used it fits with the text, simply write, "No change needed." If not, revise your possible sentence to fit the text.

1. 250 is world 69 million in Equador.

2. Parents only make $27 dollars.

3. Chemicals on trees.

4.

5.

Figure 7.5 Possible Sentences Example. See Appendix G for a blank template.

you can no longer attend school." The teacher did not tell them that their possible sentences should be what could possibly be found in the article, so they should all be related to one another.

As the problem became immediately apparent, we regrouped and tried again, this time giving the students more specific instructions: "Students, here are some words I've taken from one article. After thinking about these words, with a partner, write three to five sentences that might possibly be found in the article. Use three or four of these key words in each sentence. Remember, you are writing sentences you might see in one article. After you read the article, we'll look at your sentences to see how closely you predicted what might be in the article."

Students started again, and this time, they said things like, "Oh, this won't be about me liking bananas. They can't go to school because they have to pick bananas," and "This is in Ecuador. Where is Ecuador?" These students accurately predicted much of what they did read in the article and by the time they had all shared their possible sentences, they were eager to begin reading. They wanted to discover if their thinking was correct and they wanted answers to the questions their discussion had generated. One student asked, "Can we read now? I want to see who made these little kids do all this work."

In the following photograph, you see me working in this classroom. At this point, the students had already written their possible sentences and read the article. Now, they were returning to the article to decide if their sentences were accurate. Look at this short exchange between Darien and me:

> **Darien:** I wrote, "They used sharp heavy knives and climbed banana trees and no longer could attend school," and that's what the article said, so that sentence was true.
>
> **Me:** Yes, that was true.
>
> **Darien:** And I said, "The ten-year-old made twenty-seven dollars a day," and that was in there, too.

Figure 7.6 Darien and I discuss which of his predictions are correct. See Appendix G for a blank Possible Sentences template.

Me:	Did the article say the ten-year-old makes twenty-seven dollars a day? [*Darien returns to the article.*]
Darien:	Oh, the *father*. Not the kid. The father made that much each day. That seemed like a lot for a kid, but it's not for a father.
Me:	That's right. It was the father. But how often did the father make twenty-seven dollars? [*Darien reads that passage again.*]
Darien:	Wait! It's twenty-seven dollars a week. Not even a day! That's a big difference. He only got twenty-seven dollars a week. That's why his kid has to work. They should pay the parents more.

One Important Question

In that classroom, as I moved from group to group, I asked students to show me the sentences they thought they needed to revise. I was listening for how well they could use evidence from the text to justify their thoughts. My final question, presented to the full group, was "Did Possible Sentences help you as you read the article?"

Darien spoke up: "Usually, I read stuff and it's interesting, but I don't really think about it. This time, we got to do our own thinking and then we had to figure out if I was right. I liked that. I try to pay attention when I'm reading, but this made me start thinking before we started reading, and that made it easier."

Darien's comment reminds us that we can't measure text complexity solely by looking at sentence length or vocabulary. Darien thought the reading was "easier," and that was because he was more engaged. Nothing in the text changed. It was Darien's interaction with the text that changed and that made the reading easier.

Word Splash

A similar scaffold, Word Splash, also encourages students to predict what the text might be about by studying words and phrases from the text. You create the "splash" of words (see Figure 7.7), perhaps using a site such as WordClouds.com and share with students. In small groups, they write sentences using these words.

Figure 7.7 Sample Word Splash

I also let students create their **own word** clouds for essays they write. They upload their short essays to WordClouds.com. The resulting word cloud quickly reveals words used most often. They can then ask themselves if the point they were trying to make is reflected in the cloud that is created. That's an easy way for them to quickly see what word they have used most often.

Tea Party

Like Probable Passage and Possible Sentences, Tea Party offers students a chance to consider parts of the text before they ever actually read it. Unlike those two scaffolds, which present students with key words from a text, Tea Party allows you to extract entire sentences or phrases from the text.

Each student will receive one sentence or phrase that you have written on an index card. If your class has twenty students, then choose seven sentences and write each one on three index cards. If your class has thirty students, you might decide to find eight sentences. Now each sentence will be repeated about four times.

Each student receives one index card, and then students move around the room, sharing their cards. Jen Ochoa, an eighth-grade teacher in New York City, told me that sometimes she doesn't want her twenty-four students walking around the room. She tapes an index card to each desk after putting desks into groups of four. Then students sit at their desks and read their sentences to one another. When she rings a timer, the students move to another group of desks and read those sentences. After about three minutes of time to discuss those sentences, the process repeats until all return to their own desks.

Once students are back to their small groups, they write a group gist statement based on the sentences. After they read, they return to their predictions to consider what the sentences meant in the text.

I first saw this strategy while I was working with the writing project at the University of California, Santa Barbara. Sue Perona explained the scaffold and said she called it Tea Party because students were up and talking with one another, much like one would do at a party. "Why Tea Party?" I asked. She explained she was sure her principal would not approve of Cocktail Party.

This was before the Tea Party became a political party. More recently, one high school student told me, "I don't like politics, so I'm not doing this." I told him the activity now had a new name: Do What You Have Been Asked to Do. He laughed and said he preferred the other name.

👥 Step Inside a Classroom

I was teaching an eighth-grade class. We were about to read a poem titled "Grandmother Grace" by Ronald Wallace (1983). I distributed an index card to each of the thirty-three students. Each card had one phrase on it. I had chosen fifteen different sentences or phrases; some were repeated three times and a couple were repeated only twice (see Figure 7.8). After giving each student a card, I asked everyone to move about the room, sharing their cards with one another. Their goal was to hear enough cards that they could eventually write a prediction about the text.

You can find this poem in Appendix H on page 352.

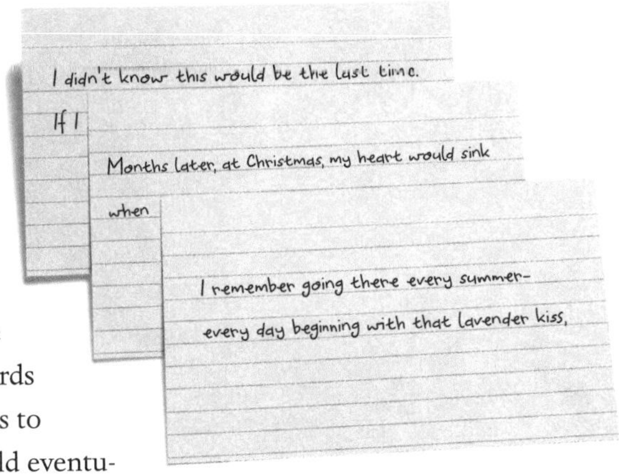

I didn't know this would be the last time.

If I

Months later, at Christmas, my heart would sink

when

I remember going there every summer—
every day beginning with that lavender kiss,

Figure 7.8
Sentences and Phrases from the Poem "Grandmother Grace" on Index Cards

Once students returned to their small groups, they began discussing the cards:

Student 1: This one, this makes me think of my grandmother—see, "spit-moistened hankies." That just sounds like a grandmother. And my grandmother, she's always trying to clean up my little sister's face by spitting on a napkin and cleaning her up. How gross.

Student 2: That is, like, so unhygienic. I mean, spit. Gross.

Student 3: Yeah, but old people do it all the time. So maybe he's with his grandmother and she keeps trying to kiss him and clean him up and stuff?

Student 1: I think he's sad.

Student 2: Why?

Student 3: See here, see it says, "I didn't know this would be the last time." I think she died and now he misses her.

Student 2: So, like, at first he didn't want to kiss her, but then she died and now he feels really bad because he didn't kiss her. Yeah.

This student is using prior knowledge to make connections.

Notice this student's direct use of the text to help make an inference.

With little information from the index cards, this student has accurately linked causes and effects and created a sequence of events.

One Important Question

After students have read the text, ask them which one sentence from all the cards most helped them make an accurate prediction. If their gist statement was far from the text, have them look at the text and choose a sentence that would have helped them make a more accurate prediction. In either situation, you are giving students a chance to reread and a chance to explain their thinking. Figure 7.9 shows one group's gist statement.

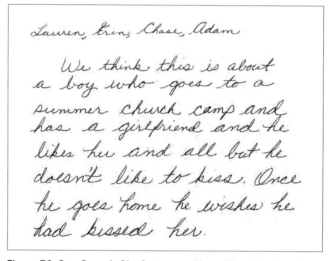

Figure 7.9 One Group's Gist Statement About "Grandmother Grace"

Knowledge Rating Charts and Thematic Clusters

Both Knowledge Rating Charts (Blachowicz 1986) and Thematic Clusters (Tinkham 1997) offer students the opportunity to consider what they know about individual words or the topic or theme before they read. This information, in turn, helps you decide where to focus your prereading vocabulary instruction.

When using a rating chart, students judge their knowledge of a word along a continuum from "I've never heard the word" to "I know it and use it all the time" or other descriptions you prefer. Thematic Clusters allow students to think about a topic or theme and then consider what they know about that topic and cluster topic-related words around categories. Students can use these scaffolds just as easily as they read and after they have completed studying a unit.

 ## Step Inside a Classroom

In a sixth-grade science class, the students were beginning a unit on the Milky Way. First, the teacher wanted to see what students more generally knew about the Milky Way. She gave each small group of two to three students a piece of chart paper and had them create categories (see Figure 7.10). They added information for each section. This information was based solely on their prior knowledge; there was no searching the internet for information. As each group shared their chart paper, the teacher could determine what most of them knew and she could determine concepts that no one mentioned.

Then the teacher had individual students complete a Knowledge Rating Chart for terms they would be reading; a completed chart is shown in Figure 7.11 (see page 100; see Appendix I for a blank template). This self-assessment helped students identify their depth of knowledge for key vocabulary.

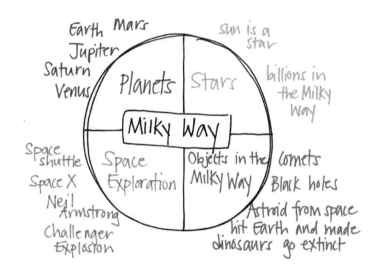

Figure 7.10 One Group's Thematic Cluster for the Milky Way

One Important Question

When using either of these scaffolds, remember to ask students how the prereading focus on the topic or individual words affected their thinking. You will hear some students respond, "It showed me which words I thought I knew but didn't." You'll also hear some say, "I don't know." Let's take that as an honest assessment and not a dismissal of your question. Point out something for them: "I see that you recognized that you didn't know what a corona is. I like how you realized that. What about now, after you've read this section? What's your understanding now?" When students default to "I don't know," we need to step in and help them discover they do know something. You are building their confidence and that's important. You can't improve competence without improving confidence.

Knowledge Rating Chart

How Well Do I know These Words?

Vocabulary Word	I have never heard this!	I have heard it but couldn't explain it. (Describe where you have heard it.)	I have an idea what it means. (Explain what you think it might mean.)	I know what this means and could explain it. (Provide your explanation.)
1. Comet			It's a big rock with a tail in space.	
2. galaxy			This is space.	
3. solar system			One part of the galaxy is a solar system.	
4. revolve				To go around something
5. orbit			When something goes around something	
6. black hole		X		
7. corona	X			

As you are selecting words for your rating chart, be sure to include a few terms that you expect students will know. They should write what they do understand in the correct area.

Figure 7.11 After completing their Thematic Cluster charts in small groups, students completed Knowledge Rating Charts on their own. Be sure students complete this chart again after they read. See Appendix I for a blank template.

Dear George,

   I was always so impressed at how well you listened to what I said about stories before we read them. Then, I heard you tell someone in the hall, "Yeah, if you listen to her before we read the story, then it's OK if you don't read it or don't really understand it. She's already told you all the important parts." So, while I was busy providing meaning for you, you were busy figuring out what you needed to remember so that you didn't actually have to comprehend anything on your own. We were quite a team, George, indeed.

Dear George,

You stood by my desk after class and said that your mom told you she would help you read the next few chapters of *Bridge to Terabithia* at home if I would give you a list of things you could do when you didn't understand something. "My mom wants to know how she should help me. I told her I'd get a list."

I didn't have a list. I would have given it to you if I'd had one, I promise. But I didn't have a list.

Clarifying Meaning

STUDENTS WHO STRUGGLE WITH READING OFTEN
fail to see reading as an active process. As Gene, a twelfth grader, said,
"What do you mean, active? You sit. You turn pages. What's active about
that?" I asked him what he thought skilled readers did while reading. He
responded, "Do? I don't know. They just read it. And then they answer all
the questions. That's what makes them good readers, because they can
answer the questions."

"So why do you think they can answer the questions?" I asked.

"I don't know. Why do some people win the lottery? Why are some
people always invited to the really popular parties? There are just some
things we aren't supposed to know the answer to. It's just the way
things are."

Gene's response, sadly, presents a worldview many accept: It's just the
way things are. In terms of reading, sometimes that attitude develops as
kids watch highly skilled students in class move (apparently) effortlessly
through a text. They see only the outward signs of comprehension—peers
correctly answering questions. What they don't observe are all the times
skilled readers reread a passage or a sentence, all the times they ask themselves, "What's going on here?" They don't hear that internal dialogue a
skilled reader has with the text or with herself while reading.

Three Readers Navigating the Same Text

I gave three eleventh graders a very difficult poem titled "Huswifery" by Edward Taylor (ca. 1685) and asked them to read it and then, one at a time, talk with me about what they did to make sense of this poem.

Huswifery

Make me, O Lord, thy Spinning Wheel complete.
    Thy Holy Word my Distaff make for me.
Make mine Affections thy Swift Flyers neat
    And make my Soul thy holy Spool to be.
    My Conversation make to be thy Reel
    And reel the yarn thereon spun of thy Wheel.

Make me thy Loom then, knit therein this Twine:
    And make thy Holy Spirit, Lord, wind quills:
Then weave the Web thyself. The Yarn is fine.
    Thine Ordinances make my Fulling Mills.
    Then dye the same in Heavenly Colors Choice,
All pinked with Varnished Flowers of Paradise.

Then clothe therewith mine Understanding, Will,
    Affections, Judgment, Conscience, Memory,
My Words, and Actions, that their shine may fill
    My ways with glory and thee glorify.
    Then mine apparel shall display before ye
That I am Clothed in Holy robes for glory.

                 —Edward Taylor

First, Karen told me this:

After I read it the first time, I thought, "Boy, I don't get it."
I decided to read it again, and this time much more slowly.
That second time, I found all these words I didn't know. I
decided to look at the footnotes to see what they could tell

This is a difficult poem for any reader. I don't often share this poem with students, but I wanted to see how different kids worked through a very complex text.

Karen is a highly skilled reader who enjoys reading. Notice that she immediately discusses what she did the second time that she read it that she did not do the first time.

She also used Sketch to Stretch (discussed on page 120) to help her visualize this poem. Her prior knowledge helped her create a sketch.

She concludes by explaining that she kept reminding herself to move to the bigger issue, "What is he really trying to say?" She recognizes that even if she doesn't understand every word, she might grasp the larger meaning.

*me. They explained some of the terms, especially the terms
about a spinning wheel. That helped a lot. Then, I decided
to sketch a spinning wheel and see if I could label the parts.
I sort of remembered what one looked like from the story
"Rumpelstiltskin." After I did that, I read it again. Some of
it made more sense, but I still kept asking myself, "What is
he really trying to say?" All the way through, I kept saying,
"How is this part related to that part?" It was a hard poem.*

Then Ama said,

*This poem makes you think all the way through it. I started
reading it and thought I'd better slow down. By the time I
got to the end of the fourth line, I knew I was lost. At first,
I went back and just started trying to reread each little part,
each word, until I figured it out. But then I decided I needed
a big picture of the whole thing, even if there was a lot I
didn't understand. So, I just read all the way through it, just
to get an idea of what it was about. Then I went back and
started rereading. I could see right away that a big part of my
problem was not knowing all the words. Some of the words
were spinning wheel terms, and I saw that those were defined
at the bottom of the page. But some of the words were just
regular words but used in a different way, like affection. And I
kept wondering why there were capital letters in the middle of
sentences. That bothered me a lot because I never could figure
it out. I finally made a list of what I didn't understand and
then tried to figure out each part.*

Ama is also a highly
skilled reader. Like Karen,
she uses rereading as a
strategy for improving
her comprehension. She
identifies two types of
vocabulary problems:
unknown words and
known words used
in unusual ways.

Ama's need to focus
on every detail that
confused her slowed
down her process.
Eventually, she grew tired
of trying to figure out
everything and stopped.

Finally, Michael shared his thoughts with me:

*This poem was too hard. It made no sense. None at all. I
read it, but it made no sense. I'm not sure what you want me
to say because I don't know what you mean—"What did you
do to make this make sense?" I read it. But it didn't make
any sense.*

Michael is a dedicated
student who wants to
please. That said, he
becomes frustrated quickly
and then gives up.

The next day, I shared Karen's and Ama's responses with Michael. He was amazed. "They did all that? You didn't say anything about doing that other stuff." Gene (from the opening paragraphs) and Michael are not alone in their misunderstanding of what it means to construct meaning.

I offer a closer examination of talk in Chapter 18.

To help them, we must allow the invisible process of comprehension to become visible. That suggests bringing more conversation into the classroom as students are reading. All the talk you can encourage, though, won't solve struggling readers' problems if the text is too hard.

When the Text Is Too Hard

Let's begin with some definitions. A text is considered to be a frustration-level text when the student reads it with less than 90 percent accuracy. Independent-level texts are those that students can read with more than 95 percent accuracy with no help. Instructional-level texts are those that students can read with 90 to 95 percent accuracy.

When the text is at the students' frustration level, then all that happens is that readers are, obviously, frustrated. In middle and high school settings, this is often the case when students are required to read textbooks. If a student reads at a third-grade level and the textbook is for eighth graders, we cannot expect that student to read that text independently. When this is the case, teachers often do one of the following:

1. Teachers do not expect students to read the textbook; instead, they tell students what they need to know.

2. If the print version of the textbook is available digitally, they encourage students to read the digital version. This allows students to click on unknown words to hear them pronounced and to hear (or read) a definition.

3. If an audio (text-to-speech) version of the textbook is available, teachers encourage students to listen while they follow along.

That first option might help students learn material, but students are learning without any reading. This option does not address the reading problems some students face and does not help them overcome difficulties.

Teachers often use the second option because digital environments are ubiquitous. However, in a meta-analysis of thirty-eight experimental studies that included a total of 171,055 participants, Delgado et al. (2018) found that "digital environments may not always be best suited to fostering deep comprehension and learning. The straightforward conclusion is that providing students with printed texts despite the appeal of computerized study environments might be an effective direction for improving comprehension outcomes" (33). Clinton's (2019) review of studies reached the same conclusion when considering expository texts: digital reading does not encourage the concentration that paper reading does and therefore may not be preferable over print texts.

The third option is perhaps the best option. Repeated studies show that audio texts improve comprehension of the text being listened to particularly when students follow along while listening. Winn et al. (2006), Moorman et al. (2010), and Stodden et al. (2012) found that less skilled readers comprehend texts better if they listen and follow along than if they only read the paper text. As your district considers materials for students, especially for content areas, confirming that the print content is available in audio form is more beneficial than making sure it is available digitally. This is particularly true if you work with readers who will find the grade-level version of the material too difficult for instructional- or independent-level reading.

Scaffolds for During Reading

When students are reading texts that offer a challenge, but not too much of a challenge, then you can support them with scaffolds that allow them to struggle successfully through the text (see Figure 8.1). If the text is at students' frustration level, but for some reason you still must share it with students, then the strategies presented next are helpful only if your students are listening to the text while reading it (see recommendation 3 from the previous page). These scaffolds help students clarify confusions, think about literary elements, and identify the author's purpose and bias.

The goal is to help students become independent readers. An independent reader is one who, in part, knows what to do when the text is

Don't confuse *independent readers* with an *independent reading level*. The former is a term that describes the mindset of a reader who can clarify confusion and uses evidence from a text to support their own thinking; the latter is a term meant to describe how many words students can decode accurately in a text with no support from others.

confusing. Dependent readers, by contrast, depend on you or someone else to solve their misunderstanding (or lack of any understanding). To move dependent readers toward independence, the first thing we must do is share with them a list of fix-up scaffolds they can use when something in the text has confused them. While such scaffolds might seem unneeded to you, remember how you felt when reading "She Unnames Them" (pages 45–48) or "Huswifery" (page 104)—a list of "try this" options might have been helpful.

DURING-READING SCAFFOLDS

If students need help with...	**Then** use...	**See** page...
Clarifying confusions (such as making an inference, understanding cause-and-effect relationships, following a sequence, or understanding relationships)	Fix-Up Anchor Charts	109
	Read, Rate, Reread	111
	Think-Aloud	118
	Sketch to Stretch	120
	Syntax Surgery	122
Character or plot development	Fiction Signposts	126–27
Seeing the relationship between conflict and character or plot development		
Understanding symbolism		
Identifying theme		
Recognizing author's purpose or bias	Nonfiction Signposts	128
Noting evidence (or lack of evidence) in a text		

Figure 8.1 During-Reading Scaffolds

Fix-Up Anchor Charts

One of the best scaffolds you can offer your struggling readers is a reminder of all the things they can try when the text is tough. You are trying to break their habits of giving up or turning to you. What's worked for me is to make an anchor chart that I refer to often (see Figure 8.2). Other teachers, though, have shared that their students benefit most from bookmarks the students make from card stock. These bookmarks list the fix-up strategies and students keep those bookmarks near as they read.

Early in the school year, you might have only two fix-up strategies on your list: *reread* and *read confusing parts aloud*. I like to start the list with "Read a portion aloud" and "Ask myself what was confusing." Then I add "Remember to reread a section." From there, we'll add "Talk with a friend," "Look up a word," "Study the pictures and charts," "Read on and then reread." As the year progresses, you can add specific scaffolds that you have taught students: Somebody Wanted But So (see page 137), Sketch to Stretch (see page 120), and Signal Words (see page 60).

When students discover something particular that works for them, let them add that to their own charts or bookmarks. I had one student who discovered that a bookmark placed under each sentence as he read helped him keep his focus. That was a great fix-up strategy for him. Another once mentioned, "I left my phone in my mom's car, and so while I was doing my homework, I wasn't texting anyone, and I understood everything so much faster. I hate to say it, but a fix-up strategy for me might be to stop texting while reading." A list of fix-up strategies is not static and is best when students help create it.

Figure 8.2 Fix-Up Practices Anchor Chart

👥 Step Inside a Classroom

I agreed to provide a professional development workshop for ELA teachers at a ninth-grade campus the week before school began. I'm usually hesitant to do this work that critical week because I think teachers would prefer to be in their classrooms doing what they need to be doing to get ready for students. The principal assured me that teachers would attend only if they wanted to attend, and she promised that this request came from teachers. So, there I was, in a San Antonio area school on August 14.

It was a great day of learning for me and hopefully for teachers. The principal had told the truth: teachers attended my session only if they wanted to attend and several teachers had been with me in other workshops and were excited to learn more. We were a group of eleven and eventually left the library, our meeting space, to instead visit their classrooms. One teacher was excited to show everyone the fix-up chart she had made over the summer. It was big enough that students could read it easily from any place in the room. It had ten "Try This!" practices that students could use immediately without instruction from the teacher. And, it was colorful.

After we all complimented her work, I asked her if she would be willing to take it down so that it was not up when students arrived. I suggested that once her students had been in class for a couple of days that she do some brainstorming with her them about what might be helpful to do when the text is tough. From that list, I explained, she could then turn to her completed chart, perhaps adding anything else students suggested. I wanted the chart to move from being part of her classroom decorations to a critical instructional tool.

She held her ground and promised that she was sure her students would notice it and use it. She promised she would point it out to them. A few weeks later, she called, laughing, and said that when she asked her second period students how often they used the fix-up chart, most responded, "What chart?" When she pointed it out, one student responded, "Oh yeah. I really love the purple marker you used." She told me that the next week she and her students created a fix-up list together. Yes, that meant she created a list with each class. Then, she combined the lists and made only one chart for her room, explaining to students that suggestions from first period class were written in one marker color and suggestions from another class were written in another color marker.

I don't have a photo of her chart, but I did jot down her ideas. Her Try This! list included reread, read on, read aloud, underline confusing parts and figure out why you are confused, talk with a friend, draw a picture, look up hard words, study examples and charts, think about what you already know, think about the title/chapter title/section title.

Anchor charts help anchor learning; they give students a place to look and something to think about or consider when they need help. They are most effective when they are created with students.

One Important Question

I try to keep the list of suggestions I offer to students short. Ten suggestions are enough. And that might be too many for some of your students. For students who need help with focus, create a list with them that has only three to five ideas. Start the work by asking, "What helps you the most when you are confused?" It's OK if some students keep returning to the same fix-up suggestions. The point is not to have a lot of tools in the toolbox; the point is for students to know how to use the tools they have.

> *"The point is not to have a lot of tools in the toolbox; the point is for students to know how to use the tools they have."*

Read, Rate, Reread

Millis and King (2010) found that rereading passages helped students understand expository texts, especially to clarify connections; Anderson (1980), Barnett and Seefeldt (1989), and Garner and Reis (1981) reported that repeated readings improved comprehension of texts; Rawson, Dunlosky, and Thiede (2000) concluded that repeated reading improved metacomprehension. Some have found this is because working memory improves; other studies show it is because repeated reading improves access of long-term memory; and some have shown this is because concentration improves with each rereading. Though the readings might vary, the outcome does not: repeated reading helps us clarify something we initially did not understand.

More recent research (Callender and Mcdaniel 2009), however, points out that for less skilled readers, repeated reading of a passage of an academic text is more helpful when the rereading does not occur immediately after the first read. For instance, rereading a passage about volcanoes on Monday and then on Tuesday is more beneficial than reading the passage twice, the second reading happening immediately after the first, unless that rereading is to clarify a specific confusion the student has identified. Separating the readings by a metacognitive task (jotting notes, identifying confusions, thinking about ways to solve that confusion, sketching a scene) improves

While rereading is a very helpful strategy for clarifying confusion, occasionally it is helpful to read on. If students tell you that after rereading they still can't figure something out, encourage them to read on—no more than a couple of pages—to see if that helps.

the value of the second read. Struggling readers who immediately reread a text with no reflection do not benefit as much as skilled readers who immediately reread a text. Callender and Mcdaniel suggest that is because more skilled readers are doing metacognitive work as they read and less skilled readers are not.

Often, though, when I tell some students to reread something, they do not think "reading the same stuff again" does them any good. That is partly because they operate under the misconception that skilled readers read something once, read it somewhat effortlessly, and get it the first time, every time. Rereading doesn't look any different from reading, so struggling readers don't see how many times proficient readers pause, loop back a few sentences, reread up to a point, reflect, start over completely, and then perhaps proceed slowly. Moreover, as we discuss texts with students, we rarely bring up the issue of how often we reread, why we reread, how the rereading differs from the reading, or how we know what sections to reread. Therefore, less skilled readers don't hear teachers or other more skilled readers talk about the sentences, passages, or even chapters that they sometimes reread several times to construct meaning. We need to help these students understand that rereading is something that skilled readers do and that it is an important way to clarify confusion.

To help them understand the value of rereading, take students through a Read, Rate, Reread exercise early in the school year as discussed next.

▲▲▲ Step Inside a Classroom

I often use "Sonrisas" with high school students and Langston Hughes' "Mother to Son" with middle school students. If needed, you can read these aloud as students follow along. Whatever you use, keep it short and make sure that it is not too complex.

Read, Rate, Reread is an exercise you can use to show students how rereading can change their understanding of a text. In a high school class I visited, the teacher distributed "Sonrisas," a poem by Pat Mora (1966; see Figure 8.3) and told students to read it three times and each time to rate their understanding on a scale of 1 to 6. If they didn't understand it at all, they were to rate their understanding as a 1, and if they could write the SparkNotes for the text, they were to give themselves a 6. Each time they read the poem, they were to rate their understanding.

After students had finished their third reading of the poem, the teacher asked students to raise their hand if their score had gone up after any of their readings. All students raised their hands. He then asked why they thought each reading improved their comprehension.

Directions: Read the following poem three times. After each reading, in the space under the poem, rate your understanding on a scale of 1 to 6, with 1 being low and 6 being high.

Sonrisas

I live in a doorway
between two rooms, I hear
quiet clicks, cups of black
coffee, *click, click* like facts
    budgets, tenure, curriculum
from careful women in crisp beige
suits, quick beige smiles
that seldom sneak into their eyes.

I peek
in the other room senoras
in faded dresses stir sweet
milk coffee, laughter whirls
with steam from fresh tamales
    sh, sh, mucho ruido,
they scold one another,
press their lips, trap smiles
in their dark, Mexican eyes.

—*Pat Mora*

Rate Your Understanding

First-read rating: _____

Second-read rating: _____

Third-read rating: _____

Figure 8.3 Read, Rate, Reread for "Sonrisas"

The students who struggle with comprehension said their numbers shot up from (for example) 1 to 4 to 6. More skilled readers said they moved from a 2 to a 1 to a 3 or 4. In other words, a little bit of improvement meant more to less skilled readers than it meant to more skilled readers. Expect that to happen and reassure all students that improvement is improvement. The point isn't to get to a 6. The point is to ask yourself why rereading changed your understanding.

At first, students offered an expected explanation: "Because I reread it." The teacher rephrased his question: "What happened the second or third time you read the poem that did not happen the first time you read it?" Once he worded the question that way, then answers were more specific. Figure 8.4 illustrates one student's explanation for his increasing score.

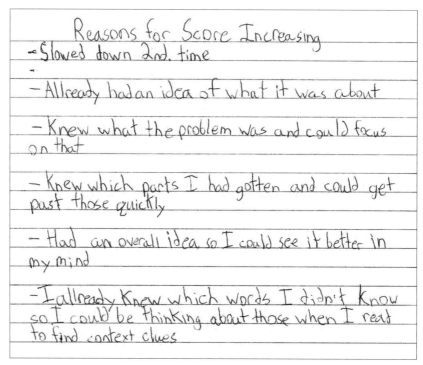

Reasons for Score Increasing
- Slowed down 2nd. time
- Allready had an idea of what it was about
- Knew what the problem was and could focus on that
- Knew which parts I had gotten and could get past those quickly
- Had an overall idea so I could see it better in my mind
- I allready knew which words I didn't know so I could be thinking about those when I read to find context clues

Figure 8.4 One Student's Explanation of Why Rereading Improved His Comprehension of a Text

? One Important Question

I propose that each time students reread, they revise their understanding of the text. The first read of a story, a chapter, a poem, a novel, a web page, a letter, an editorial cartoon—any sort of text—yields the first draft of understanding. Readers revise that draft through every rereading. That process of reading, revising, reading, revising leads me to suggest that the reading process is more like the writing process than we might have realized. For instance, both reading and writing depend upon revision. We've all seen enough student writing to know that at some point the revision of the writing begins to have a reverse effect; the revision, rather than making the writing better, makes it worse. "Stop!" we cry out. "Use the previous revision."

"The first read of a story, a chapter, a poem, a novel, a web page, a letter, an editorial cartoon—any sort of text—yields the first draft of understanding. Readers revise that draft through every rereading."

But with reading, every revision means an additional layer or dimension of understanding, whether that is another question, new connections, a sudden clarification, or better understanding of one particular word. Viewing the act of reading as revision reminds students that meaning emerges or is clarified with subsequent rereadings. This is especially true when students revisit books they have read.

Viewing the act of reading as revision reminds students that meaning emerges or is clarified with subsequent rereadings.

We know that young children want to hear the same book repeatedly. We all enjoy hearing the same song each time it comes up on our playlist. Many people want to watch a favorite movie from time to time. Art lovers like to sit in front of their favorite painting on any occasion. Why not let that seventh grader reread a favorite book for a book report? If your response is that students won't actually reread the book, then the problem is with the assignment, not the book. If students do reread a book for an assignment, ask them to discuss what they noticed in this reading that they had not noticed in a previous reading.

In a Houston-area middle school, one history teacher agreed to try an experiment with me. They were studying the Civil War, so he gave students a copy of a Before, During, and After Reading sheet I wanted to see students use (see Figure 8.5; see Appendix J for a blank template). Then, he gave each student a copy of the Gettysburg Address. On September 12 (see student's second column), he read the speech aloud and asked students to respond to one of the prompts at the top of column 2. This particular student numbered the prompts in column 2 and then provided an answer for each prompt:

1. All of it.

2. Nothing.

3. It was short so I thought it would be easy.

4. What does it mean?

As you study the remainder of column 2, you'll see that the students then read this on their own five additional times. Each time, students recorded thoughts, and you can see that each time he read the speech, this student understood more. He moved from wondering if this is the same Civil War they were discussing in his class (yes) to wondering if we are all equal.

Name konney Selection the Gettsburg Address pages ________

What the text tells me *before* I read	My thoughts and questions *as* I read	My ideas *after* I read
❑ Who is the author? What do I know about this author? ❑ When was it written? Is that important? ❑ What is the title? What does that suggest? ❑ Are their chapter titles? ❑ Is there vocabulary I need to know before I read?	1 o What parts are confusing? 2 o What parts remind me of another text or something in my own life? 3 o What parts surprised me? 4 o What questions do I have?	o My SWBS statement(s) o What do I think about what I just read? o What do I think the author was trying to say? o The most interesting part was…? o I'm still confused about…. o The names/dates/events I most need to remember are…
→ Abraham Lincoln → When he was president → ?	1 All of it 2. Nothing 3. It is short so I thought it would be easy 4. what does it mean? 9-12 Is this the Civil war from history class? 9-14 Are they at a field? Is it a centery? Does this mean they made a nation? Is it US? 9-16 Is this a speech? It sounds like a speech? It says we won't rember what is said hear but we do. Why? 9-19 So, he's saying that it was made, that settled were all are equal but the Civil war was over not being. Scare lee? 9-20 So we have to rember the reson we had the war or they will died in vane. 9-22	S The fathers → W the country to be freed equal → B it wasn't → S there was the Civil War A. Lincoln → and the people to rember all that died → he wrote this speech and it is very good I think Lincoln was saying we had all ready forgoten why we got made as a contry so we had a war and we can't forgot agin. Most intresting → last line
Vocabulary	score? proposition consecrate	

Figure 8.5 Before, During, and After Reading Student Think Sheet. See Appendix J for a blank template.
(The SWBS [Somebody Wanted But So] strategy mentioned in the third column is discussed on page 137.)

What this sheet does not capture is the conversation students had after reading this six times. All said that they liked getting to think about something for more than one day, and as one student explained, "Every day at school, you are always on a new page or learning something new. It is always hurry, hurry, hurry. I liked that with this, I got to keep thinking about something. And look at what I figured out. I did pretty good."

You are often so rushed to make sure you cover all that benchmarks and standards and progress markers that time becomes a precious commodity. What if many of the struggles our students faced could be solved by simply slowing down, giving them time to figure things out, letting them linger over words and thoughts for more than one class period? What if our best strategy were to do less?

When you are concluding your discussion about the power of rereading, be sure to ask one final question: "When should you reread?" Students discussed this in small groups and then created personal reasons for rereading that they kept in their reading notebooks. In Figure 8.6 you'll see one student's final list of when to reread.

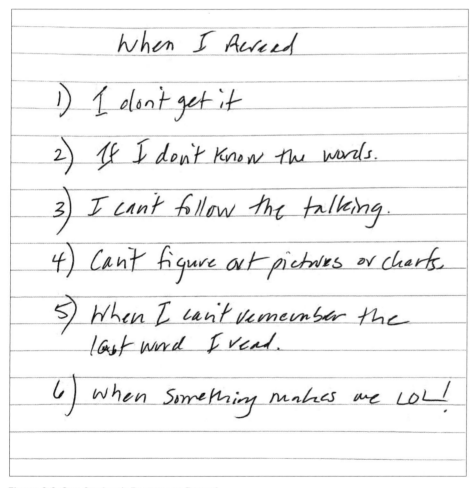

When I Reread

1) I don't get it

2) If I don't know the words.

3) I cant follow the talking.

4) Cant figure out pictures or charts.

5) When I cant remember the last word I read.

6) when something makes me LOL!

Figure 8.6 One Student's Reasons to Reread

Think-Aloud

The Think-Aloud strategy (Davey 1983; Olshavsky 1976–77) helps readers think about how they make meaning. As you model a Think-Aloud, you are showing students how you think about a text. Your language illustrates how you might

- Predict ("I think that . . .")
- Visualize ("This passage helps me imagine that . . .")
- Make comparisons ("This reminds me of . . .")
- Monitor understanding ("This part was confusing because . . .")

A Think-Aloud is different from an explanation. In a ninth-grade class studying the poem "Sonrisas," the teacher explained one part of the poem:

> *The poet isn't saying that someone literally lives in a doorway. The first stanza is about the person looking at women in suits doing one type of work, and the second stanza is about the person looking at women in faded dresses, trying not to laugh as they work.*

That was not a Think-Aloud; that was an explanation. The teacher paraphrased the poem. Let's look at a Think-Aloud for the same poem:

First, the teacher offers a generalizable lesson: visualizing is important and thinking about the setting helps you visualize.

> *When I read, I visualize what is happening. That's easier to do if the author—in this case a poet—gives me information about the setting. Visualizing the setting is always important. This poem tells me that someone is in a doorway. That's a part of the setting. And the author tells me what the person standing in the doorway hears: "click, click." Sounds are part of the setting. The person hears people saying, "sh, sh," to each other. Thinking about what's happening in both rooms helps me make a comparison. When authors show us differences, I know I need to pay attention to those differences.*

And now the teacher moves into another generalizable lesson.

This is a more effective Think-Aloud because the teacher used generalizable language. He told kids that visualizing the setting is important and then moved to text-specific language as he gave examples from the poem. Then he went on to explain that it is important to pay attention to comparisons, another generalizable lesson. Generalizable lessons are what students learn to use as they read any text. Text-specific examples show them how that lesson appears in that one text.

👥 Step Inside a Classroom

I sat at the back of the classroom, watching a teacher talk with one student about a book the teacher and I had both recently read, *Angel of Greenwood* (Pink 2021). The teacher had added it to her classroom library and one student had chosen to read it. The student approached the teacher with a question:

Student: This part was confusing.

Teacher: What does it say?

Student 1:   "After three hours sitting cross-legged in the tight circle of seven girls, Angel and Isaiah had only covered the first few pages of *The Secret Garden*. They could barely get through a paragraph without the girls asking the meaning of new words or even deeper questions about wealth and privilege" [193].

Teacher: OK. What's your confusion?

Student: I thought Isaiah was a guy. But it says the girls can't get through a paragraph. So, is Isaiah a girl?

> Notice that the teacher does not immediately explain the sentence. She asks the student to identify her confusion

Teacher: Remember the Think-Aloud I did at the beginning of class? What did I say was helpful to do if you get confused?

Student: Like, try to see it?

> Now the teacher offers the student something she can do on her own to clarify the confusion.

Teacher: That's right. If you visualize the setting, that might help you understand the text.

Student: Yeah. [*Student studies the text.*] So, Angela and Isaiah are in a circle. And I guess the girls are sitting in the circle with them. It says it is a tight circle. So, it's, like, small? They are all close together? And there's, what, a book? *The Secret Garden*. So, wait! So, Angela and Isaiah are reading the book to the girls. Oh! And the girls are asking questions. Not Isaiah. Now I get it.

> As this student tried to visualize the scene, she was in fact rereading. Did visualizing improve her comprehension, or did rereading help? Or was it visualizing while rereading? I'm not sure. But the student now has a strategy to use when she's stuck because the teacher did not immediately offer an explanation.

Teacher:	That's right. What did you do to figure that out?
Student:	I had to, like, really *see* the scene. Then I could understand it.

One Important Question

A Think-Aloud is not an oral explanation. It is a step-by-step analysis of what you noticed in the text that helped you visualize, connect, compare, or any of the other things skilled readers do as they read. To help students transfer Think-Alouds you model to texts they read, be sure to end each Think-Aloud with one final question: "What did you hear me share that you could do as you read?" If students aren't sure (and some won't be), remind them of the lesson you want them to generalize to other texts, for instance, "When I'm confused, I pause to visualize the text. This means I'm looking at where characters are, what they are doing, what they see and hear. Visualizing can help me understand what is happening." You must emphasize the generalizable lesson or your Think-Aloud won't help students as they read on their own.

Sketch to Stretch

Sketch to Stretch (Harste, Short, and Burke 1988) is a scaffold that helps readers visualize what they are reading. Students read a passage and then pause to sketch what they see in their mind's eye. Giving students time to share their sketches with others allows them to expand their thinking as they return to the text to explain their drawing. Sketch to Stretch is based on the research of transmediation.

Transmediation is the translation of content from one medium to another. Such an activity allows students time to focus their concentration on a specific scene or passage and reflect on meaning. Sketch to Stretch allows students to move content from words to images. While Harste, Short, and Burke suggested using Sketch to Stretch as an after-reading activity to offer a more metaphorical understanding of content, I see more benefit in using it during reading to encourage students to clarify confusion. When they use it during reading, students create literal representations of the text. They go directly into the text to use the author's words as evidence for their drawings.

Step Inside a Classroom

In a high school science class, students were reading about the relationship between pollution and the decline of ocean life. From the book *World Without Fish* by Mark Kurlansky (2011), they read about the growth of healthy coral reefs. Many of the students did not understand how coral reefs were formed. The teacher asked students to pair up and find a passage within a particular chapter that best helped them understand how coral reefs develop and grow.

One group chose this passage:

> *When the polyps attach themselves to rocks on the sea floor, they reproduce by dividing and growing, connecting to one another to create a colony that acts as a single organism. As colonies grow over hundreds and thousands of years, they join with other colonies and become reefs. (15)*

Math teachers have long used Sketch to Stretch, though they may not have called it that. Asking students to create a diagram that illustrates the word problem is Sketch to Stretch.

A look at Figure 8.7 on the following page (see Appendix K for a blank template) reveals that their sketch is not detailed. Squiggly circles represent the sea polyps that attach to rocks on the sea floor to create coral colonies. A vertical line through the polyps represents division. A timeline marked "100s years" shows the colony's growth to make a reef.

Though their work lacked detail, one student explained, "Drawing it and labeling stuff helps me see it." When students first begin using this scaffold, you need to remind them to pause and sketch what they are having trouble visualizing. The more they use this scaffold, the more likely they are to use it on their own as they need it. After several months of using Sketch to Stretch, on student told me, "I don't need paper anymore. I can sketch it in my mind."

❓ One Important Question

When kids are confused, it might seem illogical to tell them to sketch what they don't understand. And that would be illogical if we did not demand they use the text to support their drawing. It is important, therefore, to begin by asking students to underline the lines that are most confusing. You want to narrow their focus. But end your conversation with students by asking students how visualizing helps them understand the text. Students

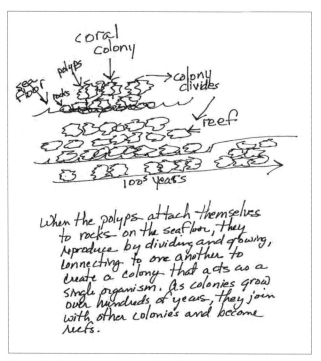

Figure 8.7 Sketch to Stretch with a Nonfiction Passage. See Appendix K for a blank template.

who struggle with comprehension need to think about how a strategy helped them think about the text; otherwise, using the strategy will not become a purposeful part of their reading process.

Syntax Surgery

Syntax Surgery (Herrell 2000) was initially used as a way to help English language learners understand the English syntax. Teachers would write a sentence on a sentence strip and cut it up (thus the name Syntax *Surgery*) and then students would put it back into order. This does help students think about word order and that is very helpful for English language learners.

I like expanding the use of Syntax Surgery and eliminating the need to cut up sentences. Choose a passage, put it on your whiteboard, and then underline phrases, circle words, and draw arrows from one phrase to another to show how parts of a passage are related. See Figure 8.8 for examples of several types of Syntax Surgery.

Connections to Make with Syntax Surgery

Problem Students Encounter

Don't see the antecedent

The problem: Often, inattentive readers will think the antecedent for a pronoun is the nearest noun. That's not always true.

Other times, these readers see pronouns that are similar (*they, them, theirs*) and think they all refer to the same noun.

Don't recognize synonyms or similar terms

This is a typical problem with social studies texts as authors describe a single event, or a group of people, or a landmass with synonyms or similar terms.

Don't recognize context clues

We find that trying to define an unknown word with context clues is sometimes easier if students first do Sketch to Stretch (see page 120) and then from their sketch, draw lines that connect words.

Don't infer omitted words

Authors will omit words that are implied by the context. Struggling readers do not realize that all they need to do is insert the words as they read.

Don't use signal words to help with meaning

Noticing what signal words actually signal is a critical context clue. Too often we forget that explicitly showing students how signal words work solves many comprehension problems. Here are a few types of signal words you should teach:

Restatement signal words

Illustration signal words

Category signal words

Don't understand role of dashes, commas, parentheses, or colons

Often terms are defined, illustrated, or expanded in information that is found between dashes, commas, or parentheses or after a colon. While highly skilled readers often seem to intuit what these punctuation marks signal, less skilled readers benefit from our showing (not telling) them how they work.

NOTE: These same symbols work differently in math, and students need to be taught that. A dash in a math problem is a minus sign. Parentheses suggest which operation occurs first.

Solving the Problem

A geometric proof is a step-by-step explanation that uses definitions, axioms, postulates, and previously proved theorems to draw a conclusion about a geometric statement. There are two of them: direct and indirect.

The platoon began marching south. They were tired and their backs hurt. But their orders were clear and they had been delivered with some urgency.

The Americans who remained loyal to the British Crown were often called Tories. These Loyalists stood in opposition to those who wanted independence from England. Seen as "royalists," the King's Men fought against the Patriots, even though they lived alongside them.

The big rock rose straight up from the middle of the fastflowing water. The boaters had to paddle hard to one side to avoid hitting the monolith.

Twelve men volunteered for the mission. Several were chosen.

men

An isthmus is also called a peninsula.

By way of demonstration, the teacher circled all the pronouns.

There were several species of dogs: collies, labs, poodles, and Rhodesian ridgebacks.

clue!

Dactylonomy, counting on one's fingers, is what young children might resort to if they forget their math facts.

[We could have as easily put dashes or parentheses around "counting on one's fingers."]

Two outcomes were critical, food shortage and water shortage.

Figure 8.8 Common Types of Connections to Make with Syntax Surgery

👥 Step Inside a Classroom

More and more, it is possible for students to write in their textbooks or their digital texts. This certainly makes Syntax Surgery something students can use on their own.

You will model Syntax Surgery by letting students see you analyze a passage that you are projecting so all can see it. You can move students from the "I do" to the "we do" phase of instruction by then distributing several short passages, double-spaced, that you want them to annotate through their own surgery.

In Figure 8.9 you can see how a student used Syntax Surgery to help her think through the poem "Sonrisas" by Pat Mora (1966). Earlier in the year, when using Syntax Surgery, this same student often drew intricate doodles on the side of her paper. The teacher, though, persisted in modeling connections she made and eventually this student had enough confidence to move from doodling to connecting.

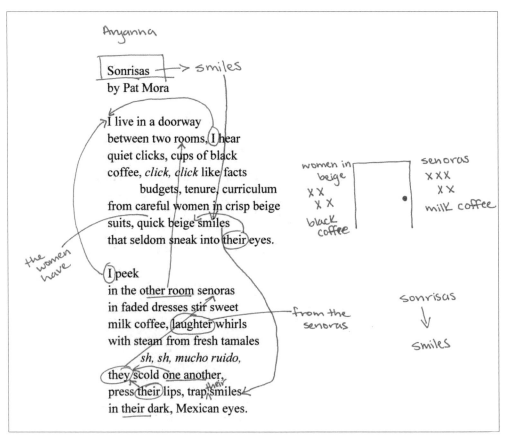

Figure 8.9 A Student's Syntax Surgery for a Passage from "Sonrisas"

Syntax Surgery can be a valuable tool for clarifying confusion *if* you model this throughout the year and with different types of texts. Line breaks and punctuation are particularly important in poetry, so don't forget to use Syntax Surgery with poetry. As students use this, remember to ask them, "What did this help you understand?" Students who expect that meaning arrives in their mind with no work—who think it's that brass ring to be grabbed—need to be reminded that meaning making is hard work. Syntax Surgery makes that work visible.

 ## One Important Question

Early in a school year, you will be the person modeling syntax surgery for students. After you have modeled something, remind students to make their own annotations that indicate how they are analyzing a passage. They need to practice what you have modeled.

As students work on a passage, always remember to ask, "What have you noticed as you have studied how words are connected [for example, nouns to pronouns] that has helped you understand the text better?" This question encourages their executive function thinking.

Notice and Note Signposts

When reading novels, students work to identify the author's theme. When reading expository texts, students should recognize the author's purpose or bias. Bob Probst and I have written extensively about a scaffold we developed that helps students accomplish both of those objectives, first in *Notice and Note: Strategies for Close Reading* (2013) and then in *Reading Nonfiction: Stances, Signposts, and Strategies* (2016). Both books discuss, in detail, how to teach students to notice features in a text. We call those features *signposts*. Recognizing these signposts helps students read closely to either understand theme or recognize author's purpose or bias. We teach six literary signposts in *Notice and Note* and five expository signposts in *Reading Nonfiction*.

There are six signposts that help students think carefully about literary elements (see Figure 8.10). The five signposts in Figure 8.11 help students think about author's purpose or bias as they read expository texts.

FICTION SIGNPOSTS

If you need to teach this literary element . . .	**Then** help students notice this signpost . . .	**By** using this teaching language . . .
Character development	Contrasts and Contradictions	When authors show you a character acting in a way that contrasts with how you would expect someone to act or that contradicts how that character has been acting, you know the author is showing you something important about that character. You'll want to pause and ask yourself, "Why would the character act this way?"
Plot development	Aha Moment	When a character realizes or finally understands something, then you want to pause because you know this realization means something. It might be showing you something about character development or a new direction of the plot. You'll want to ask yourself, "How might this change things?"
Internal conflict	Tough Questions	You know that when a character pauses to ask himself or a friend some really tough questions, then you are getting a glimpse of what's bothering him the most, and those questions often show you what the character will struggle with throughout the story. When you see these tough questions, stop and ask yourself, "What does this question make me wonder about?"
Theme	Words of the Wiser	When a wise character—who is often older than the main character—shares his or her understanding, insight, or advice on an issue or topic, stop and think about that. These insights or this advice usually reveals something important about the theme. Ask yourself, "What's the life lesson, and how might it affect the character?"

Figure 8.10 Fiction Signposts

continues

FICTION SIGNPOSTS

If you need to teach this literary element . . .	Then help students notice this signpost . . .	By using this teaching language . . .
Symbolism Plot development Character traits	Again and Again	When you see repetition in a novel, you can bet that it's important, but you might not know, right away, what it means. Repetition might give insight into the setting or a character or perhaps a symbol of some sort. You have to ask yourself, "Why does this keep happening again and again?"
Character development Plot development	Memory Moment	When we share a memory with someone, it's usually because that memory has something to do with what's happening at that moment; the memory of the past helps explain the present moment. So, when an author has a character pause to think about a memory or share a memory with someone, I know that the memory can tell me something about what's happening right now. That memory might give me insight into what bothers or motivates a character; it might help me understand something happening in the plot; it might even give me information about the theme. When you notice a Memory Moment, stop and ask yourself, "Why might this memory be important?"

Figure 8.10 Fiction Signposts, *continued*

NONFICTION SIGNPOSTS

If you need to teach this literary element . . .	**Then** help students notice this signpost . . .	**By** using this teaching language . . .
Determine main idea Recognize hyperbole Draw conclusions Recognize bias	Extreme and Absolute Language	When an author uses language such as *the worst, everyone knows, all must agree, without any doubt, all, none, never*, or *totally*, then you want to ask yourself why the author has chosen such extreme or absolute language. Why did the author say it that way?
Make cause-and-effect connections Make comparisons Infer author's purpose Draw conclusions Recognize bias	Contrasts and Contradictions	When the author shows you how things, people, or ideas contrast or contradict one another, or shows you something that contrasts or contradicts what you already know, you need to stop and ask yourself, "Why is this important?"
Draw conclusions Find facts Make comparisons Recognize bias	Numbers and Stats	When the author uses specific numbers or provides statistical information such as *twice as big* or *three times as fast*, then you need to stop and ask yourself, "Why did the author use these numbers and what do they help me see or wonder about?"
Determine point of view Make cause-and-effect connections Separate fact from opinion Recognize bias	Quoted Words	When an author chooses to quote someone, you need to ask yourself why the author quoted that person. And if the author doesn't tell you who is quoted but says things like, "Some scientists believe," or "Lots of people say," then you need to ask yourself why this author was so vague.
Identify unknown words Use context clues Recognize bias	Word Gaps	When the author chooses to use a word or phrase that you don't know, you need to ask yourself why they needed that particular word. Is it a technical word? Are there any clues in the passage that will help you figure it out? Does the author compare the unknown word to something (for example, a dagger is like a knife)?

Figure 8.11 Nonfiction Signposts

As you teach the signposts, you'll find it helpful to make anchor charts to display that explain each signpost (see Figures 8.12a and 8.12b), and you might want to distribute bookmarks that explain all the signposts, such as the ones shown in Figures 8.13 and 8.14 on the following page. This book is not meant to explain these signposts in detail as Bob and I have dedicated entire books to that purpose. Please turn to those books for detailed explanations and sample lessons.

Figure 8.12a and 8.12b Anchor Charts for the Fiction and Nonfiction Signposts Contrasts and Contradictions

Figure 8.13 Nonfiction Signposts Bookmark

Figure 8.14 Fiction Signposts Bookmark

Step Inside a Classroom

In a third-grade Solon, Ohio, classroom, one student explained how learning about the signposts helped her think about a text:

> *I like to read these books* [pointing to the cover of a series book] *and after I learned Again and Again, I saw that it said*

a lot that she liked to be "right smack dab in the middle of everything." When I kept seeing that, it made me think, "Hey, that's like her character trait, like she wants to be involved."

In Brent Gilson's seventh-grade classroom in Alberta, Canada, his students noticed all the signposts as they read the book *Wonder* by R. J. Palacio (2012). Together, students identified the literary signposts they noticed and explained why they were important (see Figure 8.15).

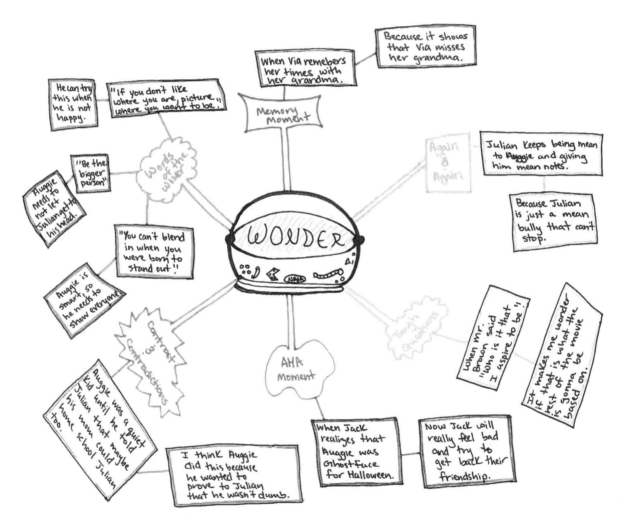

Figure 8.15 Student Analysis of *Wonder* Using Fiction Signposts

One Important Question

Students who keep the signposts in mind as they read find that this attention to the text does help them think closely and carefully about theme or author's purpose. Be careful not to turn this into a hunt. Don't ask students to "find" five Contrasts and Contradictions and three Aha Moments. Instead, encourage them to be aware, to think, and to notice the language that authors are using. And once students have noticed something, ask them that most general question: "What does that make you wonder about?"

What During-Reading Scaffolds Accomplish

All of the scaffolds mentioned here have one thing in common: they all focus students' attention on clarifying their nascent understandings. Often that is done through rereading; sometimes it is done though talk in collaboration with other students. And sometimes clarification comes as students are annotating the text. Rereading; talking; annotating: each requires giving students time to pause and think, or as Bob would say, "time to hesitate and hypothesize."

Dear George,

As your class finished reading *The Pigman*, I asked if John and Lorraine were responsible for Mr. Pignatti's death. Two students immediately started talking, each offering an opinion. I watched you stare at them. After class, you slowly gathered your books, appearing to want to ask me a question. "What's up, George?" I asked.

"How'd they know all that? I mean, this book didn't say whether or not they did it. How'd they know all that stuff to say?" You looked so bewildered.

"Well, George, they read it," I answered. "Did you read it?"

I watched you frown, resigned. "Yeah, but I must've read wrong. I never get the same stuff they get." I wish I had known what I know now, George. You could have answered that question, that one and many more.

Dear George,

The year I was in eighth grade, we read *A Tale of Two Cities*. I'll never forget that we had to draw a portrait of each character and answer twenty-five questions for each chapter. Each chapter. Twenty-five questions. Reading that book became a labor, a time of copying questions and then writing the shortest answers I could write.

Years later, I found myself teaching you, and one day I realized that I, too, had told you all to draw portraits of the main characters from the book we just finished. ("They love to draw, so they will have fun," I rationalized to myself.) Then I had you answer questions—not twenty-five, but probably too many. ("This will show me what they understand," I convinced myself.) You turned in your folder with all your work for this novel. No portraits. No answered questions. Just an empty folder.

"Where's your work, George?" I asked. You shrugged. "Did you do any of it?" I asked. You shrugged again. "Come on, George. Why didn't you do any of it?"

"It was stupid," you said.

Later, I told Anne what had happened. "So, was it stupid?" she asked. I shook my head no. "Why not?" she asked.

"Because his answers would have shown me what he understood about the story," I said.

"Really?" she responded, then asked, "Instead of asking George what he did understand, shouldn't you be helping him figure out how to understand?"

"We had already finished the story, Anne," I said. "I needed him to show me what he understood."

She peered at me over the tops of her glasses, her signature move when I obviously had more to consider. I borrowed your gesture and shrugged.

Extending Understanding

ANNE WANTED ME TO RECOGNIZE THAT EVEN though George had closed the book, his thinking about the book in many ways was only beginning. That first year of teaching, students shared what they had already comprehended by answering questions. Occasionally I had them do something "creative" such as design a better book jacket or provide a new ending to the story. Mostly, though, once students had completed the text, I considered comprehension to be the product of their reading. If I had viewed comprehension as a process, then I would have realized that the thinking students do could extend into this time called after reading. This is the time to entertain new thoughts, to revise understanding, to further connections.

Scaffolds for After Reading

This chapter, therefore, examines after-reading scaffolds that help students continue to think about what they have read. As you study these, you will recognize that all of these strategies could have gone into Chapter 8 with the discussion of during-reading scaffolds. At any point in reading a text, we pause, thus creating an after-reading moment. How did I decide which strategies to include in Chapter 8 and which ones to discuss here?

The scaffolds in the previous chapter focus on clarifying confusion or noticing something while reading. These scaffolds lean more toward doing something with the text students have read. Of course, during those "doing something" moments, confusion is clarified. Because comprehension is a process, delineations from one phase of the process to the next are blurred. This artificial division allows for parallelism in a table of contents (Before Reading, During Reading, After Reading) but you should not see them as strict recommendations on when to share something with your students. All the scaffolds presented here help students with a variety of skills, all overlapping. The chart in Figure 9.1 illustrates which skills a particular scaffold most supports.

AFTER-READING SCAFFOLDS

If students need help with . . .	Then use . . .	See page . . .
Summarizing Making cause-and-effect connections Recognizing conflict	Somebody Wanted But So (SWBS)	137
Sequencing	SWBS	138–39
	Genre Reformulation	141
	Retelling	145
Questioning the text	Three Big Questions	149
	Reciprocal Reading	149
Discussing character development	Semantic Differential Scales	153
	ABC Boxes	156
	Poster	153
Making an inference	It Says, I Say, And So	157
Making an inference Making connections Drawing conclusions	Book, Head, Heart (BHH)	160

Figure 9.1 After-Reading Scaffolds

Somebody Wanted But So

Summarizing a text appears overwhelming for many students. Some grow silent when asked to summarize while others restate everything in the story following the "and then this happened" structure. Somebody Wanted But So, or SWBS (MacOn, Bewell, and Vogt 1991), offers students a scaffold to guide their thinking about a summary. Primarily used for narrative texts—whether narrative fiction or narrative nonfiction—SWBS helps students focus on who the *somebody* is, what that somebody *wanted*, *but* what happened to keep something from happening, and *so*, finally, how everything worked out.

SWBS also moves students beyond summary writing. As students choose names for the "Somebody" column, they are really looking at characters and trying to decide which are the main characters. To fill in the "Wanted" column, they look at events of the plot and immediately talk about main ideas and details. When they move to the "But" column, they are examining conflict, and the "So" column moves them to resolution.

Sharing an anchor chart such as the one in Figure 9.2 helps students understand this scaffold.

Figure 9.2 Anchor Chart for Somebody Wanted But So

👥 Step Inside a Classroom

After reading "Thank You, M'am" by Langston Hughes, students worked in pairs to write SWBS statements for Roger and Mrs. Luella Bates Washington Jones, the two characters in this short story (see Figure 9.3; see Appendix L for a blank template). This class of seventh graders had struggled with writing summaries. After the teacher briefly explained the SWBS scaffold using the Humpty Dumpty example, students were willing to give this a try. She distributed the template and let them discuss:

Somebody Wanted But So

Name_____   Date_____

Text_____   Class_____

Somebody	Wanted	But	So
Roger	Wanted to steal the lady's purse to get money	But once she taught him a lesson he felt bad	So he was so shocked of all she did he could only say thank you.
The Lady	Wanted to go home after working hard all day	But a boy tried to steal her purse to get some money	So she took him to her home and fed him and gave him the money and taught him not to steal.

Figure 9.3 SWBS for "Thank You, M'am" by Seventh Graders. See Appendix L for a blank template.

Eric immediately sees that Shonda's first statement would leave them with an incomplete summary.

Shonda: I think it is *Roger wanted some shoes but he didn't have any money so he tried to steal some from the lady.*

Eric: Yeah, that could work, but then we would have to write more, like another SWBS, to explain the rest of what happened.

Shonda:	She said we could do that.	
Eric:	Yeah. But maybe we could just write it bigger, you know, like get the bigger point? Like, he wanted money, but the bigger thing was he started feeling bad when she was so nice to him.	Eric is figuring out the internal conflict Roger felt.
Shonda:	That's right. It said he didn't want her to not trust him. That seems like when he realized he wanted her to like him.	Compare Shonda's thinking here with her first statement. She's using the text for evidence and thinking about internal conflict. When she began, she offered an incomplete summary statement.
Eric:	So maybe he wanted to steal her purse for her money, but then she took him home and fed him and told him to wash up, and then he felt bad.	
Shonda:	Or just she taught him a lesson and he felt bad . . .	And now Shonda is helping Eric distill his language.
Eric:	That's good. [*Pause.*] And that, like, shocked him.	Eric and then Shonda both compliment each other and build on Eric's use of the word *shocked*.
Shonda:	I like that. That's real good. He was shocked. Like, why would she treat him so good? He was shocked so much that all he could say was "thank you."	

Students worked for about fifteen minutes, and then as a large group, they shared their statements. Some wrote very specific statements, such as "Roger wanted some blue suede shoes but didn't have any money so he tried to steal a purse from a lady when she was walking home." One group wrote, "Roger wanted to fit in but he wasn't really a thief so he won't forget the lesson Mrs. Luella Bates Washington Jones taught him." As students listened to each other's statements, they realized that "some of these [were] exactly what happened in the story and some [were] bigger, like the lesson you learn from the story." As you listen to what students say or read what they have written, you'll determine which students are thinking literally and which ones are thinking more abstractly.

The SWBS scaffold almost always encourages conversations about character differences and character motivations. It also helps students identify main ideas and details, recognize cause-and-effect relationships, make generalizations, identify character differences, and understand how shifting the point of view emphasizes different aspects of the story.

Students don't need to work in groups or use the template Shonda and Eric used. Figure 9.4 shows a student-created SWBS chart for several characters found in *The Crossover* by Kwame Alexander (2014).

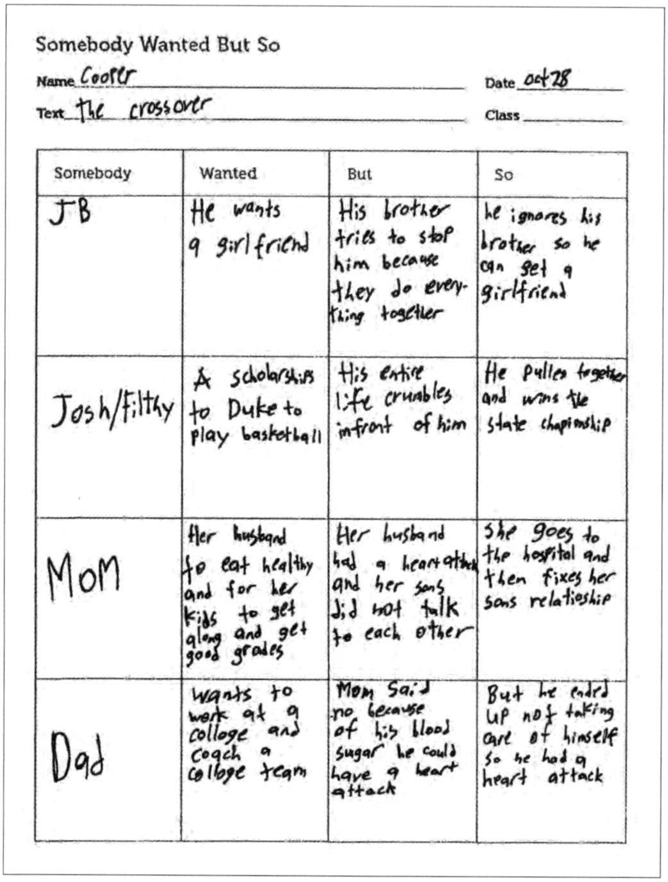

Somebody	Wanted	But	So
JB	He wants a girlfriend	His brother tries to stop him because they do everything together	he ignores his brother so he can get a girlfriend
Josh/Filthy	A scholarship to Duke to play basketball	His entire life crumbles infront of him	He pulles together and wins the state chapionship
Mom	Her husband to eat healthy and for her kids to get along and get good grades	Her husband had a heart attack and her sons did not talk to each other	She goes to the hospital and then fixes her sons relatieship
Dad	wants to work at a college and coach a college team	Mom said no because of his blood sugar he could have a heart attack	But he ended up not taking care of himself so he had a heart attack

Somebody Wanted But So

Name Cooper   Date Oct 28

Text The crossover   Class

Figure 9.4 Student-Created SWBS Chart for *The Crossover*

❓ One Important Question

After reading *The Giver*, a sixth grader wrote, "Jonas wanted to live in his community but it was a really bad place so he had to leave." He looked at his statement and said, "Boy, Lois Lowry is a great writer to have gotten a whole book from this one line."

When you use SWBS with long texts, you will want students to write statements at different points in the text. They can connect their statements with transition words such as *then, later, next, at the same time, however,* or *and.* Also, if you want to see if students understand which characters face which conflicts, on the SWBS template, you can complete the "But" column, and then let students complete the rest of the chart.

As students finish their discussion of SWBS, ask one final question: "How did the SWBS scaffold help you think about this text?" Expect your students to respond with comments such as "I thought more about how different characters wanted different things" or "It made me think about what the problem was" or "It helped me think about what happened" or "It was hard to get this whole book to one sentence, but it was fun, too." You ask this final question to help students realize that SWBS isn't something they did in class on a Wednesday; it's a scaffold they can use anytime to help them think about a text.

After several months of using SWBS, a ninth grader reported, "This is so weird. I got home and told my mom, 'I want to go outside, but I have homework so I'll have to stay inside.' My brain thinks in SWBS thoughts all the time now."

Genre Reformulation

Genre Reformulation, also called Text Reformulation or Story Recycling (Feathers 1993), is a strategy in which students transform a text from one genre to another. Whether students turn expository text into narratives, poems into newspaper articles, or short stories into patterned stories such as ABC books, reformulating texts encourages students to identify main ideas, cause-and-effect relationships, and themes while at the same time sequencing, generalizing, and making inferences.

Genre Reformulation is based on the research of transmediation, which is the same research that supports Sketch to Stretch (see page 120). When we take something in one form and turn it into another form, we tend to remember it better. I've also found that this particular scaffold is most valuable when used with expository texts (see Figure 9.5), though some students use it with narrative texts (see Figure 9.6). I offer students five pattern texts to use for their reformulations:

1. *If-Then Structures*: Use any of the books in the If You Give . . . series, by Laura Numeroff. This focuses students' attention on causal relationships.

2. *Repetitive Book Structures*: Use *Brown Bear, Brown Bear, What Do You See?* by Bill Martin Jr., as the example of a repetitive pattern. This focuses students' attention on sequencing.

3. *ABC Structures*: While you can bring in almost any ABC book, you can also simply show this pattern: *A is for _____ because _____.* This focuses students' attention on main ideas and details.

4. *Cumulative Text Structures*: "This Is the House That Jack Built" and *The Piñata That the Farm Maiden Hung*, by Samantha Vamos, offer examples

of cumulative texts. This focuses students' attention on several skills: sequencing, making causal relationships, and noticing main ideas and details. It is, as the name suggests, cumulative.

5. *Fortunately-Unfortunately Structures*: "Fortunately, I set my alarm clock last night. Unfortunately, I forgot to turn it on. Fortunately, my little brother woke me. Unfortunately, he used his new water pistol." These linked texts focus students' attention on cause and effect and sequencing.

ABC Reformulation

Silk Routes

Ancient Chinese trade route

Black Death was spread along this route

Carried goods and ideas between China and Rome

Diverse religions such as Buddhism and Christianity spread along it

Established during Han Dynasty

Fruits and furs were traded along this route

Gunpowder was sent along this route

Sand Routes

Ancient African trade route from Western Africa across Sahara all way to Mediterranean Sea

Beads, along with cloth, ivory, and slaves were traded along this route

Caravans with 1,000 to 10,000 camels carried the goods to be traded

Desert of the Sahara could not have been crossed without camels

Economy of Africa improved because of the trade across the Sahara

Forty days were needed to cross the Sahara on camels

Gold from mines of West Africa and traded made Ghana and Mali wealthy

Sea Routes

Ancient sea routes for trading from Alexandria and China

Boats carried spices, large goods, and ideas from East to the West

Chocolate and coffee also traded along these routes

Danger of rough seas made the merchants drive up prices of goods the boats carried

Europe and Indian trade route became important after Crusades cutting out the Arab merchants

Financial wealth was made from all the trade over the Indian Ocean and Mediterranean Sea

Figure 9.5   A student created this Genre Reformulation of an article about the Silk Road, the Sand Road, and the Sea Road. This side-by-side ABC reformulation allowed the student to quickly compare the three routes.

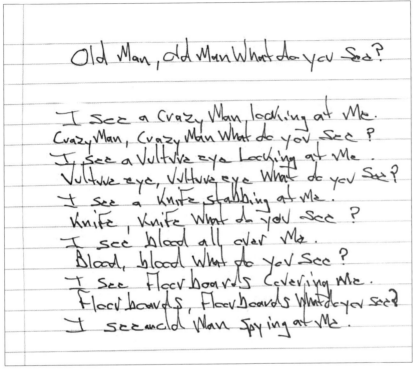

Figure 9.6 A high school student reformulated "The Tell-Tale Heart" into a repetitive pattern.

👥 Step Inside a Classroom

A tenth-grade class was studying Christopher Columbus. The teacher shared a passage about this explorer and other European settlers from the book *Everything You Need to Know About American History Homework: A Desk Reference for Students and Parents*, by Anne Zeman and Kate Kelly (2005):

> In 1492, Native American life began to change dramatically. Christopher Columbus, an Italian who was captain of three Spanish ships, "discovered" what Europeans called a New World. He thought he had reached the Spice Islands near India. He called the people he met "Indians." Soon after, other European nations sent explorers to the Americas.

> *At first, Native Americans welcomed the Europeans. They introduced the Europeans to tomatoes, corn, potatoes, and tobacco. Europeans introduced Native Americans to guns, sugarcane, and horses. They also brought diseases new to the Americas—the common cold, measles, and smallpox, to name a few—which killed many Native Americans.*
>
> *When Europeans began to explore and later settle in North America, they used guns to take whatever they wanted. They thought they had the right to do this. When they built villages and cities, they often cleared forests. These forests were the homes of many of the wild animals the Native Americans hunted.*
>
> *Some groups, like the Cherokee, took on European ways, but the settlers wanted their land anyway. Most tribes that survived were forced to move west. Today, most of the remaining American Indians live there. Some have sued the government to repay them for the land that was taken from them or granted to them by treaties that were broken. (42)*

She then asked students to reformulate the text into any pattern they wanted. One group chose the ABC pattern and, after working for a while, asked if the words they used had to be in the text. When she asked them what they meant, they explained, "We have some words from the text we want to use, like 'F is for forests that the settlers cleared' and 'W is for wild animals that lost their homes,' but we also want to say, 'A is for awful because what the European explorers did to the Native Americans was awful' and 'X is for eXtremely sad because the way they were pushed off their land was eXtremely sad' and 'Z was for zealot because the European settlers were like zealots in getting what they wanted.'"

I was listening and told them I was impressed with their word *zealot*. They said, "We are, too! We didn't have a Z word, so we had to search for one. We found *zealot* and it said, 'Someone who has strong opinions and tries to make others have those same opinions.' That sounded exactly like what the European settlers did to the Native Americans."

The teacher rightly told students they could extend beyond the words they could find in the text as long as they could explain their choices. One student told the teacher, "You are a zealot when it comes to expanding our vocabularies." Soon, all in the class decided this was their new favorite word.

One Important Question

Genre Reformulation helps students read closely as they work to reformulate the text. As one student offered, "This is hard. It makes my brain hurt." It is hard; therefore, I don't ask students to do this often. But once students internalize a pattern, you'll be pleased to see that some students use a favorite pattern—especially the ABC pattern—for portions of a text when they want, as the student did in Figure 9.5. The question I always return to is "What did you have to do as you were reformulating this text?" Students always answer, "Reread."

One student explained, "I like ABC because it looks like it is going to be easy, but it's not. You end up reading the passage, like, a million times and then you find an *A* word and then you keep reading and there's another one and then you have to figure out which one is best. It's a lot, but it is fun thinking, like solving a puzzle. But, wow, you have to do a lot of rereading."

Retelling

"So tell me what happened in the story," I said to Easton.

"Well, uh, well, it was like this man or, um, this guy, and, and they, the guy and his, uh, brother goes to, to uh, well, they, like, leave and then some stuff happens."

Stuff happens. That about summed up the story as far as Easton was concerned. While I'll admit that the general notion that "stuff happens" in a story is accurate, the phrase seems to lack the specificity most of us want in a discussion about a piece of literature. But this level of summary is what many students offer us on a consistent basis. To move students past the "stuff happens" response, consider using a scaffold called Retelling (Tierney, Readence, and Dishner 1995). A retelling is a specific way of offering an oral summary of a text. Students use a rubric or checklist to help them think about setting, characters, main events, conflict, and resolution.

I find that this structured format for briefly summarizing a narrative text helps struggling readers organize their thoughts. Provide students with a rubric such as the one shown in Figure 9.7 for them to keep with them as they retell the text. Then move them from retelling to summarizing, by then having them write a SWBS statement. As students score themselves or others, or as you score their retelling, they plot their scores on the Retelling Progress Chart (see Figure 9.8).

Retelling Rubric

Name _____ Date _____

Text _____ Class _____

Directions: Use the following checklist to rate the retelling. For each item below, circle a number from 0–3 in the appropriate column. On this scale, 0 means the retelling didn't include the item at all, and 3 means the retelling completely and successfully included the item.

Does this retelling

1. have an introduction that includes the story's title and setting?	0	1	2	3
2. give the characters' names and explain how the characters are related to one another?	0	1	2	3
3. identify the antagonists and protagonists?	0	1	2	3
4. include the main events?	0	1	2	3
5. keep the main events in the correct sequence?	0	1	2	3
6. provide supporting details?	0	1	2	3
7. make sense?	0	1	2	3
8. sound organized?	0	1	2	3
9. discuss the main conflict?	0	1	2	3
10. explain how the main conflict problem was resolved?	0	1	2	3
11. connect the story to another story or to the reader's life?	0	1	2	3
12. include the reader's personal response to the story?	0	1	2	3

Total Score _____

Comments from listener about the retelling:

Suggestions for the next retelling:

Figure 9.7 Retelling Rubric. See Appendix M.

Retellings Progress Chart

Name _____ Class _____

	Sept.	Oct.	Nov.	Dec.	Jan.	Feb.	Mar.	Apr.	May.
R13									25
R12									23
R11								20	
R10							18		
R9						17			
R8					13				
R7				16					
R6			14						
R5			12						
R4		9							
R3		8							
R2	7								
R1	6								

Figure 9.8 Ian's Retelling Progress Chart. See Appendix M for a blank template.

Step Inside a Classroom

In late September, Amelia gave the following retelling after reading Lois Lowry's *Number the Stars:*

> *OK, there are soldiers and the family, it escapes, but the soldiers are going to catch . . . Well, they hide stuff in a casket and the dogs— first, she is supposed to take this basket to the boat, and then, like, uh, the dogs and soldiers stop her. And the basket, it, like, has hidden stuff—OK—but the cocaine kept the dogs from sniffing it and then her friend gave her the necklace and she kept it.*

This retelling lacks organization, details, and continuity. It reveals that Amelia had trouble sequencing events as well as organizing her thoughts to present important facts: characters, setting, main ideas, conflicts, and supporting details. Her teacher, therefore, began modeling retellings, gave Amelia a rubric (outline) to follow when she gave retellings, and provided lots of opportunities to practice retelling. More than four months later, Amelia gave the following retelling of Katherine Paterson's *Bridge to Terabithia*.

It was these two kids and they wanted, you know, to race. OK. Wait.

This is a retelling for Bridge to Terabithia, *which is about a boy and a girl and, uh, they are friends and, uh, one dies. And it was at the beginning of the school year. OK. One of the kids, a boy, and his name was Jess and he wanted to win the race, so he was, like, running every day and then at school he met this girl and she was new and they are in the country.*

In the country, that is the setting. And the girl's name is Leslie. So, Jess and Leslie are the main characters and the setting is the country. And there are some other characters. Like Marybelle and Jess' parents and his other sisters and Leslie's parents. And so then they become friends and when they go into the forest over to a little island she says to imagine that he is the king and she is the queen and they name the land Terabithia and they, like, go there to play. He likes it but doesn't tell anyone that they go there. And they are not boyfriend and girlfriend but just friends. And that is, like, cool. And his dad is mean to him.

That is one of the problems of the story, that his dad doesn't like that he does art but Jess likes to do art. And his dad treats his sisters, like, really nice and Jess is like, you know, jealous about his dad. So then one day Jess goes with his teacher to look at some art pictures and Leslie goes to play without him, and she is killed because the bridge to their island is just a tree that has fallen over this creek. OK. It is really raining, and she drowns. And so then Jess has to find out and he is really sad and then he is worried it is his fault and stuff and his dad was almost kind of nice to him, well, just a little.

Amelia stops herself to provide an introduction for the listener.

She remembers to provide the setting and adds characters' names purposefully instead of in a haphazard approach.

Notice that now she specifically identifies the setting and now identifies the main characters.

While she rambles a bit, she also correctly identifies a conflict in the book: Jess struggles with his dad.

In this final part of her retelling, Amelia identifies the main problem and tries to provide a closing statement.

OK, that's another problem—that Leslie has died. This is like the main problem. And then Jess takes his little sister there to play, but he makes the bridge safe and he tells her about Terabithia. And so that is the end. And the main problem was that Leslie died and the other problem, but not the main problem, is that Jess' dad doesn't want him to do art. And there was a bully, but that was earlier and that was not a main problem.

When we compare Amelia's two retellings, one in September and the other in February, we see growth in several areas. The structured retelling offered her a path forward for her thinking. Most importantly, Amelia liked seeing her growth. She commented, "With the retelling chart, I keep seeing how I'm getting better and I can see that sometimes I forget things, like to say who is the main character. Without this, I would be talking and forget what I had said. This [the rubric] keeps me focused and helps me remember what I need to be discussing next. It is good."

 ## One Important Question

As students are retelling a text, listen for what they do well and listen for what they omit. Your final question should address omissions you hear: "I noticed that you did an excellent job explaining the setting, main characters, and events. You did a very good job of keeping the events in the correct order. I see, though, that on this one and other retellings, you aren't connecting what you've read to any other texts. Making that type of connection can help you think about how books are similar and different. What can I do to help you with this?"

When I asked Amelia that question, she responded, "I don't really do that because I don't know what it means. Can you explain it to me?"

I told her I had read *Bridge to Terabithia* and while I had not read any other books just like that one, I had seen the movie *The Wizard of Oz* and . . . she interrupted me there.

"Oh, I watched that movie. And yeah, it is like *Bridge to Terabithia* because Jess had went to Terabithia and that's where he had adventures and that's what happened with that girl, um, Dorothy, she went to Oz and then she just wanted to be home. [*Pause.*] That's a little, not exactly, but a little like Jess just wanted his dad to love him. Oh, so when you think about other books, you can maybe think more about the book you are reading. I get it now."

When we notice what students consistently omit in a retelling, we learn what we need to model for them. We let their needs guide our instruction.

The Three Big Questions

Louisa Moats, author of numerous texts, including *Speech to Print: Language Essentials for Teachers*, third edition (2020), explains, "There is no replacement for a teacher who can generate a good discussion and get kids to really ponder what they've read and the whys and wherefores and connect those meanings to their own lives" (Reading Rockets 2014). I agree with Dr. Moats on this point: good discussions encourage students to ponder what they have read and to connect what they have pondered to their own lives. That's the essence of a responsible and responsive reader.

And though Moats asserts that there is no replacement for the teacher who can generate a good discussion, research reveals that student-generated questions about a text improve comprehension more than teacher-generated questions (Taboada and Guthrie 2006; Joseph et al. 2015; Duke and Pearson 2017). Teaching students to ask the same good questions teachers would ask is a difficult task. One method that has proved effective is a strategy called Reciprocal Reading.

Reciprocal Reading requires that teachers model what it means to summarize, question, clarify, and predict when reading. Then they place students into small groups of four or five and assign roles: the big boss, who leads the discussion, the summarizer, the predictor, the clarifier, and the questioner. It might be helpful to distribute cue cards with prompts such as "Ask questions to help your group get started. Start your question with *who, what, when, where, why, what if*, or *how*" or "Clarify anything that doesn't make sense to your group. If you need to look up a word, do so." Students then run their own discussions as the big boss turns the group's attention to what they need to read. Everyone then speaks, using their prompts, and then they read some more and the process continues.

While this strategy is successful when implemented carefully, I've found that too often students miss some steps, students are bored by the repetitive process, and teachers do not have the time to listen in with each group to make sure all understand how to help classmates predict or summarize. Yet, I want what Dr. Moats advocates—that robust discussion that focuses the students' attention on the text and their own lives. The Three Big Questions scaffold avoids the pitfalls of Reciprocal Reading while encouraging responsible and responsive reading and discussions that improve comprehension (Beers and Probst 2016).

The Three Big Questions (see Figure 9.9) offer students the chance to focus on specific parts of the text (What is surprising?), clarify confusion (What does the author think I already know?), and consider how the text challenges their understandings (What changed, challenged, or confirmed what I already know?). Students mark up the text as they read with an exclamation point when surprised, a question mark when confused, and a *C* for passages that change, challenge, or confirm their thinking. Then, when they have finished reading, they share their thoughts with others.

For those of you who teach primary grade children, ask "What surprised you?" as you are reading aloud to students, but ask it only when you are ready to listen to a lot of surprises! Then change that second question, "What did the author think you already knew?" to "What confused you?"

Figure 9.9 Three Big Questions Anchor Chart

Three Big Questions Think Sheet

Name _____ Topic _____

Summary: In two or more sentences, explain what this text is about:

_____
_____
_____
_____
_____

What surprised you?	What did the author think you already knew?	What challenged, changed, or confirmed your thinking?

Figure 9.10 Three Big Questions Think Sheet. See Appendix N.

If you aren't sure what this second question means, take a look at the first sentence of this chapter. If you don't remember who Anne is, then you might be confused. The author (me!) thinks you remember something that perhaps you don't. Finally, with our youngest students, change the final question to "What did you learn?"

👥 Step Inside a Classroom

When Tara Smith was a sixth-grade teacher, she created a template for her students to use as they answered the Three Big Questions (see Figure 9.10). Notice that Tara added a place for her students to write a summary of the text before they commented on the Three Big Questions. For many students this would be very helpful.

The student work shown in Figure 9.11 does not require a template. This student drew a box, used icons to represent the Three Big Questions, and then added her comments. Templates are nice, but I like that students can make their own three-column box and use this as they want. Finally, Figure 9.12 on the following page offers a third method for collecting responses. This teacher asked her students to record their thinking on sticky notes and then those were placed at the front of the room.

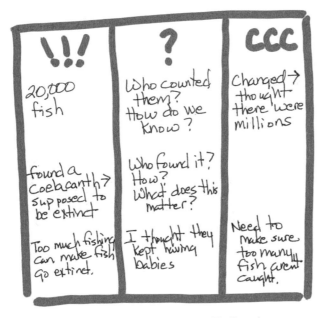

Figure 9.11 Student Work Using Three Big Questions

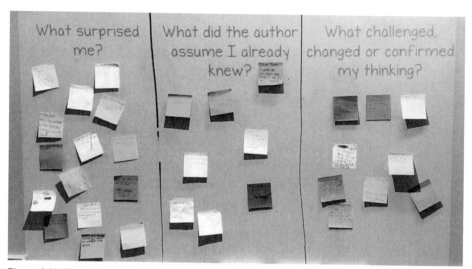

Figure 9.12 Three Big Questions on Sticky Notes

As I've talked with students about the Three Big Questions, I've heard a variety of comments:

- I like these questions. It's my thoughts.

- Answering the teacher's questions is not so interesting. This is more interesting because it is, like, what surprised me!

- I never thought about how something is changing my thinking before. Now I think about that a lot.

- I hate the Three Big Questions. It looks like there are just three things, but one surprise always leads to another one. It is easier to just answer the teacher's questions.

 ## One Important Question

While these questions are helpful for all levels of readers, they are particularly helpful for struggling readers who often doubt their ability to offer the "right" answer. These questions, though text dependent, do not have a specific answer the teaching is waiting to hear. This dialogic nature (see Chapter 18) encourages students to participate in the conversation. As one student said, "It's my surprise! The teacher can't say it wasn't a good answer." The second

"Reading doesn't change us, but it gives us the opportunity to change ourselves."

Look at the amount of writing this one group of four students generated. This took about twenty minutes. From that writing, students then were ready to write their own longer essays.

Figure 9.13 Student Responses Using Poster Activity

question—What did the author think you already knew?—gives students the opportunity to share where they need more background knowledge. It's the third question, though, that you want to be sure becomes your final question: What has changed, challenged, or confirmed your thinking? Reading doesn't change us, but it gives us the opportunity to change ourselves. End your conversations with this question to remind students that reading empowers them.

Semantic Differential Scales

Semantic Differential Scales help students think about how characters have changed over time.

Semantic Differential Scales place opposite character traits (strong / weak, optimistic / pessimistic) at opposite ends of a scale. Then students to decide how much of the trait a character possesses. Figure 9.14 offers a Semantic Differential Scale for the two characters in Langston Hughes' short story "Thank You, M'am." Students can use the scale to track character development by rating a character both at the beginning and at the end of the story.

These pairs of words work well for Semantic Differential Scales:

strong / weak
kind / cruel
brave / cowardly
honest / dishonest
bold / shy
wise / foolish
selfish / unselfish
happy / sad
mature / immature
sharing / stingy
forgiving / vindictive
motivated / unmotivated
careful / daring

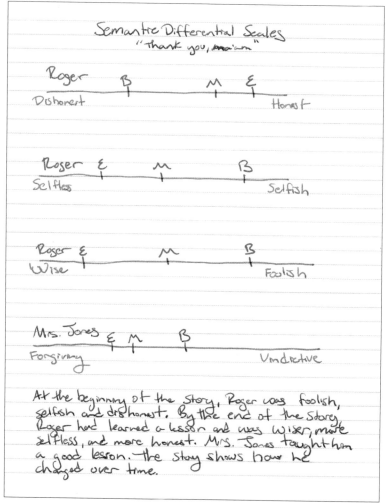

Figure 9.14 Semantic Differential Scale for "Thank You, M'am." See Appendix O for a blank template.

👥 Step Inside a Classroom

Student 1: Why did you say that Roger was more selfish than dishonest at the beginning of the story? He tried to steal her purse. That's pretty dishonest.

Student 2: Yeah, but when she asked him, "If I turn you loose, will you run?" he said yes. I think he was honest but just really wanted the money. So, since he was always honest when she asked him questions, I thought it was only that one thing that made him dishonest.

Student 1: Oh, that's good. I should change mine. Is that OK? Do you think I can change mine?

Student 2: I guess so. I mean, isn't that why we discuss this, so if we figure out something, then we can change our minds?

Student 1: Good. So, I thought that the woman, she really didn't change at all.

Student 2: Right. She was awesome from the beginning. Like mean but nice all at the same time. Hey, that's two good words: *mean* and *nice*. Those would be hard because she was kind of mean—she kicked him in his blue jean sitter and dragged him down the street. That's funny, his blue jean sitter.

Student 1: Yeah, it is like she is acting mean toward him because, like, tough love.

Student 2: So, it's interesting that she is, like, the same all the way through . . .

Student 1: [*Interrupting*] But not really because it says that she did things when she was young, too. So, if you rate her just on how she is in this story, but if you look back to when she was younger, she was more like Roger.

Student 2: Maybe that's why she gets him. She used to be like him.

In this brief discussion, what I notice is that both students used evidence from the text to make a point. Student 2 pointed out that the woman kicked Roger in his blue jean sitter. Student 1 reminded her partner that the woman had done things when she was young, too. As students discuss their ratings, you will find they often turn back to the text to confirm their thoughts.

In this classroom, the teacher eventually made bookmarks with word pairs for students to keep with them as they read. He stopped making the scales for students and asked them to keep the words in mind as they read, marking places in the text that helped them decide. Then, he moved them from the bookmarks to using ABC Boxes. This scaffold—boxes with the ABCs written in them (see Figure 9.15)—offers less support than Semantic Differential Scales as students now must choose their own words. I like that ABC Boxes let students compare and contrast two or more characters easily.

Across the room, this was another conversation:

Student 3:   Here's mine. [*With Bs and Es grouped in middle for all four comments*]

Student 4:   Mine are by *dishonest* and *selfish* for Roger. [*Bs and Es grouped at far-right end*] I think he was just pretending to be all nice so she would give him the money.

Student 3:   I don't think so. He said he wanted her to trust him.

When reading *Starfish* by Lisa Fipps, one student used ABC Boxes to trace the development of the main character, Ellie. He explained he didn't do this for Catalina because "she stayed the same."

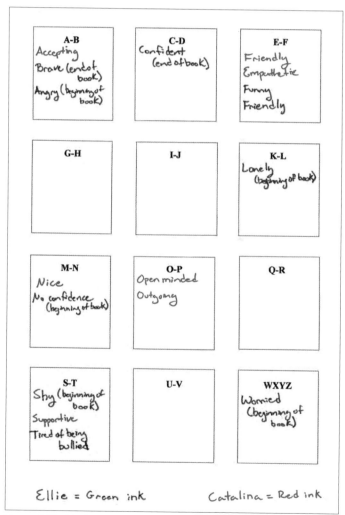

Figure 9.15 ABC Boxes Comparing Two Characters. See Appendix P for a blank template.

Student 4:   Yeah, but I don't think he meant it. He was just saying that. You know how you just say stuff. Anyway, it's a better story if you know that maybe he's going to sneak back in and steal everything.

Student 3:   I don't think he's going to do that. He's told the truth to her too many times.

Though these readers were responsive, a couple needed more work on becoming responsible readers.

I've included a template for the ABC Boxes in Appendix P, but you can make this on your own. You can also let your students create this, though that will take them the entire class period.

One Important Question

As students discuss why they rated characters the way they did, end your talk by asking students why it's important to think about how characters are changing over time. Character development is tied to plot development, conflict resolution, and ultimately theme. Students who recognize the development are more likely to understand the theme. Remember, if you have students who need help noticing how characters are changing, teach them the signpost Contrasts and Contradictions (see page 126).

It Says, I Say, And So

Some readers have difficulty making inferences or they offer an inference that is not grounded in evidence from the text. (To read more about how to help students make inferences, look at Chapter 6.) It Says, I Say, And So is a scaffold that helps students organize their thoughts as they move from considering what's in the text to connecting that to their prior knowledge (see Appendix Q).

Students complete a chart that has four columns. In the first column, you supply a question you want students to answer. In the second column, students find the information that helps them answer the question. In the third column, they write their thoughts. In the final column, they combine what was in the text with their own thoughts to offer an answer.

👥 Step Inside a Classroom

I was working with tenth graders who were reading the poem "Mother to Son" by Langston Hughes. I had students draw four columns on their own paper and then they wrote this question in the first column: "Why do you think the woman is telling her son about her life?" (see Figure 9.16). This question is not answered directly in the text, so students must make an inference to answer it.

Mother to Son

Well, son, I'll tell you:
Life for me ain't been no crystal stair.
It's had tacks in it,
And splinters,
And boards torn up,
And places with no carpet on the floor—
Bare.
But all the time
I'se been a-climbin' on,
And reachin' landin's,
And turnin' corners,
And sometimes goin' in the dark
Where there ain't been no light.
So boy, don't you turn back.
Don't you set down on the steps
'Cause you finds it's kinder hard.
Don't you fall now—
For I'se still goin', honey,
I'se still climbin',
And life for me ain't been no crystal stair.

—Langston Hughes

Students worked with a partner to answer the question. While the completed chart in Figure 9.16 is impressive, it is the students' conversation that provides insight into their thinking:

Student 1: It doesn't say why she told him.

Student 2: Maybe she just wanted to tell him, like, to motivate him.

Student 1: [*Pause.*] Is he a little kid?

Student 2: Maybe a teenager. Like he's old enough to understand what she's saying.

Student 1: Why'd she say a crystal staircase?

Student 2: Like crystal, crystal is like glass, like if you have a glass staircase it would break.

Student 1 is slow to engage deeply, starting with pointing out there is no direct answer, moving to asking about the son's age, and then asking why the staircase is crystal.

It Says, I Say, And So

Question	It Says	I Say	And So
1. Read the question.	2. Find information from the text that will help you answer the question.	3. Think about what you know about that information.	4. Combine what the text says with what you know to come up with the answer.
Why do you think the woman is telling her son about her life?	The poem says that she tells him "Don't you turn back" and "Don't you set down on the steps."	She saw him giving up and wants him to know she never gave up.	She is telling her son about her life because she sees him not doing things and she wants him to know that even when things are hard, you have to keep going because she did and now she has a better life.

It took about fifteen minutes of class time for students to make this chart. I was a visiting teacher, so I don't know if this was typical for this class, but it often took my own students a lot of time to complete tasks such as this. There's a template in Appendix Q you can use to move them more directly to the important work.

Figure 9.16 It Says, I Say, And So Chart for "Mother to Son." See Appendix Q for a blank template.

Student 1: Oh. I get it. A glass staircase. [*Pause.*] Hey, it's a Contrast and Contradiction because, look—because, look, it says that it doesn't have tacks and boards and stuff. Like her staircase isn't all perfect, like crystal. So, why would she tell him that?

Student 2: Oh, so that's the question; see in column 1? Why is she telling him about her life?

Student 1: Because here, here it says that he was going to sit down and right before it, he was going to turn around. Turn around, that's like giving up.

Student 2: [*Pause.*] He has to, she wants to tell him—oh, it's like now maybe things are better and he might think that everything was always good, but it wasn't because her life had been hard, like with a staircase that had tacks and stuff.

The day before, we had discussed Contrasts and Contradictions, and the C and C anchor chart was on the wall. I was glad to see the student make the connection, which was why I had chosen this poem.

Now the student is moving directly to the text for evidence. This is the same student who previously said the text didn't say anything about this.

After discussion, this student now reaches important conclusions.

The It Says, I Say, And So chart kept students focused on what they needed to do to answer the question. This is a scaffold, so it's something you hope you can remove as students progress through the year, but don't rush to do this.

Students who have difficulty making inferences often move directly from the question to their own thoughts without pausing to consider what the text has offered. This chart reminds them to begin with evidence from the text. If you need to, be willing to point out lines or passages that will help them focus their thinking.

One Important Question

As students use this scaffold, you are impressing on them that an inference begins with what's in the text. When you talk with students, end your conversation by asking one final question: "Why is it important to begin your thinking with evidence in the text?" If we can help students learn that an inference is not an opinion, then we are one step closer to creating responsible readers.

Book Head Heart

I'll conclude this chapter with what is perhaps the most important framework we can ever offer students, a framework that reminds students that as we read, the goal is to move from what's in the text to what we will take to heart (see Figure 9.17). Called the BHH framework (Beers and Probst 2018), it reminds students that we read texts—all sorts of texts—so that we can take something to heart, though we always begin with what's in the text.

In this era of truth decay and high-stakes tests, our inclination will be to focus instruction only on responsible reading—reading that attends to what is in the text. I would never want us to overlook the importance of having students look to texts—fiction and nonfiction—for evidence to support their thinking about that text. We must always ask ourselves questions about the text: What was the text about? What was the author's purpose?

But we also want students to do more than extract from a text. We want them reading closely, considering their own thoughts as they learn from the text. To move students toward that type of responsive reading, ask students questions such as "What surprised you?" and "What did the signposts that you noticed in the

Figure 9.17 An Illustration of the Book Head Heart (BHH) Framework

text make you wonder about?" and "What changed or challenged your thinking?" When we teach students to read responsively by wondering about what they are learning, they are more likely to see relevance in the text.

Finally, though, the reading that is most valuable to us and to our students will be reading that in some way touches us—touches them—on an affective level. This reading offers us something we want to consider for a longer time, lessons we want to hold on to, ideas that help us see ourselves and others in a new light. That won't happen with every text, but we should encourage this reading when we can. When Bob and I first wrote about the BHH framework in *Disrupting Thinking*, we were dismayed at the number of middle school students who told us they rarely wondered what a book meant to them. By high school, most students told us that they never had the time to think about how a book might affect them. One student told us, "What did I take to heart? If it's not for a test, we don't worry about it." When we asked this same student if he liked to read, he responded, "Not

really. I did when I was a kid, but now . . . now reading is just something you do to finish an assignment or get ready for a test."

Whether you let students put comments on sticky notes, or you ask your students to write comments on a graphic organizer, such as Buffy Hamilton did in her middle school classroom (see Figure 9.18), BHH is a framework that will remind us all, students and teachers, that ultimately we read so that we are connected to ourselves, to others, to the past, and perhaps to the future. When we let those squiggly marks on a page move from the book to our head to our heart, we stand for a moment alongside others and journey into the lives of others. This is the reading that helps make us more than we ever thought we could be. This is the journey we should want for all students.

Figure 9.18 Students in Buffy Hamilton's high school class use a BHH template to help guide their small-group conversations. See Appendix R for a blank template.

Dear George,

I picked up a note you had been writing during class. It was late spring and you, like all the students, were more interested in counting how many days until school was out than anything I might say. I expected your note would be to a buddy, asking him what he wanted to do that day after school, or maybe even what his summer plans were. Instead, I found a note to your grandmother. In part, it said, "Grandma, I need to know if I can come live with you. Maybe if I was in a diferant school things wuld be diferant. Its just to hard here. If I culd come live with you I culd help you with stuff and I wuld be real good. I think I just need a place to start over."

I thought you'd been thinking about ending the year. Instead, you were looking for a way to begin again. I wonder how many times I misread your thoughts, misunderstood your actions. I wonder how long it took me to understand that endings and beginnings are always connected.

Part 3

Word Work

Dear George,

   You handed me your social studies book. "Can you help me understand what I'm supposed to do?" you asked, pointing to an activity at the end of the chapter: "Evaluate the reasons for the development of the Silk Road. Justify which reason was most critical."

   "What do you need to know, George?"

   "How do I evaluate? What does that mean? And what does it mean to justify?"

   "Well, justify means to explain with reasons."

   "Why didn't it say that, then? Maybe I could do that. It's like it's written in code and no one taught me the code."

CHAPTER 10

Tier 1, Tier 2, and Tier 3 Vocabulary

WE'VE LONG UNDERSTOOD, THROUGH RESEARCH OR common sense, that when kids know a lot about a topic, they comprehend that topic more easily than students who don't know much about that topic. A landmark study, often called the baseball study, showed that low-skilled readers who knew a lot about a topic (in this study, baseball) understood a passage about baseball better than high-skilled readers who knew little or nothing about baseball (Recht and Leslie 1988). Topic knowledge is important.

We also know that the vocabulary a student uses to discuss a topic indicates their knowledge of a topic. If you ask students to tell you all they know about climate change and some say, "It's about things getting hotter," and others discuss *emissions, greenhouse gasses, CO_2, cattle production*, and *renewable energy*, plus they understand the difference in *weather* and *climate*, you generally can predict which students know more about that topic. Interestingly, even knowing some vocabulary associated with a particular topic helps students understand the topic more (O'Reilly, Wang, and Sabatini 2019). The student who says, "Climate change means things are getting hotter," will struggle more through a text than the one who already knows what *emissions* and *greenhouse gasses* are, and the one who knows all those words previously listed will struggle the least.

But how do we help kids learn all the words they need to know? First and foremost, kids will never learn enough words through any direct

- Chapter 10 (this chapter) discusses tier 1, tier 2, and tier 3 words.

- Chapter 11 focuses on scaffolds for preteaching vocabulary.

- Chapter 12 examines context clues and word parts.

instruction we can offer. They will learn the most words through the reading they do. We'll look at research around volume of reading in Chapter 16. Second, while we can never teach all the words kids need to know, that does not mean we should avoid vocabulary instruction in our classes. What's critical is knowing which words to teach. Knowing what to teach means asking specific questions. Too many times, my only question was "Do you know what this means?" Once I learned to ask more nuanced questions, then I understood what I needed to teach (see Figure 10.1). And third, we need to understand different categories—tiers—of words we might teach.

Once you have an idea of what students do and don't know about words, then you can begin to decide which scaffolds might work best with your students (see Figure 10.2).

QUESTIONS TO DETERMINE WHAT STUDENTS KNOW ABOUT WORDS

If you want to know if students . . .	**Then** ask . . .
Have *any* knowledge of a particular word.	Have you heard this word? What do you think it means? What do you think this word does? For instance, does it describe something or someone? Does it seem to be the name of something?
Can share a synonym for the word.	Finish this sentence: This word means the same as . . . .
Can identify which words in the text confused them.	Can you show me the specific words that caused you a problem?
Understand one definition of a word but not others.	Can you use this word in another way than how it appears to be used in this passage?
Use roots or affixes to help understand unknown words.	If you look at this part of the word, how could that help you figure out the meaning?
Can use the context clues.	Which part of the sentence might offer a clue to the meaning?

Figure 10.1 Questions to Determine What Students Know About Words

VOCABULARY SCAFFOLDS		
If students need help...	**Then** use...	**See** page...
Gaining basic knowledge of words	Linear Arrays	188
	Word Clusters	188
	Word Axes	187
	Semantic Maps	186
Identifying which words in the text confused them	Syntax Surgery	122
Understanding multiple meanings of words	Words Across Contexts	173
	Understanding Homographs and Homophones	171
Using roots or affixes to help understand unknown words	Roots and Affixes	198
	Vocabulary Trees	199
Using the meaning of the sentence to help build understanding	Context Clues	193

Figure 10.2 Vocabulary Scaffolds

Tier 1 Words

The words we use and read can be divided into three groups: tier 1, tier 2, and tier 3 (see Figure 10.3). Let's look at each group. Tier 1 words are those very common words that we all seem to know and learned by listening to others use them. These high-frequency words are the words of everyday language—*food*, *sky*, *baby*, *street*, *tree*, *happy*, *car*. The vast majority of these words do not have multiple meanings and don't require instruction unless you are working with English language learners. Remember, English language learners do have a tier 1 vocabulary in their primary language. For that reason, it is very helpful to encourage them to create personal dictionaries that connect English tier 1 words to their primary language vocabulary.

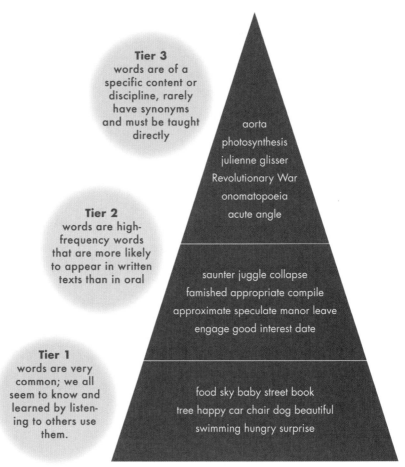

Tier 3 words are of a specific content or discipline, rarely have synonyms and must be taught directly

aorta
photosynthesis
julienne glisser
Revolutionary War
onomatopoeia
acute angle

Tier 2 words are high-frequency words that are more likely to appear in written texts than in oral

saunter juggle collapse
famished appropriate compile
approximate speculate manor leave
engage good interest date

Tier 1 words are very common; we all seem to know and learned by listening to others use them.

food sky baby street book
tree happy car chair dog beautiful
swimming hungry surprise

Figure 10.3 Tier Words Triangle

Tier 2 Words

Tier 2 words are high-frequency words that are more likely to appear in written texts than in oral conversations. Tier 2 words

- are used across disciplines
- can support or impede comprehension
- often have multiple meanings
- add precision and detail to the content
- are often abstract

Furthermore, what is considered a tier 2 word for some might be a tier 1 word for others. In the children's picture story book *Rosie Revere, Engineer* children hear about characters who *"chuckled* at Rosie's inventions" and discover when Rosie is *"dismayed."* Children who listen to that book repeatedly in preschool and kindergarten (and beyond) embrace those words as a part of their tier 1 vocabulary. Students who do not encounter texts using those words probably do not hear them from parents and caregivers on a regular basis. Those words, when eventually seen in texts, are, for those students, tier 2 words that must be learned.

In written texts, students encounter words that offer a precision that oral language often lacks: *saunter* (not *walk*); *juggle* (not *carry*); *collapse* (not *fall*); *ecstatic* (not *happy*); *manor* (not *house*); *famished* (not *hungry*); *appropriate* (not *OK*); *approximate* (not *about*); *compile* (not *gather*); *invariably* (not *always*); *occur* (not *happen*); *speculate* (not *guess*); *chuckle* (not *laugh*); and *dismayed* (not *sad*).

> The scaffold called Linear Arrays aids in teaching this type of tier 2 words. Linear Arrays are discussed in Chapter 11 (see page 188).

When our less skilled readers don't read, then they lose an important method of learning tier 2 words. There are simply too many tier 2 words for us to efficiently and effectively teach all of them through vocabulary lists. That's why volume of reading is necessary to reading comprehension.

Homographs

What do the following words have in common?

- leave
- good
- interest
- date
- type
- fast

> *Homographs* are words that are spelled the same but have different meanings (stalk of plant and stalk a person). *Homophones* are words that sound the same but have different spellings and different meanings (profit and prophet). *Homonyms* can be either homographs or homophones. Some define homonyms as words that are spelled the same but have different sounds (row the boat and the loud row).

Perhaps one commonality among these words is that they could all be linked to create the plot of a Harlequin romance. More appropriate to this chapter, though, is the common thread that these are all words with multiple meanings. They are homographs. *Leave* can mean to remain (Please leave the book there.) or to be absent from a place (She is on leave from her job.). *Good* can be a moral value (She is a good person.) or a level of skill (They did a good job.) or something you can count on (The car was good for another year.).

Many words with multiple meanings become problematic because students know the common definition but not the less common definition. As they try to use the common definition, when meaning breaks down, too often less skilled readers give up. Remember the sentence *The old man the boat*? Knowing the less common definitions of *old* and *man* is necessary for that sentence to make sense. Consider the word *fast*. What's the first definition that will occur to your students? Most will probably offer "moving fast." Fewer—if any—will offer "in a firm manner." Some who observe Ramadan might more readily provide "to go without food."

Now think of the word *run*. Students easily understand "They run a mile every day." What happens, though, when another definition is required: "The newspaper decided to *run* my article" or "He will *run* the meeting efficiently" or "The play had a great *run* on Broadway"? Students with reading difficulties often default to the one definition they know. When that definition doesn't make sense in the context, for them, reading is once again "dumb."

Some words with multiple meanings don't have a more common meaning used in most everyday language. Think about words such as *custom, buckle, racket, prune, reservation, patient, novel, marker, bank,* and *grave*. I've offered some examples of the first three words here. What examples would you offer for the rest?

Hugging was their custom until COVID.

They gladly paid the custom so they could continue on the trip.

That dress was custom-made.

The buckle on the belt was brass.

The board will buckle from all the weight.

He should buckle those things together.

Hand me that tennis racket.

All this racket is giving me a headache.

Their racket was against the law.

Wide reading will expose students to the multiple uses of words. You can make discussion of homographs a part of class time by choosing a homograph from a text students are reading and then extending their understanding of that word by using an exercise I call Words Across Contexts. With this exercise, you ask students to consider one word and to think about how the meaning changes as the context changes. For instance:

What would *jersey* mean to

   a. A rancher?

   b. Someone from New England?

   c. A football player?

What would *bank* mean to

   a. Someone standing near a river?

   b. Someone who wants to save money?

   c. A pilot?

What would *bolt* mean to

   a. A carpenter?

   b. A weather forecaster?

   c. A runner?

What would *engage* mean to

   a. A couple?

   b. Someone chosen to do a job?

   c. A mechanic?

What would *novel* mean to

   a. A writer?

   b. A creative problem solver?

You can find a template for Words Across Contexts in Appendix S.

While you can go online to find many lists of words with multiple meanings, I've included one I've compiled in Appendix C. Share one or two of the words with students at least a few times a week and let students discuss all the meanings they know.

Academic Vocabulary

Some tier 2 words are words students will encounter in their classes, in textbooks, and on state-mandated tests. They include words such as *essay, persuasive, argumentative, evidence, formulate, opinion, interpret, conclude, generalize,* and *evaluate.* (See Figure 10.4 for an example.)

There is no definitive list for these words. New Zealand researcher Averil Coxhead (1998) analyzed many college textbooks looking for the words used most often across all disciplines. She then separated the list she'd compiled into ten sublists. Sublist 1 words occurred most often across all texts;

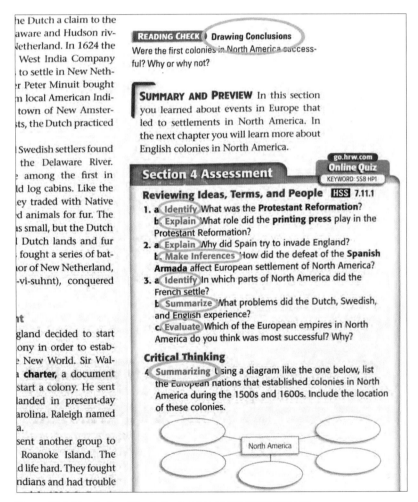

he Dutch a claim to the aware and Hudson riv- Netherland. In 1624 the West India Company to settle in New Neth- r Peter Minuit bought n local American Indi- town of New Amster- ts, the Dutch practiced

Swedish settlers found the Delaware River. e among the first in ld log cabins. Like the ey traded with Native d animals for fur. The s small, but the Dutch Dutch lands and fur fought a series of bat- or of New Netherland, -vi-suhnt), conquered

nt

gland decided to start ony in order to estab- e New World. Sir Wal- a **charter,** a document start a colony. He sent landed in present-day arolina. Raleigh named a. sent another group to Roanoke Island. The d life hard. They fought ndians and had trouble

READING CHECK **Drawing Conclusions**
Were the first colonies in North America successful? Why or why not?

SUMMARY AND PREVIEW In this section you learned about events in Europe that led to settlements in North America. In the next chapter you will learn more about English colonies in North America.

go.hrw.com
Online Quiz
KEYWORD: SS8 HP1

Section 4 Assessment

Reviewing Ideas, Terms, and People **HSS** 7.11.1
1. a. **Identify** What was the **Protestant Reformation**?
   b. **Explain** What role did the **printing press** play in the Protestant Reformation?
2. a. **Explain** Why did Spain try to invade England?
   b. **Make Inferences** How did the defeat of the **Spanish Armada** affect European settlement of North America?
3. a. **Identify** In which parts of North America did the French settle?
   b. **Summarize** What problems did the Dutch, Swedish, and English experience?
   c. **Evaluate** Which of the European empires in North America do you think was most successful? Why?

Critical Thinking
4. **Summarizing** Using a diagram like the one below, list the European nations that established colonies in North America during the 1500s and 1600s. Include the location of these colonies.

North America

Figure 10.4 Vocabulary Words from a Social Studies Textbook

sublist 10 words occurred least often. I've included sublists 1, 2, and 3 words in Appendix T. This list has been widely circulated and studied by other researchers, and it often forms the basis for vocabulary study in schools (Gardner and Davies 2014; Nagy and Townsend 2012).

Even though I have included the words of the first three sublists, I do not recommend that you distribute these lists and tell students to learn them. I do, however, recommend using the lists as a starting point for creating the academic vocabulary list appropriate for your school. Delete or add words as needed. How will you decide what those words are? Look through your textbooks across content areas. What words appear in the assignments? What words are used in the prereading pages of a chapter? Look at any test-prep information you use with students. Study the sample test items. What words appear repeatedly in questions, directions, sidebars, captions, intro-ductory material? You should find that words such as *summarize, analyze, extend, generate, sequence,* and *define* appear across textbooks. Such a list is helpful only if you and colleagues agree to use the academic words with students. When students hear all teachers use the words that they also see in all their textbooks, then they learn them faster.

Step Inside a Classroom

The high school principal asked me if I could spend some time working with the faculty on vocabulary development for students. I asked if I could begin this work by visiting some classrooms. In particular, I wanted to hear the language *teachers* were using. Here are some examples:

> **Teacher A:** "Let's talk about how these events were alike and different."

> **Teacher B:** "As you look at these two plants, with your partner, discuss their similarities and differences."

> **Teacher C:** "We've been talking about types of angles. What common characteristics do all angles share and what are their unique properties?"

> **Teacher D:** "As you talk with your partner, compare and contrast these two characters."

In this school, data analysis of standardized tests revealed that students had trouble with items that asked them to compare and contrast. The teachers (and principal) were confused because teachers across disciplines made sure students had practice doing that. But look at the language students heard as they moved from one class to another: *alike and different; similarities and differences; common and unique; compare and contrast.* Less skilled readers often do not connect or cluster all the terms to realize they all mean the same thing.

Look at other language from these same teachers:

Teacher A: "Tell me why these events are important."

Teacher C: "Draw a picture that would explain why this way of solving the problem works."

Teacher D: "Decide who you think the main character is in this story. Share quotes from the text for support."

Again, everyone on the faculty agreed that teaching students to provide evidence was important. In one class, though, that meant students were asked to *tell why*; in another they were told to *explain*; in the still another they were to *decide* and *share*. As I shared these examples with the faculty, some said they often used the academic language words but not every day.

Others said they altered their language based on the skill level of students. I asked if that meant a teacher actually told some students to "tell why" and then turned to others and asked them to "provide evidence." After a moment, some said that was what they do: "I guess if I think my kids don't know what some words mean, I use easier words."

We all want to use language that helps our students be successful, and we all want to respect the language choices our students make. Simultaneously, if one measure of success is through performance on state-mandated tests, we want them to be able to understand and use the academic language of those assessments. We help students accomplish this by connecting our own tier 1 vocabulary ("show me") to the academic tier 2 vocabulary students might read on tests ("demonstrate" or "provide").

Perhaps one of my favorite teachers I've ever met was the physical education teacher from that school. He understood that his language made a difference, too. "Students always love their PE teachers. We get to wear shorts and blow whistles and tell kids to move their butts. Plus, we have them moving, and kids love to be active." With his popularity, he recognized that his language carried much sway. When I returned to the school a month after that first visit, he had embraced the idea of using academic vocabulary. He explained that he now told students to "stop the sauntering and sprint with intensity" or "endeavor to accomplish the undertaking." He said he enjoyed thinking of a new way of saying something, and kids were making a list of all his "weird statements." He shared that even though the kids missed him saying, "Move your butts," they now laughed when he told them, "Progress quickly your derrieres."

Tier 3 Words

Tier 3 words are the words of a specific content or discipline. While we can teach some tier 2 words by linking them to more common tier 1 words, tier 3 words rarely have synonyms and must be taught directly: *photosynthesis, aorta, Revolutionary War, acute angle, onomatopoeia, julienne, glissade.* Unless you spend time cooking or dancing (or with those who do), you might not know those last two terms. Tier 3 words are low-frequency, rare words and are best taught when students encounter them in a text.

Often, we think tier 3 words should be the focus of vocabulary instruction, especially in content area classes. I'm going to suggest these words must have some instructional time, but not the majority of time.

▲▲▲ Step Inside a Classroom

The middle schoolers were studying issues around the environment. They were about to read an article about the role the dung beetle plays in affecting greenhouse emissions. Here's an excerpt from the *National Geographic* article:

> *Sadly, like many animals these days, dung beetles are in decline. Roslin said that in Finland, for example, more than half of dung beetle species are threatened or near endangered.*
>
> *The reasons include the lack of diversity in both dung and pasture that goes with fewer but more intensively managed farms, and the reduced quality of the dung—which nowadays contains more chemicals, such as anti-parasite drugs given to farm animals. (Holland 2013)*

The teacher had pretaught *anti-parasite*, explaining that he doubted his students had seen this term prior to reading this text. I agreed. It's a rare term, a tier 3 word. *Anti-parasite* is not fully defined in context, but the context does provide some clues: it's a drug that's a chemical and it's given to farm animals. His focus on that one term, however, did not help the students who did not know the more useful tier 2 words: *decline, endangered, diversity, intensively,* and *managed.* Students will understand far more of those two paragraphs if they know the meanings of those words than if they know the definition of *anti-parasite.* Don't spend too much time on tier 3 terms because they occur infrequently. Spend your instructional time on tier 2 words.

I discussed that with the teacher. He countered, "But I can't spend all my time teaching all those words. I don't know how to do that. Have them write definitions? I'm a science teacher. This is a unit on the environment. When do I teach vocabulary?" He wasn't defensive; he was thoughtful and curious. We studied the passage and he decided kids probably knew *threatened, endangered,* and *diversity.* He decided he needed to focus on what an *intensely managed farm* would be. That, he thought, was doable.

Then, as the students discussed this passage, we both discovered something neither of us had anticipated. Those words were not the problem (though no one knew what an intensely managed farm was). The problem was an inference the students needed to make. Look at passage again:

> *Sadly, like many animals these days, dung beetles are in decline. Roslin said that in Finland, for example, more than half of dung beetle species are threatened or near endangered.*
>
> *The reasons include the lack of diversity in both dung and pasture that goes with fewer but more intensively managed farms, and the reduced quality of the dung—which nowadays contains more chemicals, such as anti-parasite drugs given to farm animals.*

As the students discussed the second paragraph, several asked, "Reasons for what?" The students didn't know what *reasons* referred to. Both of us, skilled readers, had inserted what the author had omitted without realizing it: "The reasons *for the decline of the dung beetle* include the lack of diversity . . ." These kids needed help with an inference.

Figure 10.5 Encouraging conversation can improve comprehension.

Now the teacher was overwhelmed. "I can teach some words, but now I need to teach them how to make an inference, too? How do I do that? When is that supposed to happen?"

I pointed out that in this case, if we had considered the text from a struggling reader's point of view, we might have noticed the omission. We could have asked the question, "Reasons for what?" and let students discuss what they thought for a minute or two. But that won't happen if we don't slow down our own reading of what students will be reading. We can't skim the chapter or remember what the chapter said from last's year reading of it or tell ourselves we don't need to reread whatever novel we are teaching next. After all, we read that when it first came out. We must read carefully what students will read. Are there discipline-specific words that are not defined in the context? If so, we need to teach those. Which tier 2 words matter the most? Are there some inferences that we've made that might cause students to struggle to the point of frustration? Can we help them think through those passages?

Don't think the classrooms I visit are filled with students who are always engaged and ready to be learning. Some girls couldn't stop laughing over the word *dung*; one boy kept asking if dung beetles liked to sing "I Want to Hold Your Hand," and three wondered if I would be back the next day. Their question was not offered with hope.

When we give students time to work together to share their thinking, about words, about inferences, about what has confused them, they often resolve confusion themselves. In that classroom all we needed was one small group to say, "Oh, is it . . . ?" These two students thought it meant *reasons for the decline of the dung beetle*. Others looked back to the text and decided that was right. Remember, the smartest person in the room is the room. The more you let ideas from individuals or groups percolate to the surface so all can consider them, the more everyone benefits.

Dear George,

One day, you burst into class laughing. "Knock, knock," you said.

"Who's there?" I answered.

"Cantaloupe."

"Cantaloupe who?"

"Can't elope tonight. Dad's got the car." You laughed hard and without slowing, you continued, "OK, do this one. Knock, knock."

"Who's there?"

"Cash."

"Cash who?"

"No thanks, but I would like some peanuts!" You interrupted your laughing to make sure I understood the pun: "Get it? It's cashews, you know, like cashews that you eat. *Cash who* and *cashews*." Before I could say anything, you turned to share these jokes with others. For that moment, language was fun, and you wanted to share what you had figured out with others. I still laugh when I see cashews. Cash who?

Dear George,

How many times that year did you say to me, "What's this word mean?" and how often did I respond, "Look it up"? I hate to tell you, but that was my stock advice to students for several years, more specifically until my fifth year, when one student wrote, "Luke, warm the water," for the definition of *tepid*. I asked her to explain that to me. "Well, I looked up *tepid* and the definition was lukewarm. I figured that was a misprint because I had never heard the word *lukewarm*. I thought the glossary was giving me an example. So, I wrote, 'Luke, warm the water.'"

When a student actually thought "Luke, warm the water" was the definition of *tepid*, I was finally motivated to do more than hand kids another vocabulary list or ask Anne to buy another set of vocabulary workbooks. The answer wasn't in a better list or a different workbook. The answer began with research I needed to know.

Preteaching Vocabulary

RESEARCH HAS REPEATEDLY SHOWN THAT TEACHING the meaning of critical words that appear in a passage helps students understand that passage (Stahl and Fairbank 1986; Wright and Cevetti 2016; McQuillan 2019). Lubell (2017) explains that "instead of requiring students to memorize lists of words, teachers can build vocabulary by teaching vocabulary words as they appear in the student's reading." This teaching of critical unknown words that students will encounter in a text is particularly helpful for less skilled readers (Lehr, Osborn, and Hiebert 2004).

Preteaching Vocabulary Helps Until It Doesn't

Preteaching specific words before students read a text helps them understand *that* text, but that knowledge doesn't help them understand other texts unless that targeted word shows up again. Direct instruction of vocabulary helps students understand one passage, but overall, this is not an efficient way to help students learn all the words they need to know to comprehend texts.

This is not new knowledge. In 1987, Nagy and Herman reported that "it is highly unlikely that teaching individual word meanings could ever produce more than a very slight increase in general reading comprehension" (31). Wright and Cevetti's (2016) review of research found that Nagy and Herman's conclusion, reached about thirty years earlier, was correct.

"If the goal is to improve reading comprehension of any text, then the sheer number of words that would need to be taught and the time that it would take to teach all those words would make teaching individual words an inefficient use of classroom time."

If the goal is to improve reading comprehension of any text, then the sheer number of words that would need to be taught and the time that it would take to teach all those words would make teaching individual words an inefficient use of classroom time. What helps the most? Wide reading (discussed in Chapter 16).

These findings have serious implications for how we spend time in the classroom. If teaching specific words won't help students comprehend a text that doesn't have those words, should we spend our time teaching specific words? The answer is yes because such instruction will help with *those* texts. If we are preteaching some vocabulary, then choosing the rights words is critical.

Deciding Which Words to Preteach

It is most valuable to teach a few words that are central to the topic or theme. As you are selecting words, don't skim the text for all the uncommon words you think your students won't know. Instead, slow down, read carefully, and consider which words are critical for students to be able to understand the central message. If those words aren't defined in the text (and often they will be), define them before students read.

Step Inside a Classroom

I was visiting a seventh-grade classroom. Students were reading an article from *National Geographic*. One passage said,

> *Garana and her family have lived in their one-room house for two years. It's one of the thousands of mud-brick homes in the Shamshatoo Afghan Refugee Camp. The camp holds about 50,000 Afghan refugees. They are people who have fled from war or drought in Afghanistan. (Page 2002, 18)*

The seventh-grade teacher had pretaught the word *refugee*. When I asked why, he explained that he thought few of his students would have seen the word, though he did think some might have heard it on television. I pointed out that the word was defined in the text. "Yeah, but I don't think they'll notice that. Or they won't realize that's the definition," he explained. If that was true, perhaps it was because students had had a steady diet of teachers doing the work the students should have been doing as they read. When we define words that are explained in the text, we teach students to depend on us, not the text.

"When we define words that are explained in the text, we teach students to depend on us, not the text."

As students talked about this passage, there was a different word that confused many: *camp*. This word, unlike *refugee*, does not have a definition or example provided in the text. Students knew the more common definitions of *camp*—the verb meaning to pack up a tent and head into nature to spend the night and the noun meaning a place kids might go in the summer: church camp, science camp, scout camp, day camp, YMCA camp. Some shared that in the summer they go to their "grandparents' camp." They did not, however, know the less common definition needed to understand what was happening to Garana and others.

In this passage, *camp* meant a place where people are detained or confined, usually with harsh conditions. As students discussed this, one said, "Oh, this is a bad camp. Like we read last year about concentration camps. Do you think they call them camps so people will think they are going someplace fun?"

Camp looks like an easy word, so the teacher left it alone. That was the wrong choice. As you select words, ask yourself if the word is already explained in the text. Choose words that are not explained (or are explained poorly) and that help students think about the overarching problems, issues, events, concerns, and so on.

Scaffolds to Preteach Vocabulary

Instruction as simple as telling students what a word means can help students understand the text. While that brief instruction is helpful, some research indicates that when we help students think more deeply about that word, they have a better chance of remembering it. Following are a few scaffolds for taking a closer look at words.

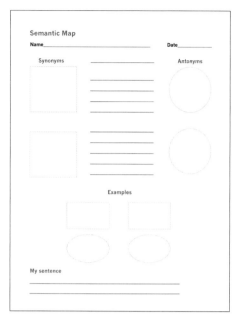

Figure 11.1 Appendix U: Semantic Map

Semantic Maps

Students can use a Semantic Map to think about what a word *is* and what it *isn't*, as well as use it to record examples and nonexamples of the word (see Figure 11.1). A few tips when working with Semantic Maps:

- Don't distribute a list of twenty words and tell students to complete twenty semantic maps.

- Do let students work with one or two others to complete a map that helps them understand specific words.

In one eighth-grade history class, a group of students looked up the definition of the word *pluralism* and made a Semantic Map for it (see Figure 11.2), while another group made a map for *individualism*. Then groups shared their maps. This takes some class time, but such focus helps students think deeply about a word.

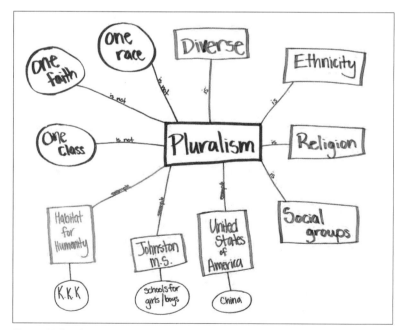

Figure 11.2 A Semantic Map of Pluralism

Word Clusters, Word Axes, and Linear Arrays

As you teach one word, cluster it with other words that share a similar meaning. For instance, the word *abode* can be clustered with other words that have to do with housing: *house, residence, dwelling, domicile, home, habitat.* Students can enlarge that cluster by adding words that suggest temporary outdoor structures: *lean-to, tent, hut, shed;* multiple-family dwellings: *apartment, condo, tenement, high-rise, dormitory;* and words that suggest expensive homes: *manor, villa, chateau, estate, mansion.* The constant clustering and combing of clusters helps students see relationships among words. We can help students think about clusters by using a Word Axis or a Linear Array (see Figures 11.3, 11.4, 11.5, and 11.6).

Word Axis

Students use a Word Axis template to arrange words along an *x*-axis that moves from informal to formal and a y-axis that progresses from less to more (see Figure 11.3). Students can place the instructional word anywhere along the x- and y-axes. For example, if the target word is *startling*, first begin with the easier word *amazing* placed at the intersection. Students then brainstorm other words that have a similar meaning to *amazing* and add them to the axes after deciding if each word means more or less than *amazing*, and if each word is more or less formal than *amazing*. Then students look up the definition of the instructional target word (*startling*) and decide where to position it on the axis. They now have a visual representation of where this word fits in their understanding of words with a similar meaning (see Figure 11.4).

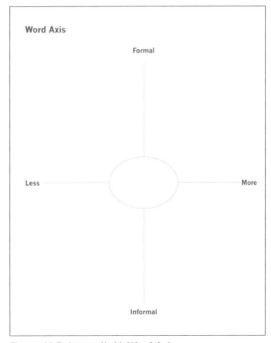

Figure 11.3 Appendix V: Word Axis

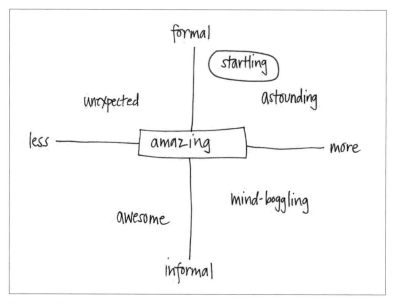

Figure 11.4 A Word Axis for *Amazing*

Linear Array

Students use a Linear Array to arrange a cluster of words along a continuum to help their understanding of an instructional target word. In this first example of a Linear Array, the teacher chose the target word *tepid* and the endpoints *coldest* and *hottest*, writing only the endpoints on the array. Next, she asked students a brainstorming question: "What are all the words you know that relate to the temperature of water?" Then, students arranged those words on a horizontal line, moving from the endpoints *coldest* to *hottest*. Finally, the teacher placed the instructional word, *tepid*, on the array above the line between the words *cool* and *warm*—her placement of the word gave students an immediate understanding of its meaning (see Figure 11.5). If students are working on Linear Arrays in small groups on their own, they will place the instructional target word on the array after looking it up; your job is to determine what the initial brainstorming question will be and what the endpoints of the linear array will be.

In the next example of a Linear Array, the teacher wanted ninth graders to learn the target word *immaculate*. As with the previous example, thinking of the question that will spur students' initial brainstorming is your first step, followed by thinking what the endpoints will be. In this case, the teacher asked, "What are all the words you know that could describe how messy or clean your room is?" Then, students arranged the words they brainstormed along the array from the endpoints *trashy* to *perfect*. The target word, *immaculate*, appeared at the far end of the array (see Figure 11.6).

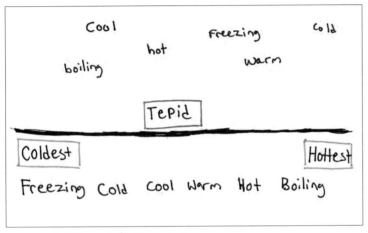

Figure 11.5 A Linear Array, Example A

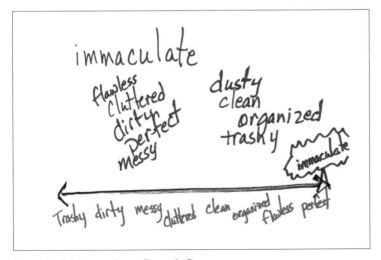

Figure 11.6 A Linear Array, Example B

189

Dear George,

No one ever wants to relive that seventh-grade year. It's so tough in so many ways. But how I wish you and I could step back in time and do that one again. We could have done so much in so many areas, including vocabulary; instead, I pushed you through the red level of that workbook we used. Toward the end of school, as we finished the last vocabulary unit, you asked if we were done with that vocabulary book. As I stood in the doorway, talking with an eighth-grade language arts teacher, I nodded my head yes. You walked to the garbage can and threw it away and muttered something I'm probably happy I didn't understand. The other teacher told you that you couldn't get rid of it that easily. You asked her what she meant. She explained that in eighth grade you'd have the yellow-level book.

"Same stuff?" your small voice asked.

"Yep," her throaty voice replied.

Your eyes welled with tears that you quickly wiped away. "I give up," you whispered and sat down, head on folded arms.

"It'll be OK," I said, kneeling beside you.

"Really?" you asked. "Which part will be OK? Not knowing how to do these stupid books or not knowing how to read or not knowing any of the answers that any teacher ever asks? Just which part do you think will be OK?"

Your words caught me by surprise. Over all my years of working with teachers and students, I have always been surprised by the honesty we all sometimes share with one another. In a workshop filled with hundreds of teachers, one lone teacher stood up and offered to us all her frustration: "Sometimes I don't do more because I don't know what else to do, and sometimes, I'm simply too tired to do more." She sat down. The room was quiet. Some teachers looked down; some glanced at her; and almost every teacher nodded. One teacher sitting beside her reached over to hold her hand. In that one moment, all those teachers understood her feelings of exhaustion and frustration. In 2021, a twelfth grader told me, "I want to care about what I'm doing, but I just don't. It seems like school is about hurry, hurry, hurry. But hurry to where? I'm afraid of what I'm supposed to do after school." Those two people, one a teacher and one a student, like you did that day long ago, reminded me that at our core we all want—we all need—to be heard.

Dear George,

"What's this word?" you asked.

"*Determination*," I said. "Do you know what that means?" I asked.

"Nope."

"Do you want to talk about what it means?"

"Nope."

As you walked off, I told you, "I'm *determined* to teach you some new words."

You kept your head down, but I saw that smile. "Nope," you said.

Context Clues and Word Parts

THIS FINAL CHAPTER ABOUT VOCABULARY ADDRESSES
two important instructional practices:

1. Teaching students to use context clues to understand unknown words

2. Teaching students to use root words and affixes to understand
   unknown words

Once, in a very unscientific study (no control variable, no written record,
no strict data analysis—just sitting in a restaurant with a lot of English
teachers in Detroit during the National Council of Teachers of English
Annual Convention), I asked about twenty teachers to ask as many teachers as they could during the next two days the following question: When
it comes to vocabulary instruction, what advice do you most often share
with students? Two nights later, we met at the same place and shared our
results over more glasses of wine. We had either fifty responses or twenty-
five hundred. I lost count. Yes, the methodology lacked rigor. What was
interesting to me, though, was the number one response: "I tell kids to use
the context clues."

When the *Context* Is the Clue

Let's consider the usefulness of this advice. Yes, we tell students to use
context clues . . . often. The problem with that is, discerning the meaning
of unknown words using context clues requires a sophisticated interaction

with the text that some less skilled readers have not yet achieved. Conversely, if they could use the context as a clue, they would be more skilled readers. Consider the following sentences:

> *The jaundiced voters doubted whether they believed the politician; like so many other politicians, this one offered promises that the voters didn't think he would keep. Their pessimistic attitude frustrated the candidate as he tried to explain that he was sincere in his promises.*

If the word we want students to define from the context is *jaundiced,* then what context clue or clues do we expect them to use? The best clue comes in the second sentence, where a synonym for *jaundiced* is offered— *pessimistic.* You probably saw that right away. But you're a reader who makes all sorts of inferences while reading. Look at what skilled readers must do to get to that clue:

- Readers must infer that *their* in sentence 2 refers to *voters* in sentence 1.

- Readers must recognize that *pessimistic* is describing *attitude* in the same way that *jaundiced* was describing *voters.*

- Then, they have to make the inference that there's a semantic connection (not just syntactic) between *jaundiced* and *pessimistic.*

- Next, from that inference, they have to see that *pessimistic* is a synonym for *jaundiced* and, from that, infer that *jaundiced* means *pessimistic.*

- If they don't know what *pessimistic* means, they must use all the information in both sentences to infer that voters aren't happy with politicians. That means they must know the words *candidate, frustrated,* and *sincere*—all tier 2 words less skilled readers might not have read enough to retrieve quickly from long-term memory.

- And, they must infer that the candidate is a politician.

All of that must happen even when there is a direct clue (a synonym) to the meaning in the sentence.

🫂 Step Inside a Classroom

While working in a high school, I gave two students the following paragraph:

> Tara's dad couldn't believe his ears. Finally, he folded his newspaper in half, set it on the coffee table, and got up from his chair to leave the room. As he got to the door, he said, "I never thought that I'd tell my loquacious daughter that she is DRIVING ME NUTS!"
>
> His daughter finally moved the phone from her mouth and said, "You say something, Daddy?" before he walked out, shaking his head.

I asked one student, an accomplished tenth grader (pre–AP English class; assistant editor for the school newspaper; all-A, honor roll student) to let me record his thinking about the word *loquacious*:

> Well, I thought I had heard that word before, but thought it was, like, to do with being loco, you know, crazy. But that, I don't know, maybe that's it, because it says "she is driving me nuts," like crazy. But then I looked back to that first sentence and where it says "couldn't believe his ears" rather than his eyes, then that got me thinking about hearing, you know, because it's usually "couldn't believe his eyes." Ears is important or the author wouldn't have changed it. And then later it says that when he said "you drive me nuts" that then the daughter, she, like, moved the phone from her mouth and that means that she was talking. And, like, talking and hearing, they have to do with each other. And my sister, oh my gosh, she is always on the phone talking, and that can drive you nuts. So, maybe, like, loquacious, it means, like, talking, a lot.

I can't begin to count all the inferences that student made to define that word from the context. But what's readily apparent is how active he was in constructing that knowledge. It's that level of activity that is sometimes missing from our less skilled readers.

Then, I asked a ninth-grade student who told me adamantly he did not like to read and admitted more quietly, "I don't read very good," to read the same passage and then talk about how he figured out the meaning of *loquacious*:

> *It's something about the girl, the daughter. And see how these words are capital—you're driving me nuts—well, that must be important because it's in capitals and it's about the girl, too. So, so, you know, if you're, like, really bothering someone you say "you're driving me nuts." So, it means, it is like, what is it when you really bother someone? You're like a pain. Annoying. That's it. Maybe it could mean annoying.*

An important difference between these two readers is that the first reader was willing to move beyond the single sentence where the word occurred to infer the meaning; in fact, he was willing not only to move beyond but also to look back to preceding sentences. He understood that context extends beyond the immediate few words after the word in question. The less skilled reader, however, viewed context in a limited manner. I suspect that was supported by many worksheet pages in which he practiced using context clues where the clue did occur in the same sentence as the target word. Those contrived practices rarely help prepare students for the types of clues they will encounter in real texts.

Note that both readers were willing to move beyond the passage to try to bring in their own background knowledge. The first reader made a connection to his own sister who talks on the phone a lot; the second reader talked about hearing the phrase "driving me nuts." The difference, again, is that the first reader made a connection beyond the sentence where the target word occurred. The second reader limited his thinking about the word to that single sentence.

The first problem we see with telling students to use context clues is that the clues are subtle and require multiple inferences from readers. Second, context clues may give some readers some idea about the word's meaning, but that usually isn't sufficient for inferring specific meanings (Vacca, Vacca, and Gove 2000; Nagy 1988; Baumann and Kameenui 1991). In other words, context clues occasionally offer the gist of the meaning, enough perhaps to complete that one reading, but not enough to allow students to define a word so that they can use it on their own in other situations.

Types of Context Clues

Does that mean we should abandon teaching context clues? I don't think so. It means we must recognize that using the context as a clue is something that requires repeated practice and might be more challenging than we originally realized. Some clues to meaning do appear in the context, though, and they are often signaled by transition words. Teach these four main types of context clues:

- definition or explanation clues
- restatement or synonym clues
- contrast or antonym clues
- gist clues

Definition or explanation clues are the most direct clues an author offers readers. With this type of clue, the author actually defines the word for the reader, generally in the same sentence. For example:

> *A symbol is something that stands for something else.*

Restatement or synonym clues are clues that explain unfamiliar words in the text by restating them in simpler terms or by using synonyms. This type of clue is often used in content area textbooks. Unlike definition clues, restatement clues may or may not appear in the same sentence as the unfamiliar word. For example:

> *Cowboys often wore chaps, leather trousers without a seat, over their pants to protect their legs from thorns.*

> *The food was bland. In fact, everyone called it tasteless.*

Contrast or antonym clues offer an opposite meaning for a word. These clues often require that students catch and understand the signal word. Like restatement and synonym clues, the contrast or antonym may appear in the same sentence or a subsequent sentence. For example:

Chad is calm and quiet, but his brother is boisterous.

Gist clues are the most subtle type of clue an author can offer readers. With these clues, the reader must infer the meaning of a particular word from the general context—or the gist—of the passage. Sometimes readers must read an entire passage before they understand the meaning of the word. For example:

> *John burst out of the woods and found himself at the edge of*
> *a precipice. Clinging to a boulder, he gazed down dizzily at the*
> *blue ribbon of river below.*

The word *precipice* isn't defined, restated, or put in contrast with other words. Therefore, readers must figure out what that word means by reading the passage and thinking about the other information in the text. "If he's gazing down, he's up high. And, if the river looks like a blue ribbon, he must be very high. Boulders are very big rocks, usually on mountains. A precipice must be someplace up high, on a mountain, at the edge of something where you can see over to what's below."

Teaching context clues requires we do just that—teach the clue that is in the context. Telling kids to use their context clues often leaves them as perplexed as if we had said nothing. Teaching requires we show them, through our own reading, how we use the clues in the context to help us understand what words mean.

Teaching Specific Roots and Affixes

We can't directly teach the meaning of all words, and sometimes the context leaves students clueless; therefore, we also must help students increase their word knowledge by teaching them how words work. In other words, let's teach them the meanings of prefixes, roots, and suffixes. When students learn those meanings, they can unlock the definitions of many words.

My work with less skilled readers suggests that they benefit from learning specific roots, prefixes, and suffixes. Students who benefit the most are those who attend schools in which teachers do some vertical planning with all the grades in the school. This way, teachers from each grade know which roots and affixes constitute the master list for the school and, more specifically, which ones will be introduced at which grade level. No longer should one teacher decide to do a unit on roots and affixes because she likes word study while the next three teachers say they just don't take the time to do that; word study should be something teachers across grades embrace so that students have repeated opportunities for learning and relearning. Start with the most common roots, prefixes, and suffixes (see Appendix W) and then move to the content-specific roots and affixes found in Appendix X.

Vocabulary Trees

Rather than handing students a list of roots with their definitions and examples of words that include those roots, let students build Vocabulary Trees (see Figure 12.1).

To build a vocabulary tree, choose which root word you want students to study and have them write it in the root of the tree. Under the root, students write its definition. In Figure 12.1, for example, the student has written *tract* in the root area of the tree with "to pull, drag" written underneath. In the trunk of the tree, students write a key word that you provide that uses that root. Under the word, students write the definition of the word. Then, in the branches that come off the trunk, students write as many other words as they find that use that root. In this case, the student found *detract*, *subtract*, *traction*, and *contract*. Students define each word and copy a sentence that uses it. This could be a sentence they heard, one they read, or one they said themselves. In the twigs off the branch, they record where they heard or found the sentence.

This works best as a group activity, something that's visible so students can add words as the year continues. I visited a school where Vocabulary Trees grew in the hallways and students could read them as they stood around lockers or add words when teachers approved of their choices. Other students have turned to digital tools to create vocabulary trees that have "bloomed" as we've watched the video play.

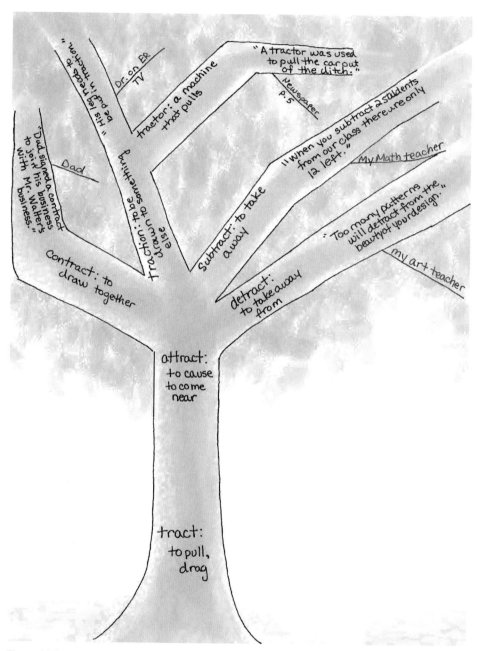

Figure 12.1 Vocabulary Tree

Dear George,

Little by little, without realizing it, you were showing me that learning words didn't have to be about lists and quizzes; it could be about curiosity and fun. So, George, this is for you:

Knock, knock.

Who's there?

Ya.

Ya who?

No, thanks. I use Google!

And one more because I miss you, George . . .

Knock, knock.

Who's there?

Hike.

Hike who?

I didn't know you liked Japanese poetry!

I'm done for the evening, George. I hope wherever you are, you also sometimes see a cashew and laugh.

Dear George,

You sat beside my desk one day after school, struggling through a short story. I read a few sentences; you read a few sentences. Your finger pointed to each word as you said it, slowly, one . . . word . . . at . . . a . . . time. For you, reading was a slow and laborious process. Many times, I found myself simply telling you the word just so you'd finish. Once, as we sat together in our classroom during lunch, eating sandwiches and reading a portion of a short story aloud that I knew you'd never get through on your own, I said, "I think it would make more sense to you if you'd just read it a bit faster."

"Now why didn't I think of that?" you replied with a slow grin and then continued your word-at-a-time approach.

I heard echoes of that conversation recently when I listened to a beginning teacher suggest to a tenth grader that he seemed to be reading very slowly. "No duh," he said. "Miss," he continued, "I'd love to read faster, but this is as fast as the reading brain works."

Slowly, like your reading, I came to understand the role of fluency in becoming an independent reader.

CHAPTER 13

Fluency and Automaticity

AUTOMATICITY IS THAT ABILITY TO DO SOMETHING quickly without conscious thought about the task.

For instance, as I typed these words, I didn't consciously think about where each key is located on the keyboard; in fact, when I try to recall the location of individual keys, I begin making errors. If you play a musical instrument, you know that once you have memorized a piece of music, your fingers know what to do. The muscle memory of what notes to strike next lets you strike the next keys automatically and play the music fluently. Should you start to concentrate on fingering or particular notes, you will stumble.

If you don't play an instrument, think about driving someplace. Have you ever arrived and wondered how you got there? Have you gotten into your car on a Saturday to run errands and then discovered, at some point, you were driving to your school? That's automaticity. And if you didn't stop suddenly or jerk the steering wheel quickly to avoid a pothole, then your driving was smooth. If we were talking about reading instead of driving, we would use the word *fluent*.

So much of what we do each day depends on us being able to do things with automaticity. You pour another glass of milk and don't concentrate on how far to tip the milk carton (or perhaps that's a glass of wine and you know exactly how far to tilt the wine bottle). You fill that glass easily, barely paying attention to your actions as you continue talking with others about your day. That automaticity allows you to think about other things as you accomplish that task.

203

On the other hand, have you watched a one-year-old take her first steps? Her concentration on the task is all-consuming. Talk and walk? No. Talk and babble a conversation? No. That little one focuses on each step. That one action takes all her cognitive energy. But soon, with practice, she will do more than take steps without purposefully lifting a small foot and carefully placing it. She will walk fluently, rushing when she needs to, slowing when that is better, and keeping a calm, measured pace when that is best. She will have found her rhythm.

The Rhythm of Reading

Reading automaticity refers to a reader's ability to recognize words without conscious decoding.

It means readers recognize words as whole units, and they recognize the words quickly and accurately. They see the word *cat* as a unit—not /c-a-t/ or even /c-at/. Sounding out words a letter at a time or syllable by syllable slows a reader and disrupts fluency, and that interrupts meaning. While this is a step that happens for most readers as they first begin to sound out words, as they build automaticity, it's not how they continue to read.

When letters appear between slash marks, say the sound of the letter, not the letter and not the word.

It's important to remember that students don't develop automaticity via decoding but rather through repeated exposure to a word they can decode. Said another way, just because students can sound out a word doesn't mean they automatically recognize it.

"It's important to remember that students don't develop automaticity via decoding but rather through repeated exposure to a word they can decode."

Decoding and decoding automatically are two different skills. I can play the guitar, but changing chords does not come automatically to me, and then playing those chords, one after another, does not come fluently. Why not? I don't practice. Automaticity requires practice—whether we are talking about playing the guitar or decoding words. When students have trouble decoding, the first thing they need to do is decode more. Their brains need to develop the muscle memory of how combinations of letters work. As students begin to decode automatically, then they can begin to read fluently. Automaticity—rapid and accurate word recognition—is a necessary condition for fluency.

Fluency

Fluency—the ability to read smoothly and easily at a good pace with appropriate phrasing and expression—develops over time as students' word recognition skills improve. When students can decode accurately, decode with automaticity, and read with phrasing and expression that brings meaning to the words, they are reading fluently (Rasinski 2004). Students lacking fluency read slowly, a word at a time, often pausing between words or phrases; they make frequent mistakes, ignore punctuation marks, and read in a monotone. This, in turn, affects comprehension. Fluency does not automatically result in comprehension; a lack of fluency, however, can impede comprehension. Fluent readers know the words automatically and therefore move easily from word to word, spending their cognitive energy on constructing meaning.

> *"Fluency does not automatically result in comprehension; a lack of fluency, however, can impede comprehension."*

Fluency and Less Skilled Readers

Let's go back to our sentence about those old folks and the boat: *The old man the boat.* To understand it, you must do more than decode the words, and you must do more than understand that *old* can be the noun and *man* can be the verb. You must read it with prosody, the phrasing needed so the text makes sense. You must read the sentence this way: The old [*pause*] man the boat. The sentence is not written with a comma (The old, man the boat) because our grammar doesn't put a comma between the subject and the predicate. Your brain, however, must add the pause. And the fluency occurs in that moment of silence. The reader who recognizes that need for that silence is a fluent reader.

When we compare fluent and disfluent readers, we see the differences listed in Figure 13.1.

👥 Step Inside a Classroom

Let's look at two readers who lack fluency, Mike and Sharamee.

Mike

When I met Mike, he was in ninth grade. He didn't play any organized sports but loved skateboarding, and when given the choice, he sat at the back of the room, hunched down into his seat. He was retained in third

COMPARING FLUENT AND DISFLUENT READERS

Fluent Readers...	Disfluent Readers...
Change their reading rate depending on the text	Read slowly and with difficulty
Use punctuation to help guide reading	Skip over punctuation
Chunk words into meaningful phrases	Read one word at a time
Read with the expression that the words and punctuation suggest	Read in a monotone
Self-correct as needed	Read through mistakes

Figure 13.1 Differences in Fluent and Disfluent Readers

grade and made barely passing grades throughout middle school. He was tested for resource classes in sixth grade and did not qualify since there was no significant difference between his achievement level and his IQ.

He was a quiet young man who appeared to have mastered the art of being invisible. He rarely brought his books to class and used his notebook as a place to cram papers that he seldom looked at again. He resisted any reading aloud and generally refused to do so by just putting his head down on his desk or saying that he forgot his book. When he did read aloud just for me, it was slow, it was halting, and it revealed an overreliance on sounding out words and little attention to comprehension.

What follows is a transcript of his oral reading of the first four sentences of "The Gift of the Magi," by O. Henry (1997), a story in his ninth-grade literature anthology. Mike's words appear in italics above the actual words from the text:

On-one d-d-do-l-l-ar and, and eight-eighty-sev-eighty-seven c-e-nts.
One dollar and eighty-seven cents.

Th-that w-was all.
That was all.

And eight-six and six cents off it was in pen-pens pens saved
And sixty cents of it was in pennies. Pennies saved

one, one twi-two at a
one and two at a

time. By b-b-bull, bulldozers, by the bulldozers the gro-groc-er and the
time by bulldozing the grocer and the

veg-vegetar-veternarian man and the but-cher, butcher, man
vegetable man and the butcher

until one, one check, one check got burned, burned up,
until one's cheeks burned

with the si-slice, im-impo-impossible . . . of par-parts-pars-i-my.
with the silent imputation of parsimony. (2)

Without doubt, this text was far beyond Mike's independent reading level and was also not an instructional-level text for him. This was a frustration-level text. But in the school I was visiting, teachers did not have the option to make sure students read at their instructional level. They read what was in an old literature book.

I asked Mike what these four sentences were about. He responded:

I don't know. [Pause.] I guess, somebody, [pause] there was,
like, a bulldozer, and somebody's check, the check it got burned
up, into parts. [Pause.] I don't know. [Long pause.] You know
I can't read this stuff.

Mike was right. He couldn't read that stuff. And he wasn't going to improve if he did not get a chance to practice with instructional-level texts that allowed him to hone decoding skills while building automaticity and fluency. He was trying to sound out words one letter at a time and sometimes a syllable at a time. With multisyllabic words, he often made up what the final syllables would be, perhaps to create a word he knew, or dropped the final syllable entirely. He read through punctuation, not pausing at periods or, conversely, pausing where there was no end punctuation. He did know some sight words as well as recognize some high-frequency words, but he got lost in the slow reading rate and the misspoken words.

That said, he did want this text to make sense. That's most apparent in the words he inserted while reading, words that were not a part of the original text. For example, where the text read, "by bulldozing," he decided the word was *bulldozer* and then inserted the article *the*, so he read it, "by the bulldozer." The insertion showed that he was attempting to make what he was reading make sense at some level. Later, he read, "one check got burned, burned up," for "one's cheeks burned." Substituting "check" for "cheek," he then inserted "got" and "up" to create the phrase "one check got burned up," a phrase that made good sense.

When he had finished reading and I asked him to tell me what the passage was about, he continued to rely on that phrase and even tried to extend the meaning—"the check it got burned up, into parts"—by changing "parsimony" into "parts." He then said, "I don't know," in an admission that the text really didn't make sense to him. These slim indicators told me that he did know that texts are supposed to make sense and he was working—at least to some degree—to make that happen.

Finally, his comment "You know I can't read this stuff," reminded me that Mike was no novice when it came to facing difficult texts. He expected that he wouldn't be able to do it, expected that I *knew* he wouldn't be able to do it, and didn't expect anything to change.

So, where do we start with a student like Mike? His most obvious problem was that decoding wasn't automatic; therefore, he was a slow, disfluent reader. Helping him with word recognition was a priority. As his ability to quickly recognize words improved, his fluency and reading rate improved. As that happened, he had more cognitive energy to spend on comprehension. Then we began to see that Mike also had a very limited vocabulary. Spending time building that vocabulary became a priority.

Sharamee

Sharamee was a seventh grader who was facing retention for that grade. She was energetic and funny and loved to talk. She willingly read aloud and always volunteered for any sort of oral reading: reading directions, reading poems, reading the morning announcements, reading minutes from the student council meetings, reading selections from her literature book. Her oral reading was very fast, sometimes so fast that her words slurred together. When asked to slow down, she would vary her rate for a few words, then speed back up. Though a fast reader who could pronounce almost any word in almost any text, she did not have a lot of expression in her reading.

Though she enjoyed reading aloud, she rarely read silently. During sustained silent reading time, she would find many excuses to not read—everything from needing to go see the school nurse to saying she forgot her book. If she did get her book opened in front of her, it wasn't long before she was writing notes or turning around to whisper to the person behind her. When asked why she didn't like to read silently, she responded, "I just like to read aloud, you know, to say the words." I asked her if, when she read silently, she heard the words in her mind. She said, "I don't know. What do you mean 'hear them in my mind'? If you want to hear it, you have to read it aloud." If *you* aren't sure what I mean by "hearing the words in your mind," then reread this sentence and try not to hear the words. Can you do it? Probably not. Skilled readers "hear" the words of a text as easily as (sometimes more easily than) they visualize a text. Many less skilled readers, however, like Sharamee, claim they don't hear anything when they read.

When her class read aloud the play *The Diary of Anne Frank*, Sharamee read the part of Anne. The teacher spent several days discussing the Holocaust, World War II, Hitler, and how some people helped Jewish people by hiding them. She talked at length about Anne and the diary she wrote. The class then spent several more days reading the play aloud. When they finished, I had the opportunity to interview Sharamee:

Me:	What did you think about the play?
Sharamee:	It was good.
Me:	Yeah? What was good about it?
Sharamee:	You know, just the play, it was good.
Me:	What did you think about Anne?
Sharamee:	About Anne?
Me:	Yeah, you know, about what she went through?
Sharamee:	I'm not sure. Like when?
Me:	Do you remember what happened to Anne?

Sharamee:	She got this diary. And there's a play. And they hid, you know, they hid, in the play. She had a sister.
Me:	Remember how your teacher told you that Anne's diary was published as a book, and how part of it was turned into the play you just read?
Sharamee:	Uh-huh.
Me:	Why do you think what she put in her diary was important enough to turn into a book or make into a play?
Sharamee:	Because, uh, well, it's a play, you know, and she wrote this diary, because of the war and then wrote a play. It was the war. She didn't want there to be a war.

Later, I asked Sharamee if she was a good reader. "Oh, yeah, I'm real good," she quickly replied.

"Why?"

"I just am. I can read real fast. The teachers always call on me to read."

"So how well do you comprehend what you read?" I asked.

No reply.

"You know, when you've finished reading," I explained, "do you understand what you were reading?"

"Well, sometimes that part's a little hard." She pauses. "But the reading part I do real good," she said.

For Sharamee, reading meant decoding. We began reading aloud to Sharamee asking her to retell what she heard every few paragraphs. We made sure she was listening to funny texts or texts with high adventure and we read with a lot of expression. When she would laugh or wonder what was going to happen next, we would talk about what in the text caused those reactions. Then, we would have her read aloud the next sections, stopping often. We would encourage retelling (see page 145) and often used Sketch to Stretch (see page 120).

Though I try hard not to say "good reader," sometimes I slip up. I did when speaking with Sharmee and she responded using the same term. I shudder when I think of students who tell themselves they are "bad" readers.

Reading Rate

Reading rates usually increase faster during the elementary school years than during the middle and high school years. Furthermore, the more a reader reads, the more her reading rate will improve. So, students in classrooms that provide big blocks of time for sustained silent reading, as well as students from home environments that encourage home reading, show more gains in reading rate than students who do little reading at school or home.

We should also expect that reading rates vary as the content changes (one might read magazines faster than physics books), as motivation and interests change, and as background knowledge changes. In fact, the ability to vary that rate is a sign of a proficient reader and exemplifies what fluency is really all about—accurate, smooth, expressive reading that allows for comprehension of the text. So, while gaining speed in reading rate is important, speed alone does not equal fluency. Fluency is also determined by accuracy, phrasing, and intonation (Clay and Imlach 1971).

Depending on the source you use, you will see that guidelines for reading rates vary for the same grade levels (Harris and Sipay 1990). Most often, these differences occur because of the difficulty or ease of passages students are reading. I like to use the range of rates offered by Barr et al. (2007) because these reading researchers provide a wide range for each grade (see Figure 13.2). When middle schoolers or high school students fall below these minimum average oral or silent reading rates, then I've got to look carefully at their fluency and automaticity and work at improving their reading rate.

TYPICAL READING RATES FOR GRADES 3–6		
Grade	Oral	Silent
3	70–120	90–120
4	90–140	110–140
5	100–150	140–170
6	110–150	160–190

Figure 13.2 Reading Rates Across Grades (adapted from Barr et al. 2007)

When Reading Rate Is Low

Why is it important to improve a student's reading rate? Let's do a little math to see how a slow reading rate affects middle and high school students. First, notice in Figure 13.2 that the typical silent reading rate for a sixth grader is 160 to 190 words per minute.

Here's the problem: You read at a rate of 60 words per minute. You have 10 pages of homework to read. Each page of homework has 500 words (social studies textbook, science textbook, literature book). How long will it take you to complete your homework?

Did you finish your calculations? You'll spend 83 minutes, or 1 hour and 23 minutes, just reading 10 pages. And that's presuming that it's 10 pages that are at your independent level. Now, let's say you have 20 pages to read—a typical amount for many high school students. Reading time is now at 158 minutes, or 2 hours and 38 minutes. That's more than 2.5 hours just to read your homework—not to complete the assignments, mind you, just to read the pages. Compare that with the student who reads about 275 words per minute (the average words per minute [WPM] rate for skilled readers in grades 9–12). That student will spend about 18 minutes reading 10 pages or about 36 minutes reading 20 pages. With little effort, you can understand how a slow reading rate can affect a student's attitude toward reading.

Improving a student's reading rate doesn't automatically mean a student's attitude toward reading will improve or that comprehension will improve. But comprehension will not improve as long as the reading rate is low and students are disfluent readers. Fluency is a necessary, but not sufficient, part of comprehension.

To determine a student's reading rate, keep in mind that you are measuring both accuracy and speed. To determine a silent reading rate, follow these steps:

1. Choose a book at the student's independent reading level.

2. Give the student some background knowledge on the book by providing a very brief summary.

3. Have the student begin reading the book silently.

4. Time the student for one minute. At the end of the minute, have the student stop reading and count the number of words that the student read in that one minute.

5. Repeat this two more times.

6. Add the three numbers and divide by three. That gives you an average silent reading rate.

7. Make sure you follow up with some general questions about what the student read. If the student can't answer questions you believe he should be able to answer after reading the passage only one time, then the rate tells you little.

I like to determine a silent reading rate and an oral reading rate. Oral rates are generally slower (we simply can't read aloud as fast as we read silently) but offer a better understanding of the phrasing, expression, and intonation that a student is using while reading. To determine a student's oral reading rate, follow these steps:

1. Choose a passage with at least two hundred words. Give the student an overview of the passage.

2. Tell the student to begin reading at a rate that's comfortable for her.

3. Tell her if she makes a mistake, she should certainly go back and correct it. Tell her that if she comes to a word she does not know at all, she should try to figure it out on her own. If she can't, you should wait about three seconds and then either tell the student to skip it or tell the student the word.

4. As the student reads, you need to follow along on your own copy and take note of all errors (technically referred to as miscues). Any miscue that is corrected should be noted as such. If the student inserts words that aren't there (text says, "drove fast," and student says, "drove very fast"), that's a miscue. If the student omits words (text says, "drove very fast," and student says, "drove fast"), that too is a miscue. If the student skips a word because she doesn't know it, or if you have to supply the word, that's a miscue. If the student simply repeats words, do not count repetitions as miscues.

5. Decide how many minutes you want the student to read (one to five minutes) and then when finished, divide the number of words she read by the number of minutes.

6. Next, tally the uncorrected miscues. Divide that number by the total number of words read. So, if the student made 9 miscues on the 150 words she read, the proportion of miscues is 6 percent. Now, subtract that 6 from 100 (100 being perfect accuracy) to get an accuracy rate of 94 percent. Remember, the instructional reading level is an accuracy rate of 90 percent to 94 percent.

7. Rate the student's fluency. I rate students on a scale of 1 to 3. Level 1 indicates that the student reads a word at a time, pauses often, still sounds out many words, uses a monotone, ignores punctuation, and lacks any sort of meaningful phrasing. Level 2 shows that the student manages some fluency in some phrases, still pauses occasionally to repeat words or sound out words, responds to some punctuation, and uses some expression. Level 3 shows good phrasing, nice expression, some repetitions mostly to correct miscues, smooth (not choppy) reading, and intonation that indicates an understanding of what the student is reading.

8. Check the student's comprehension by asking questions and asking the student to retell the passage. Remember, good accuracy with low comprehension means that the passage is too difficult for instructional purposes.

Improving Fluency

If I see that a student is scoring far below the average reading rates, then I know I must help the student with fluency. Sometimes fluency problems are not a result of poor word recognition or a lack of automaticity. Sometimes children have tracking problems with their eyes. If students constantly lose their place while reading, tracking might be a problem. If you suspect this, make sure you let parents know immediately so they can get their child to the ophthalmologist.

Other students are simply easily distracted. They aren't paying attention to what they are reading—whether silently or orally—so they lose focus. If you hear a lot of "ums" in between words while students are reading aloud, that may be the problem.

And still other students slow down as they read an unfamiliar text. If that's the case, consider doing more prereading activities to help students prior to reading the activity. When the issue is, however, that students simply have not developed the fluency they need, try the following suggestions.

High-Frequency Words

Sight words are generally considered to be those words that students need to learn by sight because they don't follow regular decoding rules (e.g., *have*, *does*, *give*, *been*). The reality is, though, all words that we decode automatically have become sight words. Often we use the term "sight word" when we mean those words that are spelled irregularly. *High-frequency* words are those words that appear so often in texts that automatic recognition is helpful. Students need to be able to recognize both irregularly spelled words and high-frequency words instantly.

Blevins (2001), building on the work by Johns (1980), Fry, Kress, and Fountoukidis (1993), Adams (1990), and Carroll, Davies, and Richman (1971), offers these numbers:

- Of the approximately six hundred thousand–plus words in English, a relatively small number appear frequently in print.

- Only thirteen words (*a, and, for, he, is, in, it, of, that, the, to, was, you*) account for over 25 percent of the words in print, and one hundred words account for approximately 50 percent.

- The Dolch Basic Sight Vocabulary contains 220 words (no nouns). Although this list was generated over forty years ago, these words account for over 50 percent of the words found in textbooks today.

There are many lists of both sight words and high-frequency words. The Dolch Basic Sight Vocabulary and Fry's Instant Words List are two of the more common lists. I've included these lists in Appendixes Y and Z.

Spend some time making sure your disfluent readers know these words. It takes very little time to call a student to a conferencing area of the room and simply run through the words. If this looks like out-of-context reading, that's because it most certainly is. I want to see how quickly students can recognize the most frequently seen words in the least contextual environment. I've found that if a student can quickly recognize *because* written alone on an index card, then he generally can recognize it in a sentence. If a student can't recognize the word in isolation, then he may or may not be able to recognize it in context. I want students to definitely be able to recognize it in context—not sometimes, not when the contextual clue is obvious enough, but all the time.

You can reinforce high-frequency words with word walls. Word walls are a powerful way to get words in front of students for constant reinforcement. Find a space on your wall where you can put up words, arranged alphabetically. Write the words large enough that students can see them easily from a distance. Also, don't build a word wall prior to the first day of class so that it is on the wall when students arrive. That word wall would belong to you. Instead, have the portion of the wall you'll be using marked and divided into a grid labeled with letters of the alphabet so that students know where to put specific words, and then build the word wall with the students. Now it's theirs. For a high-frequency word wall, I often ask students to look at a few pages of text and find some words that appear over and over. They find words like *of, a, the, at, that, but, have, very, would, about, had,* and *if* with little trouble. I (or a student) write one word on a card (again, use big print and a marker), and then we put the word under the correct letter.

"If we don't give these slowest readers time to read, they will never be anything other than a slow, disfluent reader."

Finally, help students learn high-frequency words through *lots* of reading. This is difficult because students who need help reading high-frequency words are our slowest readers, so giving them time to read means giving them books they can read and then lots of time to read those books. If we don't give these slowest readers time to read, they will never be anything other than a slow, disfluent reader.

Give Students Varied Opportunities for Hearing Texts

Students need to hear fluent reading in order to become fluent readers. Make sure as you are reading aloud to students, you are modeling good expression, good phrasing, and good pacing. Keep in mind that you can model fluent reading by reading aloud just a few pages from the chapter students are reading or the short story they are about to read. Smith (1979) reminds us that when students listen to a teacher read aloud a few pages of a text they are about to read on their own, and follow along as the teacher reads, these students then complete the story with better fluency and accuracy.

Echo reading in small or large groups improves fluency. In echo reading, the teacher reads aloud a short passage, modeling strong phrasing, and then students repeat the same passage, mimicking his reading. As with comprehension instruction, begin an echo reading lesson with specific information:

"As I read the following passage, note how I raise my voice at the end of sentences that are questions." Again, if you think your students don't need this level of practice, then move to other strategies.

Choral reading is similar to echo reading except the teacher isn't reading the passage first with students echoing afterward. Choose a few lines that offer a specific reason to be read aloud. Perhaps there's a section of dialogue between two characters, one who is whispering while the other is shouting. One part of the class can read the shouting character's words while the other responds with the whispered text. The point of choral reading is to work on a specific aspect of fluent reading.

After any type of oral reading—whether it be a read-aloud from you, echo reading, or choral reading—ask students what they noticed about how the dialogue was read, how statements and questions were read differently, how excitement was added, how a character's emotions were captured through stress and intonation. Ask what they noticed about the phrasing and the pacing. Remember, in the beginning, their answers might vary between the ever-ready "I don't know" and the frustrating shoulder shrug. Then, you have to model answers. It also might mean you aren't exaggerating the reading enough. Students must hear the features you want them to understand.

Teach Phrasing and Intonation Directly

It's one thing to model fluent reading and another to directly teach students how to use correct phrasing and intonation. You can do it by sharing a series of sentences and asking students to read them (through choral reading, echo reading, or reading by individual volunteers) following the directions you give. The goal is to show students that how you read a text can make a difference in what you understand about the text.

Don't assume that nonfluent readers naturally understand this. The reality is, they probably don't give phrasing and intonation much thought. You've got to show them directly how stress on certain words can make a difference in meaning. Try it with this example:

> *Read the following sentences aloud. In each sentence, stress the word that is underlined:*
>
> **You** *read the book.*
>
> *You* **read** *the book.*

*You read **the** book.*

*You read the **book.***

Why did your voice change as you read each sentence?

Have Students Reread Selected Texts

One of the best ways to improve fluency is through the repeated rereading of texts (Samuels 1979). Let the student read an instructional-level text aloud. You time him for a prearranged number of minutes (one to five is fine). Afterward, discuss any miscues the student made and count the number of words per minute the student read accurately.

Record this on a chart. Then let the student reread this passage two more times. As students reread, they are focusing on correcting the miscues they made previously and improving their phrasing and rate. Recording the data gives students a record of their reading-rate improvement over time.

Prompt—Don't Correct

Often when nonfluent readers read aloud, their reading is interrupted not only by their own pauses but by other students (or teachers), who tell them the word that is causing the pause. Whether we do this out of kindness, out of frustration, or because we don't know other strategies, telling the dependent reader the word encourages more dependence. On the other hand, letting the student stare at the word indefinitely doesn't help either. The alternative to correction is prompting.

Prompting means giving the student the prompt he needs to decode the word successfully on his own. The simplest prompt is "Read that again." Sometimes starting the phrase or sentence over again gives the student an opportunity to recognize a word. Other times, the prompt needs to be more explicit:

- Can you divide the word into syllables and sound it out that way?
- Do you see a part of the word you recognize?
- Can you think about the letters and the sounds they make?
- Can you try sounding it out slowly to see if that helps?

If none of those prompts helps, then you need to tell the student the word. As you do, can you remind them of certain sounds particular letter combinations make? For instance, *sh* makes the sound heard at the beginning of *shoe*; *kn* makes the sound heard at the beginning of *not*; *ph* makes the sound heard at the beginning of *fun*; *-ing* makes the sound heard at the end of *sing*. Then, have the student start that sentence again, reading the word without your prompt. Providing the word and then letting the student read on doesn't benefit the student.

The goal with prompting is to move away from correcting. I've seen students read aloud, pausing between words to wait for the teacher's nod of approval. I've watched other students read until they come to a word they don't know, pause, wait for the teacher to insert the correct word, and then read on, never saying the word that gave them trouble aloud. Correcting rarely fosters independence. Prompting so that the student is in control of figuring out the word contributes to independence. You can strengthen the power of prompting by asking students, when they've finished reading, to identify what they did when they came to a word they didn't know. Let them keep a list of strategies they use. Figure 13.3 shows you one eighth grader's list of strategies for tackling words she doesn't know.

> "Correcting rarely fosters independence. Prompting so that the student is in control of figuring out the word contributes to independence."

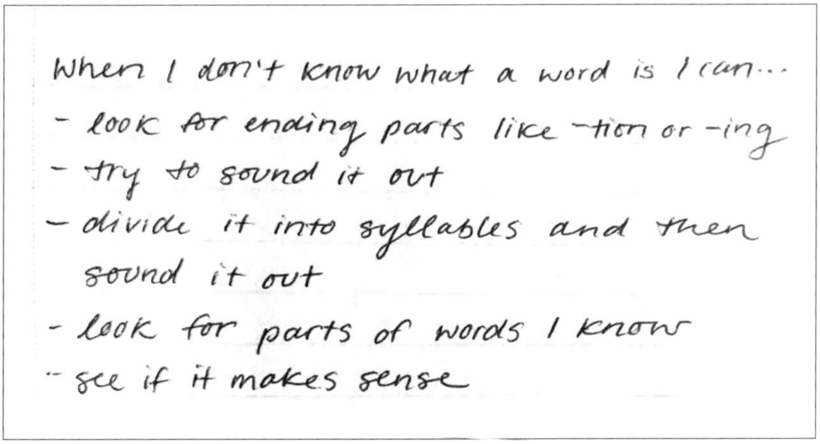

When I don't know what a word is I can...
- look for ending parts like -tion or -ing
- try to sound it out
- divide it into syllables and then sound it out
- look for parts of words I know
- see if it makes sense

Figure 13.3 An Eighth Grader's Ways for Figuring Out Words

Questions to Ask Yourself

"Disfluent readers are most often disfluent because of a lack of practice with reading. We cannot confuse teaching about reading with the act of reading."

Disfluent readers are most often disfluent because of a lack of practice with reading. We cannot confuse teaching about reading with the act of reading. Ultimately, struggling readers must have a lot of time to read at their instructional or independent level. Furthermore, we must examine our own instructional practices with these students. Ask yourself the questions shown in Figure 13.4.

Questioning My Fluency Practices

- How often do I give students instructional- or independent-level texts to read?

- How much time in my class do I give students to read?

- How often do I read aloud to students? Do I read aloud different genres? Poetry sounds different from a science text; math problems sound different from a novel.

- When struggling readers read aloud, do I correct their mistakes or prompt them to correct their own mistakes?

- What prompts do I offer students?

- How often do I use echo reading or choral reading?

- How often do I discuss with students why I read a certain passage a certain way?

- Do I remind students to transfer what they've been doing with oral reading to their silent reading?

- Do I ask students to pause while they are reading silently to reflect on how the reading sounds in their mind?

- Do I give students specific instructions before they begin to read silently about how the reading should sound in their mind

Figure 13.4 Assessing Fluency Instruction

As you reflect on those questions, you'll probably find ways to improve some of your instructional practices. What's rewarding about reading instruction is that as we become better teachers of reading, students become better readers.

Dear George,

I listened to a fifth grader read aloud. His reading was fast, too fast. "Slow down," I said. "You're going so fast; I can't understand all the words."

He was eager to share a particular part of the book with me, so he explained, "I'm hurrying to get to the good part. Just listen faster."

Just listen faster. I had to laugh. I thought for a moment about talking to him about phrasing and expression, but then, luckily, that moment passed. Instead, I realized he was urging me to keep up with him, go at his pace because he had someplace important to go and he wanted me to get there with him. Just eleven years old, he sometimes reminded me of you in that wonderful innocence that marks this thing called childhood. Like you, he needed me to listen to his words, follow his direction, and let him set the pace. As a teacher, that's tough when thirty of you sit in a classroom, all needing one teacher to listen faster, listen better. That's the part of teaching that's an art. It's the part that is not learned in a methods class; it cannot be tested in a midterm exam or evaluated during a principal's quick walk through the classroom. Listening is an art and kids, well, they always know which teachers are the ones who really listen.

Dear George,

   You were a poor speller, but honestly, because you wrote so little, I could not identify patterns of problems nor did we ever talk in depth about the errors you were making. You never asked about spelling instruction, though you often wanted to know if "spelling counted." By contrast, years later, I met William, an eighth grader. Spelling was the focus of almost all of our conversations.

   One day, William handed me this note, folded intricately so that his piece of notebook paper was now about two inches wide. Across that small space, he had written, "Open only if YOU can help."

   I stared at that, wondering what was inside. Was something terribly wrong in his life, or did he want tickets to the upcoming Garth Brooks concert? With hesitation, I finally unfolded his note. It was, of all things, a note about spelling: "I can NOT spell good. Do you no how to help with spelling?" Of all the things a student has ever told me about their lives as a learner, William remains the only one to directly reach out about spelling. On my last day with William, he handed me another intricately folded note: "You say to techers dose spelling count and thay say that spelling allways counts and thay take of if you spell it wrong but then they dont tech you to spell it right ecsept to make you take more tests. If spelling dose count so much then why dont thay tech you to do it?"

CHAPTER 14

Spelling

TWO DAYS BEFORE COVID-19 CLOSED THE NEW YORK
City school district, I was there with Bob, working with teachers. As we
walked through the hallway of one school, I stopped by a classroom door,
watching as sixth graders asked their teacher to detail some of the require-
ments for an assignment she had explained:

- "Does this need to be double-spaced?"

- "Do we submit online?"

- "How many pages should this be?"

Although the questions continued, one particular question never sur-
faced: "Does spelling count?" Early in my career, that was always a question.
I asked the teacher about that. She said that she didn't take off for spelling
anymore. "It's just not worth it, and besides, they have spell-check."

Does Spelling Still Count?

I disagree with her statement, and so does the research. Spelling does still
count, and spell-check is not the answer.

The body of research on spelling is vast. Individual studies and meta-
analyses of groups of studies conclude that decoding ability is enhanced
when spelling abilities improve (Ehri 1986; Graham and Santangelo 2014;
Moats 2005). While some argue that the meta-analyses that conclude the
benefits of teaching spelling have problems with the methodology used
in collecting the research articles (Fletcher 2020), there is agreement that
"spelling skills can impact reading ability" (Pan et al. 2021).

If we want to look beyond research that links spelling, reading, and
writing abilities, we can look to additional research about spelling and

223

jobs. Research reveals that spelling errors on job applications reduce one's chance of being interviewed for the job or being promoted if one has a job (Adecco 2022; Martin-Lacroux and Lacroux 2017). A misspelled word can put a person's application in the "no" pile. Additionally, companies that have spelling errors in advertisements are seen as less trustworthy (Stiff 2012) or even fraudulent, if the ads are online (Consumer Reports 2012). Think of the times you have decided not to open the attachment with an email or click on a link in a website after noticing misspelled words. That's the sign that something is wrong. That marketing person who writes, "Do you need a brake?" and isn't selling brakes but instead is selling a new line of herbal teas has hurt the company.

Another body of research has focused on what readers think of authors who misspell words. Adults and students as young as second graders think less of a writer when spelling errors are evident (Varnhagen 2000). While I think any book will have some spelling errors slip through (so be kind, dear reader), I do understand that too many errors will interfere in your reading and ultimately affect your thoughts about me (and my editor).

Yes, spelling still counts.

Those Weekly Spelling Tests

Many adults recall getting a list of words on Monday and then being tested over those words on Friday. Some remember activities spread throughout the week: repeated writing of words; defining the words; using those words in sentences. But those activities were sandwiched between getting and testing. One more activity happened on the weekends: forgetting.

Before that get-then-test instructional practice, spelling instruction in the US included pretests. A Monday pretest over a group of words began the weekly spelling lesson. Then the students could correct misspelled words and focus their attention on those words. They wrote those words repeatedly, eventually moving to writing the words, covering them, and then writing them again. This type of immediate feedback showed students which words they had learned (memorized) and which had not yet moved into long-term memory. A check test on Wednesday showed students how they were progressing. Then the test on Friday showed the results of the weekly effort.

The move from pretest–check test–final test to get-then-test did stream-line instruction, but this did not serve students well. That first pretest focused students' attention and the Wednesday check test provided needed feedback. Additionally, the original pattern for instruction (pretest, check test, final test) also included returning to words missed on the weekly Friday test for monthly and yearly review. (Perhaps you remember the six-weeks spelling test that reviewed the previously learned one hundred words?) This type of constant review helped solidify learning (Rohrer 2015). That was lost as the get-and-test approach was adopted.

And Now?

In many districts after about third grade, spelling is no longer taught. Spell-check is the answer. The problem is that this reduces the value of spelling to correctness and discounts the importance of understanding letter patterns in decoding. Plus, spell-check does not catch the most common writing error—correctly spelling the incorrect word. Students write *there* when they mean *their*, *cell* when they mean *sale*, *board* when they mean *bored*—and spell-check does not check for those mistakes.

The solution seems easy: teach students to spell. That said, teaching spelling is difficult because our English spelling patterns are filled with exceptions. We have twenty-six letters (graphemes) to represent forty-four sounds (phonemes). Individual letters can make different sounds (*g* in *gym* and *got*), and pairs of letters can make various sounds (*ou* in *though*, *couch*, *journey*, *court*, *you*). As I have previously written, "our English alphabet is at once remarkably rich and woefully inadequate" (2002, 5).

In spite of the irregularities and exceptions, much of our English lan-guage does follow rules. Instruction begins with understanding how spelling ability develops in children.

Stages of Development

Research shows us that spelling is a developmental process (Beers 1980; Beers and Henderson 1977; Read 1971; Schlagal 1989; Templeton 1983, 2002). Children advance through stages as their

Surprise! That's a different Beers!

understanding of letter-sound relationships deepens. At the earliest stage, children lack any awareness of letter-sound relationships; at the most advanced stage, children manipulate Latin and Greek prefixes, suffixes, and roots to spell words correctly. These stages are thoroughly described in *Words Their Way* (Bear et al. 2019). As we understand the features of each stage, we understand what types of instruction we should offer (Bear et al. 2019). See Figure 14.1 for an overview of the five stages.

Spelling Stages

Words Their Way, 6th edition (Bear et al. 2019) often is my go-to resource for providing diagnostic spelling assessments in English and Spanish and for activities that help move students from one level to the next.

1   **Emergent:** This stage marks children's first attempts at writing. These children are in preschool, kindergarten, and perhaps first grade. It is marked by a range of behaviors from scribbles to pretend writing (marks that look like letters but aren't) to random letters. Children at this stage put letters on a page without any attention to the letter-sound relationship. As they progress through this stage, they begin to pay attention to the sounds that particular letters make. By the end of this stage, children may write a word using its initial and final consonants.

2   **Letter Name:** Students at this stage spell using the names of letters to spell words. These students are generally in grades one and two. So, they spell *make* as *mak*. They might write the word *drive* as *jriv* since the /dr/ sound puts your mouth in a similar position as it is in when you say the letter *j*. They might spell the word *bed* as *bad*; again, the student is searching for the name of the letter that most matches the /ĕ/ sound. If you say the /ĕ/ sound (as in *bed*), then say the letter *e*, you'll see that there is very little relationship (from your mouth's point of view) between the /ĕ/ sound and the /ē/ sound. Students spell long vowel sound patterns with the name of the letter and don't worry about any sort of vowel marker that would indicate that the vowel is saying its long sound. They generally spell short vowel sounds incorrectly following this pattern: short *e* changes to *a*; short *i* changes to *e*; short *o* changes to *i*; and short *u* changes to *o*. They usually spell short *a* correctly. Digraphs and blends are often incomplete at this stage, so they spell *that* as *tat* and *hand* as *had*.

Figure 14.1 Overview of Spelling Stages   *continues*

Spelling Stages

3	**Within-Word Pattern:** At this stage, students spell short vowel sounds correctly and are attempting to spell long vowel patterns. Students are generally at this stage between grades two and four. At the letter-name stage, they might spell the word *team* as *tem*; however, you know a student has moved into the within-word stage when you see the child trying to use a vowel marker. At this stage, *team* might be spelled *teme* or *teem* and then eventually *team*. Students also begin to experiment with how to spell *r*-controlled vowels. Often, they reverse the vowel and the *r*, so they might write *brid* instead of *bird*, for example. As students move through this stage they also secure how to spell some of the more complex digraphs and blends, such as *str* and *scr*. Toward the end of the stage, they turn their attention to unusual vowel teams, such as *ou*, *aw*, and *oi*.
4	**Syllable Juncture:** Students reach this stage between grades three and eight. By this point, students are spelling most vowel patterns for single-syllable words correctly. The issue at this stage is how to spell multisyllabic words. In this stage, their attention is focused on how to add suffixes correctly, in particular when to double the final consonant before adding *-ed* or *-ing*. Students at this stage might spell *hoping* as *hopeing* and *hopping* as *hoping*. These students are also figuring out how to spell the vowels in the unstressed syllables of a word. So, they might spell *sample* as *sampul* or even *sampal*. As they progress through this stage, they move to the correct spelling. This stage marks a good time to focus on prefixes and suffixes so that students can understand why *really* is spelled with two *l*s and *misspelled* is spelled with two *s*s.
5	**Derivational Constancy:** This stage might begin as early as grade five for some or not until grade eight for others. For most, it extends through adulthood. Words studied at this stage are words that are derived from the same root. For instance, when students see the constant relationship between *compose* and *composition*, they are more likely to spell *composition* correctly. Other relationships include *haste* and *hasten*; *express* and *expression*; *design* and *designation*; *consume* and *consumption*. Students at this stage also learn about assimilated prefixes (also called absorbed prefixes). Assimilated prefixes are prefixes where the consonant has changed to match the first letter of the root to make the word easier to say. So, instead of *in-* + *literate* for *inliterate*, the letter *n* assimilates to the *l* and the prefix changes to *il-*; therefore, the word is *illiterate*. Or the prefix *sub-* changes to *sup-* so the word is *suppress* instead of *subpress*.

Figure 14.1 Overview of Spelling Stages, *continued*

Using Spelling Stages to Help Identify Instructional Practices

Understanding these stages offers us guidance for helping students. For instance, in Figure 14.2, we see how three seventh-grade students spelled twelve words. Take a look at the figure and see if you can decide each student's spelling stage.

Reed is still misspelling short vowel sounds, isn't sure how to spell digraphs or blends, and is spelling long vowel sounds simply with their letter names (*fram* for *frame*, for example). As the words become more complex (*nation* and *squirrel*), his spelling deteriorates so that he begins to omit vowels, relying only on consonants, as an emergent-level speller would. At what stage would you place Reed?

Rosa, unlike Reed, is spelling short vowel sounds correctly. Additionally, she can spell the digraphs /*th*/ (*with*) and /*sh*/ (*sheep*) and /*ch*/ (*couch*) correctly. She also has spelled the blend /*tr*/ correctly (*train*). When you look at her attempts to spell words with long vowel sounds (*sheep*, *train*, and *frame*), you see that she is not spelling those long sounds with only their letter names (*shep*, *tran*, *fram*), but instead is trying to mark those long vowel

These three students completed the spelling inventory in their own handwriting. I've retyped their words for ease of reading.

COMPARING THREE SPELLERS

Correct Word	Reed	Rosa	Jimmy
bed	bad	bed	bed
cap	kap	cap	cap
with	wet	with	with
sheep	sep	shepe	sheep
train	jran	trane	train
frame	fram	frame	frame
couch	koth	coch	couch
hurt	hrt	hert	hurt
making	makng	makeing	making
hoping	hopng	hopeing	hoping
nation	nasn	nasheon	nashun
squirrel	skrl	skwerl	squirle

Figure 14.2 Comparing Three Spellers

sounds with a second vowel. She understands something must happen but isn't quite sure what it is. She appears to have one pattern: add silent *e*. Therefore, she has spelled *frame* correctly; however, that might be lucky rather than deliberate. When we look at how she is trying to spell more complex vowel sounds (*couch* and *hurt*), we see that she still has trouble. As you continue to look through her test, you see that she continues with the pattern of adding silent *e* to words (*makeing, hopeing*) and becomes very confused by the time she reaches *nation* and *squirrel*. At what stage would you place Rosa?

Jimmy is further along in spelling development than either Rosa or Reed. We see that he doesn't have trouble until he reaches the last two words. At what stage would you place Jimmy?

Reed is still at the letter-name stage. Rosa is at the within-word stage. Jimmy is at the syllable-juncture stage.

How fair would it be for these three students to share the same spelling list? Reed needs to continue working on short vowel sounds, digraphs, and blends, while Jimmy is ready to consider how to spell suffixes and vowels in unstressed syllables of multisyllabic words. Rosa needs to learn how to spell long vowel sounds and unusual vowel sounds in single-syllable words. Giving them all the same list would mean somebody would be too challenged and someone else wouldn't be challenged enough.

"The problem, however, isn't with giving students a spelling list; the problem is giving all students the same list."

It's this one-list-fits-all mentality that results in memorizing words rather than understanding how words work. When students simply memorize for the test on Friday, that knowledge is generally gone by Monday. Sometimes we've been frustrated with spelling lists because it appears that giving students lists of words hasn't improved their spelling ability. The problem, however, isn't with giving students a spelling list; the problem is giving all students the same list.

Does that mean that if you have twenty-five students you must create twenty-five spelling lists? No! There are only five stages of spelling. And though each stage breaks into early, middle, and late, the reality is that by middle and high school, most students fall into either the within-word or syllable-juncture level. In that case, you may need only two or three lists. Spelling lists for older students should not be created based on the texts they are reading; instead, they should be related to students' developmental spelling levels. Students at the same level can work together on activities such as word sorts.

Spelling Scaffolds

Once you understand spelling stages, then you can decide what instructional practices will best help your students. The following ideas might help.

Use Word Sorts

As you plan your time for the week, set aside twenty- to twenty-five minutes for students who need help with spelling instruction to do some word sorts. Word sorts help students discover spelling rules and patterns as students literally sort words with the same spelling pattern into groups. Then students write the rule that explains why that group of words fit into one sort. A list of spelling rules that can help you create word sorts can be found in Appendix AA.

 Step Inside a Classroom

Students were in small groups. They were looking for the pattern that would help them know when to use *-ible* and when to use *-able* at the end of words. By doing the sort, students were learning a rule rather than memorizing a word. If you aren't sure of the rule, study these groups of words and see if you can explain the pattern.

achievable	edible	possible
avoidable	excitable	remarkable
believable	horrible	returnable
breakable	legible	terrible
comfortable	notable	transportable
debatable	observable	visible

First, students sorted words into two big groups: words that ended in *-ible* and words that ended in *-able*. I then told them that their *-able* words should be divided into two groups. They were stuck. I encouraged them to look at the root words. One student explained that term to the other students by telling them, "That's the part of the word that's left when you take off the ending." The students worked on that and realized that some words that had *-able* at the end had originally ended in the letter *e* (the root word for *excitable* is *excite*); other root words did not end in the silent *e* (the root word of *breakable* is *break*). Once they saw that pattern, they grouped the words into the three categories shown in Figure 14.3. Then they had this discussion:

Student 1: Oh yeah. OK. So, are we done?

Student 2: No. We have to get the rule for when you have, when you know it's *-ible* and when it's *-able*. [*Pause.*]

Student 3: So, like, if you have to take off an *e*, it's, like, *-able*. Why is it, then on this group, why is it *–able*, because they don't end in *e*?

Figure 14.3 Words for *-ible* and *-able* Endings

Student 2: But look, look at these words. OK. See, like here if you take it off, it is a word, even without an *e*. See, *remarkable*. You can take off the *-able* and you have *remark*.

Student 1: Yeah, yeah, yeah, that's it. See here. OK. All of them are words. So, add *-able*.

Student 2: OK, so if it's a word or a word if you put back on the *e*, then you add the *-able*.

Student 3: So on these, why is it *-ible*? [*Pause.*]

Student 2: Is it because these are more unusual words? You know, like *edible*.

Student 1: But *terrible* and *horrible*. That's not unusual.

Student 2: Yeah. [*Pause.*]

Student 3: Maybe it's because they don't end with *e*, you know, if you take off *-ible*.

Student 2: But some of the *-able* words don't end with *e*.

Student 1: Yeah, but if you take off the *-ible*, then, oh, look, that's, look, they aren't words; they don't make any sense.

Student 2: So, what does that mean?

Student 3: Does it mean if the word isn't really a word, then add *-ible*?

The students called me over to share their discovery. I asked them to write a rule using the terms *root words* and *suffixes* (see Figure 14.4).

"We did good, didn't we?" one asked.

Sorts take time, that's true. But when students uncover patterns and rules that govern those patterns on their own, they are much more likely to remember them. Turn to Appendix BB for word sorts you can use with students.

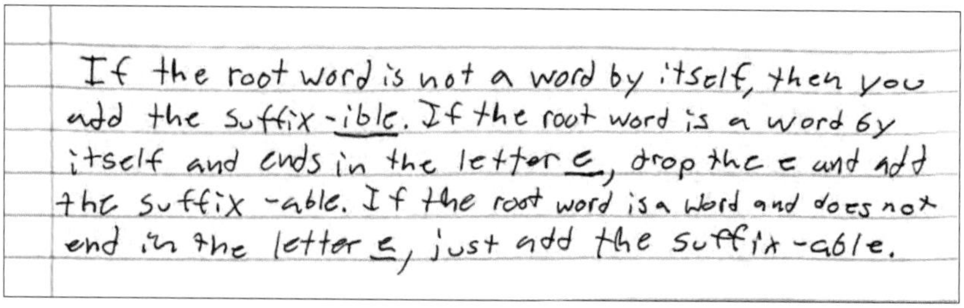

> If the root word is not a word by itself, then you add the suffix -ible. If the root word is a word by itself and ends in the letter e, drop the e and add the suffix -able. If the root word is a word and does not end in the letter e, just add the suffix -able.

Figure 14.4 Students' Rule for When to Use *-ible* or *-able*

Teach Commonly Misspelled Words

Post a list of commonly misspelled words that all students are required to spell correctly at all times. You can find lots of these lists by doing an internet search. Figure 14.5 offers one list of commonly misspelled words that I particularly like, mostly because this list was first published in 1917 in the *Merrill Speller, Book 1*. It seems some words will always cause problems!

COMMONLY MISSPELLED WORDS

ache	color	grammar	many	some	used
again	coming	guess	meant	straight	very
always	cough	half	minute	sugar	wear
among	could	having	much	sure	Wednesday
answer	country	hear	none	tear	week
any	dear	heard	often	their	where
been	doctor	here	once	there	whether
beginning	does	hoarse	piece	they	which
believe	done	hour	rays	though	whole
blue	don't	instead	read	through	women
break	early	just	ready	tired	won't
built	easy	knew	said	tonight	would
business	enough	know	says	too	write
busy	every	laid	seems	trouble	writing
buy	February	loose	separate	truly	wrote
can't	forty	lose	shoes	Tuesday	
choose	friend	making	since	two	

Figure 14.5 Commonly Misspelled Words

Teach Homonyms in Context

Some students continually confuse words like *principal* and *principle* or *to*, *two*, and *too*. I find that students get *more* confused when we distribute lists of homonyms and require them to take tests on them. Instead, when you notice a problem, correct it. If a student writes *rights* rather than *writes*, check to see if it was simple confusion or if the student really doesn't know the difference. When they don't know the difference, you might have to look for helpful mnemonics.

For instance, many a student has remembered to spell the head of a school as *principal* because the last three letters spell *pal*. Some remember to how to spell *too* correctly when they think that if you eat too much dessert, you have had more than one helping. Others remember that *where* is the correct spelling when they mean the location (see the word *here* inside *where*?). *Wear* is connected to what goes on your body—including your ear! *Their* is easy to remember as the word that shows possession if you can see the word *heir* in it. *There*, the word that focuses on location, has the word *here* in it. If discussing the building where the government works, write capitol and not capital because the governmental building has a dome, and *dome* has the letter *o* in it. With colleagues, discuss the homonyms that most often confuse your students. Next, create the mnemonic that might help your students choose the correct word.

Dear George,

   One day, William slipped me a note. It said,

> "I had this techer in fith grade and she said we wouldnt do
> spelling any more that year becase spelling isnt important becase
> any one can spell. That made me feel real bad becase my spelling
> isnt so good. I think that may be spelling isnt importunt to
> pepole who can spell good. But if you cant spell good, spelling is
> real importunt."

   William is right: when you can't spell, spelling is really
important. I gave you spelling lists, George. You gave me back
spelling tests that might or might not have had correctly spelled
words. And then we repeated that same pattern the next week.
But I never studied the patterns of your mistakes and certainly
did not know anything about the developmental nature of
spelling. I might have told you at some point about *i* and *e* after
c . . . but perhaps I did not.

Dear George,

   I wonder how many times I told you, "Just sound out the word."

   "Just sound out what?" you responded one day in frustration.

   "The word, George; sound out the word," I replied, equally annoyed.

   You stared at it and finally said, "I don't hear any sounds. I don't know what you're talking about."

CHAPTER 15

Phonics

"I HESITATE BEFORE WRITING THIS CHAPTER."

Those are the *exact* words that opened this chapter in the first edition.
In 2002, it was rare to find professional books that focused on helping older
struggling readers. It was rarer that those books addressed phonics. Instead,
books about reading in upper grades concentrated on improving comprehension. The first edition of *When Kids Can't Read—What Teachers Can
Do* was the exception as it addressed comprehension, vocabulary, spelling,
reading engagement, and phonics instruction. I mention this here because I
do not want any reader to think I've added this chapter now, in this edition,
to address the topic of the moment.

I've always seen the value in phonics instruction. Whether designing and
teaching a course in phonics for undergraduate and graduate students at the
University of Houston or writing professional books or working with teachers and administrators, I've never doubted that teaching students, especially
young students, how letters and sounds work together is important. While
I might spend more time focused on helping students comprehend a text
(as the body of my professional writing certainly would support), that is
because more often than not, the middle school and high school students
I see know how letters and sounds work. Their problem is not decoding.
Their problem is decoding with automaticity and fluency. They lack practice. And, lacking that practice, they have minimal experiences with interacting with texts, so their comprehension skills are limited. When I do work
with students who have very few decoding skills, however, those students
must learn what, through the years of school, they have missed.

So why the hesitation? To begin to answer that, let me share the
opening section of this chapter as it appeared in the first edition. I include
it here with no revisions to illustrate that even as things change, they often
stay the same.

From the First Edition

In the previous decade, educators, researchers, and policy makers studied the reading development of young children with an intensity never before experienced in this country. That attention has, depending on who is talking at that moment, either brought us greater clarity in how young children become skilled, fluent, and proficient readers or offered a smokescreen to obscure best practices. Much of this conversation has centered on the role of explicit phonics instruction, moving the great debate in phonics from journal pages to politicians' podiums. It was hard to find a candidate in the most recent national political races who did not address taxes (they all promised to lower them), hate crimes (they were all against them), and phonics (they were all for it).

At the dawning of the new millennium, that discussion intensified. In December 2000, the *Report of the National Reading Panel: Teaching Children to Read* was published (Langenberg et al. 2000). This report was intended to provide clarity to our understanding about the most effective reading instruction in early grades, specifically examining phonemic awareness, phonics, fluency, vocabulary, and comprehension. After determining a strict definition of what type of studies it would review, a subgroup of the National Reading Panel focused on thirty-eight phonics studies that used either an experimental or a quasi-experimental design in an attempt to discover to what degree a causal relationship exists between phonics instruction and reading achievement.

The hundreds of pages of the *Report of the Subgroups* and the less detailed *Executive Summary* led to a flurry of articles and listserv debates as proponents of explicit, systematic phonics instruction lauded the panel's findings and opponents criticized its focus on experimental and quasi-experimental research, the validity and generalizability of its conclusions, and the differences between the findings in the *Report of the Subgroups* and the *Executive Summary* (Garan 2001a, 2001b, 2001c; Ehri and Stahl 2001; Shanahan 2001). Tension mounted and phrases like "the war on reading" sometimes felt like an attack on individuals rather than strikes against illiteracy and aliteracy. Consequently, to talk about word recognition now, in the year 2002, means entering into a national debate that on the best of days opens oneself to national criticism and on the worst of days stands you in the line of not-so-friendly fire.

And Now Back to This Edition

That introduction from the 2002 edition is applicable today. Substitute *science of reading* for *National Reading Panel* and here we are, all over again. Today, discussions of phonics in some academic circles are rarely civil and often result in name-calling. A few educators who have spent their lifetimes working with teachers are now loudly booed by some during conventions when their names are mentioned. "We are booing," one person explained, "because we hate her." And some conferences have gone so far as to remove speakers from the program if their names are too closely associated with balanced literacy.

We should be ashamed.

Why wade into such dangerous waters? Though the majority of middle school and high school struggling readers do not struggle because they only lack word recognition skills, there are students for whom this is the problem. For these students, though they might also need help with comprehension strategies, fluency, and vocabulary development, unless we are also willing to address their word recognition deficits, we are not providing them all the instructional support they need. Thus, though I hesitate at writing this chapter, I remain committed to including it in this book. Indeed, when kids can't read, we sometimes must help them figure out the words. And that's where advocates of the science of reading and I certainly stand on common ground.

A Focus on Phonics

The term *science of reading* was used early in the eighteenth century when educators began to scientifically study the development of language skills. In *The Western Classical Tradition in Linguistics*, Keith Allan (2010) explains that the term was used to refer to studying the pronunciation of ancient languages. Leap forward to the 1990s, when the term *scientific researched-based reading* emerged as we entered into what some called the "reading wars." Scientific researched-based reading referred to the body of research that helped us all understand how the brain learns to decode words and comprehend what those words in that text mean in that situation.

When we move to the twenty-first century, science of reading reemerged in public circles as some journalists and some politicians found it helpful to say that teachers don't know reading research and therefore have not taught beginning reading with enough focus on phonics. To better understand this, I recommend reading "Conflict or Conversation? Media Portrayals of the Science of Reading" (MacPhee, Handsfield, and Paugh 2021). The authors explain that journalists have framed reading instruction in the US as a crisis with a single solution: teach more phonics. They go on to say that this type of journalistic reporting has intensified the reading wars and created division between parents and teachers, teachers and colleagues, and educators and the public.

This oversimplification of what the science of reading is has fostered concern among those who want to help children become skilled readers. A well-told story that offers an easy solution is appealing for many. For decades, many decades, parents and teachers, policy makers and educational researchers have looked at how anyone becomes a reader. State and national tests provide data that allows stakeholders to say, "Student A can answer these types of questions and Student B cannot." Low student achievement in classrooms and on mandated tests has been blamed on a myriad of factors: how phonics was taught in early years; what language is spoken at home; how much experience the teacher brings to the classroom; how much reading the child does outside of school; what the income level of the family is; how many books are in the child's home; how many minutes are spent on task; how many children are in the classroom; which materials are used; how much time the child spends on things other than reading; what background experiences the child has had; and on and on.

"It is hard to determine a single instructional solution to such complex questions, though it's that simple answer that is often wanted."

Debates on translating research into classroom practice continue as many consider what to do, how to do it, when to do it, with what kids to do it, in what order to do it, and for how long to do it (with *it* meaning anything related to reading instruction). It is hard to determine a single instructional solution to such complex questions, though it's that simple answer that is often wanted. In "Lost in Translation? Challenges in Connecting Reading Science and Educational Practice," Seidenberg, Borkenhagen, and Kerns (2021) explain that "the need for additional translational research linking reading science to classroom activities, the oversimplified way that the science is sometimes represented in the educational context, and the fact that theories of reading have become more complex and less intuitive as the field has progressed" (S119). In other words, there is no simple answer.

Beginning in 2018, the media offered a simple answer to the public by saying, essentially, "we know the science of how kids learn to read, and the science says they must learn phonics." Such statements suggested to many that teachers have ignored the science, have chosen not to teach children about letters and the sounds they make. This is not true. This reduction of all of the science that surrounds reading to one topic, phonics, is not something that educational researchers have suggested. This came from journalists who were writing or speaking to the public. The "science of reading" became a call to teach direct, explicit, synthetic phonics lessons: lessons that rely on teaching kids the rules that govern how letters and sounds work. This approach was leveraged as the "scientific" approach, and other research-based approaches—for example, a balanced literacy approach— were seen as nonscientific. The public has responded to this new "reading war," spurred on by journalists, by going to school boards demanding that their districts follow the science of reading (Williams 2022).

As we all move forward, it would be best if we:

- Recognize that there is research that supports the direct teaching of phonics rules with children up to grade 3; and,

- Recognize that teaching children to think about the words they have sounded out in the context of what they are reading also is grounded in research (Gennari, MacDonald, Postle, and Seidenberg, 2007).

As Gennari et al., explain:

> This study investigated the neural mechanisms involved in computing word meanings that change as a function of syntactic context. Current semantic processing theories suggest that word meanings are retrieved from diverse cortical regions storing sensory-motor and other types of semantic information, and are further integrated with context in left inferior frontal gyrus (LIFG). Our fMRI data indicate that brain activity in an area sensitive to motion and action semantics—the posterior middle temporal gyrus (PMTG)—is modulated by a word's syntactic context. (1278)

Or: words are ambiguous and the context is required for them to make sense. For instance, *rose* is either a flower or the past tense of the word rise; *hammer* can be either a noun or a verb; a *sling* can support a broken arm or it is a way to throw something. Context matters. But that context doesn't matter if you can't sound out *sling* or *hammer* or *rose*. Sounding out is a necessary but insufficient condition for comprehension—and comprehension is the goal of sounding out.

But explaining that the "posterior middle temporal gyrus is modulated by a word's syntactic context" isn't as catchy as saying "we know the science and the science says teach phonics." And thus, the movement that is now directing what many policymakers are now mandating: The Science of Reading. Used in this new context, the science of reading is not a body of work; it is a pretense of a solution. It's not generative; it is static. It is not a point where we can all begin; it's the place where we take sides.

And what does any of this mean as we consider older students who struggle with reading?

Phonics in the Upper Grades

The National Reading Panel's report found that phonics instruction for older readers (older meaning grade four and beyond) who are developing normally was less effective than phonics instruction in earlier grades. How does that extrapolate to what phonics instruction (type and degree) we should offer in middle and high school for low-achieving students?

Members of the National Reading Panel (NRP) have been quite clear that the *Report of the Subgroups* did not find that older struggling readers would benefit from explicit phonics instruction (Shanahan 2001). While some schools would provide anecdotal evidence that suggests placing struggling readers into explicit phonics programs is beneficial (and longitudinal data will tell us the long-term gains of such moves), most of us would agree that the phonics instruction we might offer middle and high school students should not mirror the instruction they received in elementary school. In fact, we

"It is important to emphasize that systematic phonics instruction should be integrated with other reading instruction to create a balanced reading program. Phonics instruction is never a total reading program" (National Reading Panel, 2000, 2–97).

know that students who struggle with word recognition do not become fluent and proficient readers just because we give them additional phonics instruction (Stahl 1997). The National Reading Panel (2000) found that "it is important to emphasize that systematic phonics instruction should be integrated with other reading instruction to create a balanced reading program. Phonics instruction is never a total reading program . . . Phonics should not become the dominant component in a reading program, neither in amount of time devoted to it nor in the significance attached" (2–97). As we address the needs of older struggling readers, we must look beyond phonics instruction to the larger category of word recognition and then place such instruction within the context of a classroom environment that encourages—even requires—the following:

- extensive reading at instructional and independent reading levels;

- many opportunities for discussions about the readings;

- ongoing opportunities for writing;

- a strong read-aloud program;

- direct strategy instruction in comprehension; and

- meaningful vocabulary development.

This chapter is not a chance to shame, blame, or applaud anyone on either side of the phonics debate. It is, instead, information to aid conversations with colleagues regarding phonics instruction that best serves your students. What your individual school and district choose to do should be determined by you and your colleagues, the experts in your classrooms, after careful consideration of the issue.

> *"This chapter, therefore, is not a chance to shame, blame, or applaud anyone on either side of the phonics debate."*

Commonly Used Phonics Terms

We'll begin with a list of terms. I do not present these terms and their definitions so that you might spend valuable instructional time teaching students to define *diphthong*, *digraph*, or *phoneme*. Instead, I offer these definitions to help you, the professional in the classroom, know the terminology used when discussing phonics instruction.

I made the mistake of mentioning to a ninth-grade student that a certain combination of letters was a diphthong. He perked up, "Thongs? Did someone mention a thong?"

General Vocabulary

Word Recognition: *Word recognition* is a broad term that encompasses the many ways students can access print: decoding or sounding out; recognizing prefixes, suffixes, and root words; looking for small words inside big words; knowing words by sight; using the context to figure out meaning that leads to word recognition.

High-Frequency Words: High-frequency words are words that occur often in our written language. Students need to be able to recognize these words quickly. Appendix Z offers a list of high-frequency words. You can find similar lists by searching for "high-frequency words" on the internet.

Sight Words: Some use the terms *sight words* and *high-frequency words* interchangeably, meaning *sight words* are words that readers should know by sight, without sounding them out. Others use *sight word* to mean a high-frequency word that lacks a predictable grapheme-phoneme (letter-sound) correspondence, so the word cannot be decoded following anticipated rules. For instance, *have* is often considered a sight word because the letter *a* makes its short sound instead of the long sound a reader might anticipate by looking at the silent *e*.

Decoding: This term is often used interchangeably with *word recognition*, but I suggest that's an overgeneralization of this word. Decoding refers to understanding the letter-sound code. A synonym for this word could be *sounding out*. When teachers say a student can't decode, that means the student can't recognize words via sounding out.

Phonics: The term *phonics* refers to the rules or, more accurately, the *generalizations* that help readers understand under what conditions certain letters or letter combinations will make certain sounds. You will find a list of the most common phonics generalizations in Appendix CC. The purpose of providing this list isn't so you can require struggling readers to memorize these generalizations; instead, the list is for your own knowledge.

Words About Syllables

Syllable: A syllable is a part of a word (or sometimes the entire word) that has one vowel sound in it.

Closed Syllable: This is a syllable that has only one vowel; the vowel is followed by one or more consonants; the vowel sound is short. Examples include *am*, *tent*, and *soft*.

Open Syllable: This is a syllable that has a long vowel sound with no consonants after it. They are open because there is no consonant after them. Examples include *she, by, go,* and *we.* In the two-syllable word *pretend, pre* is an open syllable (long vowel with no consonant after the syllable) and *tend* is a closed syllable (short vowel with consonants after the vowel). In the word *contrast, con* is a closed syllable (short vowel sound followed by a consonant) and *trast* is a closed syllable (short vowel sound followed by a consonant blend).

Silent E *Syllable:* This is a syllable that follows the VCe pattern (vowel, consonant, silent e). Examples include *name, rode,* and *flute.*

Words About Letters and Sounds

Graphemes: Graphemes are the letters of our alphabet. We have twenty-six graphemes in our written alphabet.

Morphemes: Morphemes are the smallest grammatical unit of speech. Free morphemes are units that can stand alone with meaning: *chair, boat, run, love.* Bound morphemes are units that must be attached (bound) to free morphemes: *-ing, -er, -ion, -ful.*

Phonemes: Phonemes are the smallest unit of sound. The word *cat* has three graphemes (*c, a,* and *t*) and three phonemes (/c/, /a/, and /t/). Remember, when a letter is placed between diagonal marks, say the sound of the letter, not the name of the letter. The word *little* has six graphemes (*l, i, t, t, l,* and *e*) and four phonemes (/l/, /i/, /t/, and /l/). The word *shoe* has four graphemes (*s, h, o,* and *e*) and two phonemes (/sh/ and /ü/). This lack of one-to-one correspondence between graphemes and phonemes makes our language a difficult one to decode. See Figure 15.1 for a list of the various phonemes in our language and example words that contain those sounds.

Vowels: The graphemes *a, e, i, o,* and *u* are vowels. Vowels can make long sounds (*ape, eat, bike, hope, tune*), short sounds (*at, bed, it, hop, run*), a sound called schwa (in *alarm,* the first *a* makes the schwa sound), an /r/ sound when the grapheme *r* follows the vowel (*car, term, bird, horn, burn*), and other sounds when combined with other vowels (e.g., *soil*).

Consonants as Vowels: The letters *y* and *w* sometimes act as vowels. *Y* functions as a vowel either on its own (*by, friendly*) or by teaming with another vowel (*say*). *W* functions as a vowel by teaming with another vowel (*cow, paw, own*).

PHONEMES IN OUR LANGUAGE

Consonant Sounds

1. /b/ (*bib*)	9. /m/ (*mat*)	17. /z/ (*zebra*)
2. /d/ (*dot*)	10. /n/ (*nest*)	18. /ch/ (*child*)
3. /f/ (*fun*)	11. /p/ (*pat*)	19. /sh/ (*ship*)
4. /g/ (*go*)	12. /r/ (*ran*)	20. /th/ (*this*)
5. /h/ (*hot*)	13. /s/ (*sun*)	21. /th/ (*thin*)
6. /j/ (*jelly*)	14. /t/ (*take*)	22. /hw/ (*where*)
7. /k/ (*kite*)	15. /v/ (*vase*)	23. /zh/ (*measure*)
8. /l/ (*let*)	16. /w/ (*wish*)	24. /ng/ (*sing*)

Vowel Sounds

25. /ă/ (bat)	32. /ī/ (bike)	39. /ow/ (mouse)
26. /ĕ/ (bed)	33. /ō/ (hope)	40. /oi/ (boy or soil)
27. /ĭ/ (pit)	34. /ȳü/ (unicorn)	41. /ô/ (ball)
2 8. /ŏ/ (hot)	35. /å/ (father)	42. /ù/ (bird)
29. /ŭ/ (fun	36. /ə/ (ago)	43. /â/ (fair)
30. /ā/ (make)	37. /ü/ (moon)	44. /ä/ (car)
31. /ē/ (meet)	38. /o͝o/ (book)	

Figure 15.1 Phonemes in Our Language

Vowel Teams: A vowel team is a combination of vowels (two or sometimes three), or a combination of a vowel and one or more consonants, that makes one single sound. For example, *ou* makes the sounds you hear in *sound, should, you,* and *though; ea* makes the sounds you hear in *team, head,* and *steak; igh* makes the sound heard in *high* and *night.* The terms *digraph* and *diphthong* are often used instead of the term *vowel team.* A vowel digraph is two vowels (and occasionally three) that create a single sound (*ee* in *sweet* and *ew* in *pew*), while a diphthong is two vowels that produce two sounds that glide into one another. The *oy* in *boy* and the *ou* in *out* represent diphthongs. The *ea* in *create* is not an example of a diphthong. See Figure 15.2 for examples of vowel sounds.

Consonants: The remaining graphemes are called consonants. Your students might be interested to know that all vowels can function in a word as a consonant. For instance, in the word *azalea,* the *e* takes on the /y/ sound; in *one,* the *o* takes on the /w/ sound; in *stallion,* the letter *i* takes on the /y/ sound. These exceptions make teaching certain rules more difficult, but they are fun to note.

Consonant Teams: When two or three consonants appear together and create a single sound, they are a consonant team. These consonant teams are often called consonant digraphs. Some consonant digraphs create a new sound, one not otherwise represented by a single grapheme. For instance, the digraph *sh* makes the sound heard at the beginning of *ship.* Other digraphs create a sound that can be represented by a single grapheme. For example, the digraph *ph* makes the /f/ sound. Still others are combinations in which one of the letters is silent: *kn-, gn-, pn-, wr-, gh-* (at the beginning of a word), and *-mb.* See Figure 15.3 on page 249 for lists of the most common consonant digraphs.

Consonant Blends: Some consonants can be combined (clustered) to create sounds that blend together. Unlike digraphs, which cannot be sounded out separately, blends can be segmented. So, you could not sound out *child* by saying /c/ /h/ /i/ /l/ /d/, but instead, you must keep the *ch* together to get the /ch/ sound. However, you can segment the cluster *tr* in *trip* to get /t/ /r/ /i/ /p/. Blends are consonant clusters (generally two, but occasionally three) that can be segmented, one from the other. See Figure 15.4 on page 250 for lists of the consonant blends.

VOWEL COMBINATIONS AND SOUNDS

Short and Long Vowel Sounds

Letter	Short Sound	Long Sound	R-Controlled	L-Controlled
a	mat	make	car	ball
e	fed	feet	term	
i	bit	bite	bird	
o	on	boat	horn	
u	us	use	turn	

Diphthong Spellings and Examples

Spelling	Example
ou	house
oy	boy
oiw	soil
ow	cow

Diphthong Spellings and Examples

Spelling	Example	Spelling	Example
ai	pain; air	ou	trouble; house
ay	day	au	author
ea	meat; head	aw	paw
ee	sweet; steer	oo	mood; book
ey	key; convey; geyser	ei	weigh; receive; foreign; seismic
oa	float	ie	relief; lie; patient
ow	grow; plow	ew	grew; sew
oi	boil	ui	fruit; guild

Figure 15.2 Vowel Combinations and Sounds

CONSONANT DIGRAPHS

Sound	Spelling	Examples
/ch/	ch	child, beach catch
/k/	ch	choir, chemistry
/sh/	ch	Chicago, chef
/sh/	sh	ship, fish
/th/	th	thank, thin, three, this, then
/hw/	wh	when, why, where
/ng/	ng	sing, bank
/f/	gh	laugh
	ph	phone
/n/	kn	knight
	gn	gnat
/g/	gh	ghost
/m/	mb	lamb

Because there are always exceptions to rules, some single consonants and consonant-vowel combinations make a sound more normally made by a consonant team. These exceptions include the following:

/zh/	s	vision
	s	measure
	g	garage
	z	azure
	ti	equation
	x	luxurious
/sh/	s	sure, sugar
/sh/	ti	nation
/sh/	ci	facial

Figure 15.3 Consonant Digraphs

CONSONANT BLENDS

Beginning of Word: R-Blends

br	break
cr	crash
dr	drip
fr	free
gr	grow
pr	print
tr	truck

Beginning of Word: L-Blends

bl	black
cl	click
fl	flag
gl	glass
pl	plate
sl	slip

Beginning of Word: S-Blends

sc	scout
sk	skate
sm	small
sn	snake
sp	space
st	stop
sw	sweep
tw	twin
qu	quick

End of Word

-ct	act
-ft	gift
-ld	old
-lp	help
-lt	colt
-mp	lamp
-nd	hand
-nk	bank
-nt	ant
-pt	slept
-sk	mask
-sp	clasp
-st	test

Three-Consonant Clusters

sch	school
scr	scream
spl	splash
spr	spring
squ	squeak
str	stream
thr	thread

Figure 15.4 Consonant Blends

Words About Word Families

Rimes: A rime is a vowel and any consonants that follow it in a syllable. In the word *cat, at* is the rime. In *sight, ight* is the rime. The rime of a word is what lets it rhyme with other words (although some words that do not share rimes may nonetheless rhyme). *Cat* and *mat* share the same rime, and they rhyme. *Bore* and *floor* rhyme but do not share rimes.

Onsets: Onsets are the consonants prior to the vowel. In the word *that, th* is the onset and *at* is the rime; in *school, sch* is the onset and *ool* is the rime. See Figure 15.5 for a list of the most commonly used rimes.

The Rime of the Ancient Mariner means "the end of this old sailor."

Read more about onset-rime on page 256.

MOST COMMONLY USED RIMES									
A		**E**		**I**		**O**		**U**	
-ack	back	-eat	seat	-ice	nice	-ock	sock	-uck	duck
-ail	pail	-ell	bell	-ick	sick	-oke	smoke	-ug	rug
-ain	rain	-est	west	-ide	hide	-op	drop	-ump	jump
-ake	take			-ight	might	-or	for	-unk	skunk
-ale	male			-ill	will	-ore	core		
-ame	name			-in	win				
-an	can			-ine	fine				
-ank	tank			-ing	sing				
-ap	nap			-ink	drink				
-ash	rash			-ip	dip				
-at	sat								
-ate	late								
-aw	saw								
-ay	day								

Figure 15.5 Most Commonly Used Rimes (Wylie and Durrell 1970)

Understanding the Terms Matters

Knowing terms such as these is important, not because we want to test students over terms—we certainly don't—but because they give educators a common vocabulary and allow us to understand questions that parents, principals, and policy makers ask about phonics. For instance, parents ask if we're going to "teach phonics." I'm not convinced that the majority of these parents are asking if we're going to teach the phonics generalizations; sometimes I'm not sure that they know what they are asking. They are simply frustrated at their children's problems with reading, and *phonics* is a word they've heard. We can't answer their questions with any degree of confidence if we don't know what the words mean. A conversation with parents illustrates this point.

👥 Step Inside a Classroom

I was the speaker at a parent meeting in a middle school. About one hundred parents and teachers came for my talk. The topic was "Helping Your Middle Schooler with Reading." At one point, a mom raised her hand and asked, "Don't you think schools ought to be teaching more phonics?" I asked her to tell me specifically what she meant. "Well, don't you think all these problems that some kids are having with reading in middle school are because they didn't learn enough phonics in elementary school?" Some parents nodded their heads in agreement.

Still wanting her to be more specific, I asked, "Which reading problems are you referencing?"

She responded, "You know. Kids just can't understand what they read."

This mom meant well. And although I don't know this for a fact, I'll bet her child was having some sort of reading comprehension problem, and she wanted a label for her child's problems. Phonics—either too much of it or not enough—often gets to carry the blame for all reading woes. As I looked around the room, I saw the principal of the elementary school that fed into this middle school and the language arts supervisor for the district. I saw middle school language arts teachers, and I saw a lot of parents waiting for my answer:

"If the issue is that students are having trouble *understanding* what they are reading, then I'm not too sure if teaching students that when two vowels go a-walkin', the first one does the talkin' will help those children understand how to make an inference or summarize what they've read or predict what might happen next in the text. If you're asking me if teaching more phonics will help students comprehend better, I have to say, I think the answer is no. Does that mean I think students don't need to understand the sounds letters make? Not at all. I think that's an important part of the reading process. It just isn't the entire process, and it doesn't mean students can automatically *understand* what they've decoded. If, however, the problem is that students have poor reading comprehension because they can't decode the words accurately, then yes, we need to make sure they understand how letters and sounds work."

She said no one had ever explained that to her. We agreed to meet later to discuss her child. Knowing words and what they mean is important. The next step is deciding which instructional scaffolds are best for your students (see Figure 15.6).

If students need help with . . .	**Then** use . . .	**See** page . . .
Decoding	Teach High-Frequency Words	255
	Teach the Most Common Phonics Generalizations	255
	Teach Common Syllables, Prefixes, and Suffixes	256
	Assess What Students Know About Sounds and Letters	254
	Teach Rime Patterns	256
	Teach Rules About Syllables	256
	Teach Schwa Sound	259
	Use Instructional Texts	259

SCAFFOLDS FOR TEACHING PHONICS

Figure 15.6 Scaffolds for Teaching Phonics

Phonics Scaffolds

Phonics is a necessary, but not sufficient, condition for reading comprehension. And with older students, what they are often missing is practice. Practice may not make perfect, but it does make one fluent. When I'm working with middle school and high school students who have trouble with word recognition, I need answers to these questions:

- How many high-frequency and irregularly spelled words can the students quickly recognize?

- Can they quickly and accurately decode single-syllable words but not multisyllabic words?

- When they are reading multisyllabic words, are they decoding the entire word slowly or not decoding it at all?

What follows are not the same suggestions I might offer teachers working with students in an intensive reading program where the focus is to teach phonics rules students have never acquired; instead, these are suggestions that teachers in regular academic settings could implement.

Assess What Students Know About Sounds and Letters

When it's apparent that students' reading problems aren't vocabulary, comprehension, or fluency issues, but instead word recognition, spend some time with those students asking them to name the letters (graphemes) in specific words. Ask them to identify what sounds those letters make. You're listening to hear what letter-sound correspondence knowledge each student has. I've met some students, especially second language learners, who don't recognize all the letters and certainly don't know all the sounds those letters can and their combinations make.

You don't need a special assessment form to do this, nor do you need a lot of time. Just point to some words and ask students to tell you what letters are in the word and what sounds those letters make. You can also show them consonant diagraphs such as *sh*, *ph*, and *th* and blends such as *tr*, *st*, and *bl* and ask students to tell you what sounds those pairs of letters make. You can show them vowel teams such as *ai* and *ee* and ask them what sound the vowels would make. Put these letter combinations into the context of a word. The small number of students who can't recognize letters and lack even a basic knowledge of the sounds those letters make probably need specialized help.

Teach High-Frequency Words

Automatic recognition of high-frequency words is critical for fluent reading. These words are often difficult for beginning readers or older struggling readers to decode because many do not follow the regular sound-letter relationships. The Fry Instant Words list offers the one thousand most common words in the English language. Fry, Kress, and Fountoukidis remind us that "the first twenty-five words make up about a third of all printed material," while the first hundred "make up about half of all written material" and the first three hundred "make up about 65 percent of all written material" (1993, 23).

The first one hundred words include *of, you, word, what, said, there, would, number, people, who, down, did,* and *part.* If students do not know these one hundred words, their reading rate slows long before they encounter less common words and multisyllable words. The Fry list of the most common words is included in Appendix Z.

Have students read the words to you from the Fry list. If they don't know them, start there.

Teach the Most Common Phonics Generalizations

Clymer (1963) looked at phonics rules to determine how often the rule stood and how often there was an exception to the rule. Most of the rules had exceptions. The common phonics rules are in Appendix CC. Some rules you know: When a word ends in the /k/ sound, and the vowel sound is short, the sound is represented with the letters *ck.* (as in *deck*). If the vowel sound is long (as in *leak*), then use the letter *k.* If there is a consonant before the /k/ sound (*milk*), also use the letter *k.* Other rules are ones you might have once known but have now forgotten: When the last syllable is the /r/ sound, it is unaccented. An example is *butter*, and an exception is *appear*.

You should be familiar with the rules and when you notice a pattern of what is slowing a struggling reader, then you might teach that rule. "I see that you are trying to give this vowel its short sound. But see that letter *r* after the vowel? That *r* controls the vowel sound and makes it sound like the *r* sound you hear in *bird* or *word*." You teach the rule that would benefit your students *if* learning the rule will correct a problem. Again, it is usually *reading* practice students need, not *rule* practice.

Teach Common Syllables, Prefixes, and Suffixes

Five thousand of the most common words share some very common syllables: *-ing, com-, -ful*. Students can improve their reading rate, and therefore fluency, if they quickly identify these syllables. You can find a list of the most common syllables as well as common prefixes and suffixes in Appendix DD.

Don't duplicate these lists and tell students to memorize them. Instead, choose some you want to teach. Make some word lists with those syllables or prefixes and suffixes. Encourage students to look for these as they read.

Teach Rime Patterns

Once called word families, rime patterns help readers identify chunks of words quickly. In the word *hop*, *h* is called the onset and *op* is the rime. Students don't decode *hop* as /h/ /o/ /p/ (which is often difficult to blend) but instead decode it as /h/ /op/. The strategy of using rime patterns to help children learn to decode by analogy (if the letters *a* and *t* sound like /at/ in *cat* then they probably sound that way in *bat, sat, that,* and *flat*) has received considerable attention (Gaskins and Elliot 1991; Cunningham 1995; Wylie and Durrell 1970; Fox 1996). Rime analysis is a helpful way for older struggling readers to build word identification and automaticity.

Figure 15.5 (see page 251) offers the list of thirty-seven rimes from which students can form more than five hundred words (Wylie and Durrell 1970). Remember, the goal is to teach students to transfer that rime pattern to other words. You can't presume that because you show them *at* in *cat*, they'll see it in *pattern* or *caterpillar* or even *bat*. If you have students who struggle with decoding, you'll need to reinforce instruction often.

Teach Rules About Syllables

When students can sound out single-syllable words, but stumble through multisyllabic words, then I find that teaching them how to divide a word into syllables can be helpful. It can also be confusing.

To understand where to make syllable breaks, students need to recognize some basic patterns. Help students see those patterns by showing them how to transform any word into a spelling pattern, or code, that uses three letters: *C*, *V*, and *e*. *C* stands for any letter that's a consonant; *V* stands for vowels; and *e* stands for the silent *e* at the end of some words (*make*, *life*). So, the spelling pattern CVVC might stand for *boat* or *meal*. CVC could stand for *cat* or *hop*. CCVCe is the pattern for *close*, while CVCC is the pattern for *fish*. Once students can see how *C*, *V*, and *e* can represent spelling patterns, we discuss how a word divides into syllables between those *C*s and *V*s (see Figure 15.7).

DIVIDING WORDS INTO SYLLABLES

1. Every syllable must have a vowel sound (not just one vowel, but a vowel *sound*).

2. Vowel teams should not be separated into different syllables: *ai, ay, ea, ee, oa, ow, oi, oy, ou, ie, ei.*

3. Consonant teams should not be separated into different syllables: *ch, ck, ph, sh, th, wh, tch.*

4. If a word has two consonants between two vowels, divide between the two consonants. So, VCCV divides as VC-CV, as in *al-bum* and *rab-bit* and *con-tain.*

5. If a word has one consonant between two vowels, divide between the first vowel and consonant. In the word *pilot*, the letters *ilo* create the VCV pattern. This word is divided as cV-CVc. *Oval* and *aloud* divide as *o-val* and *a-loud.*

6. If a word has one consonant between two vowels and that consonant is an *x*, divide after the *x*. So, VxV divides as Vx-V, as in *Tex-as* and *ex-it* and *ex-act.*

7. If the word ends in Cle (as in *possible*), the Cle form the last syllable. So, *bu-gle* and *ta-ble* and *lit-tle* and *syl-la-ble.*

Figure 15.7 Dividing Words into Syllables

The only reason I'd ever work with students on dividing a word into syllables is to help them figure out the vowel sounds. Vowel sounds are generally what cause the problem for readers, not consonants (though the letter *c* certainly represents enough sounds to give some novice readers fits). Once students can see the pattern, they can sometimes identify the sound the vowel should make in that pattern. For instance, the pattern CV means that the vowel will makes its long sound (*no, go, by, he*), while the CVC pattern results in a short vowel sound (*tap, red, sit, top, run*). See Figure 15.8 for a list of patterns and the typical vowel sounds found in those patterns. Use time teaching patterns and syllables if a particular student needs help (as opposed to practice) in decoding multisyllable words.

PATTERNS AND RESULTING VOWEL SOUNDS

Long Vowel Sounds		Short Vowel Sounds	
Pattern	Example	Pattern	Example
CV	my	VC	at
CVV	see	VCC	end
CCV	she	CVC	run
CCVV	flee	CVCC	past
CVVC	rain	CCVCC	think
CVCV	baby	CCVC	stop
CVCe	take		
CVVCe	leave		
CCVCe	these		
VCe	ate		

Note: there are, of course, exceptions to these patterns. For instance:

- CVVC is also the pattern for *head, said,* and *been*—all words with a short vowel sound.
- CVCe is also the pattern for *give, love,* and *have*—all words with a short vowel sound.
- CVCC is also the pattern for *told, bold,* and *sold*—words with a long vowel sound.

Figure 15.8 Patterns and Resulting Vowel Sounds

That Tricky Schwa Sound

The schwa sound is the vowel sound that is unstressed in a multisyllabic word. You've seen it identified in dictionaries as the upside down and backward *e*: /ə/. For example, in the word *civil*, the second *i* makes the schwa sound (/uh/). Telling struggling readers that the schwa sound is the vowel sound in an unstressed multisyllabic word usually results in glazed eyes. I tell students to remember that in many multisyllable words, those middle vowels make the /uh/ sound. If students can get through the first syllable (usually the stressed syllable) and can figure out the consonants and then just say /ə/ for the remaining vowels, they usually come close to the correct pronunciation of the word. Is this specific decoding? No, it's an approximation and some will disagree with doing that. For those folks, and perhaps for you, if your decision is to spend time teaching rules, also give students even more time with books so they can practice putting those rules into action. With multisyllable words, remind your students of the following:

1. Look for prefixes, suffixes, and consonant blends and digraphs that you already know how to say.

2. Remember that the vowel at the beginning of the word (first syllable) will follow rules you already know; other vowels might make the /uh/ (schwa) sound.

3. After you have read through the word, read it again, faster. Read it aloud. Read it in the entire sentence.

Use Instructional-Level Texts

Students need practice on word recognition with texts that are at their independent and instructional levels. When students must read certain texts that you know will cause word recognition problems, then I suggest you accept that you won't be improving word recognition with that text. Focus on what you can do with that text. I had to teach *The Tell-Tale Heart* to two eighth graders who simply could not get through the words in that text. So, I recorded the story for them, gave them headsets, and had them do a read-along, that is, follow along in the text as I read it to them. Occasionally, on the recording, they heard me say, "Stop and discuss what's happened so far." Together, they talked about characters and events. Because I took away the burden of word recognition, they were able to concentrate on meaning.

Reading aloud to students or letting them listen to the text is not a replacement for word recognition practice. It should not replace the reading students should do. However, when the text is too tough for some students, then tell yourself that with that particular text you won't focus on word recognition. Instead, focus instruction on literary elements, comprehension, or vocabulary. Then, make sure you create some time for students to practice word recognition and fluency with texts that are at their independent and instructional reading levels. Younger readers will also benefit from highly decodable texts. These are texts that are created to give students practice with particular letter patterns.

When Kids Can't Decode

Working with adolescents who have difficulty with word recognition is difficult on good days, beyond frustrating on bad days. And that's for us, the folks who already can decode. I sometimes try to imagine what it would be like to be a thirteen-, fourteen-, fifteen-, or sixteen-year-old and not know how letters and sounds work. When I think that way, I understand negative attitudes, sarcastic remarks, books left in lockers, and bored expressions that announce, "This is dumb."

"Our struggling readers first and foremost need teachers who believe that all kids can become more skilled readers; they need teachers who want to share a passion for reading with them."

For some, the reaction is to put these students into intensive, scripted phonics programs. The reality is, however, research shows that explicit phonics instruction much beyond first grade does not create fluent readers (Ehri et al. 2001). Word recognition is critical, but students can learn to recognize many words by learning about prefixes, suffixes, and rimes. They can learn some basic vowel rules (*r*-controlled, vowel teams, diphthongs) and about consonant blends and consonant digraphs without moving into scripted intervention programs. But none of that will matter if we fail to give these students plenty of opportunity to read at their instructional and independent levels, give them repeated chances to hear us read aloud while they follow along, and remind them that the goal of decoding is comprehension.

Our struggling readers first and foremost need teachers who believe that all kids can become more skilled readers; they need teachers who want to share a passion for reading with them. They need to be in classes that encourage lots of writing, volumes of reading, and many opportunities to talk about their reading and writing. And they need to know that we have confidence that they can become better readers.

They don't have confidence. I promise you that. You must have enough confidence to sustain yourself and to encourage them. I don't think I realized how important this was until one teacher told me how she really had not expected her eighth graders could get better at word recognition:

> *I left your workshop yesterday a little angry at you. When you said we had to believe that kids really could get better at word recognition, I thought, "Well, just what does she think I've believed all this time?" Last night, though, I really thought about what you said and thought about some of my students and asked myself if I truly believed I could help those students become better readers. Suddenly, I realized I didn't. I didn't have enough confidence in what I might be able to do to convince these kids they could be better readers. We were going through some motions— mostly looking at comprehension things to help them on the [state-mandated] test. That was all. Why wasn't I doing more? I asked myself. In part because I didn't know what else to do and in part because I didn't think whatever I did would make a difference.*

What you do with word recognition can make a difference. But before you can ever convince your struggling readers of that, you've got to believe it first. And perhaps that means you need to be told more often that you are what matters most.

In the twenty years between the first edition and this edition, and in the decades prior to that first edition, what has remained constant is our nation's willingness to blame the wrong phonics program on reading problems that have persisted. We need to put aside this tired debate. Let's recognize that great teaching makes the difference, not this method or that method. The landmark studies called the "first-grade studies" of the 1960s (Bond and Dykstra 1967) found that "evidently, reading achievement is influenced by factors peculiar to school systems over and above differences in pre-reading capabilities" (121–22). The researchers found that different methods of phonics instruction worked well in some classroom environments and not well in others.

As I've reflected on where we've been in phonics instruction since those first-grade studies, I've decided we are all too bound by the term *best practice*. It's a great term. Who would not want what is best for a student? And best practices are supposed to be based on research. But research must be viewed against the context in which teachers—you—teach. To take research findings and expect them all to fit into the context of any classroom is to forget that *professionals* apply what is needed in a particular context at a particular time.

Too often something labeled a best practice is handed over to teachers, who then are to use that practice without considering other factors. I suggest such an approach is not a best practice at all. Instead, I propose that any best practice is the product of four critical components: research, student data, teacher knowledge, and individual student needs (see Figure 15.9). With this vision, the students' needs drive instructional decisions, not research that did not consider the context of a teacher's individual students. And teachers are viewed as professionals who do more than blindly follow the results of a research study that might have little to do with the grade, content, or backgrounds of the students they teach.

Does phonics instruction matter? Yes. But you matter more. What you know about phonics, about research, and most critically about your students will always matter more.

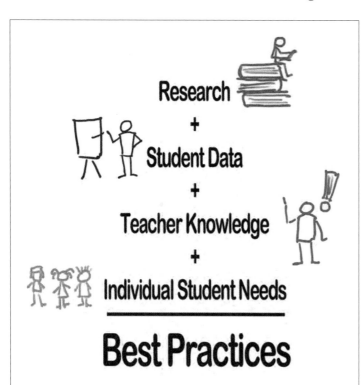

Figure 15.9 Toward a Better Model of Defining Best Practices

Dear George,

"Stay after school," I said to you. "I'll help you with this chapter."

So, that day in February, we sat side by side at a conference table at the back of the room. I listened to you struggle through words. Finally, you said, "This book is too hard. The words are too long. It's just too hard." Then you pushed the book and your notebook off the tabletop. "I just don't care," you said, not worrying that someone might hear you, for the school day had ended a good hour earlier. "I just don't care anymore," you said again, beginning to cry, hating yourself for crying, hating me more for seeing you cry. You stood up, then sat back down, completely defeated.

I sat still, not sure what to do. "George, I'll help you. You can do this," I said.

You looked up. "No. The book is too fucking hard," you said. I'd never heard that word from a kid speaking to me. I jumped up, sure I was supposed to do something, but before I could say anything, you looked at me and said, "It doesn't matter what you do to me or what you say to me. Don't you get it? It's not the fucking book. It's me. I'm just too dumb."

When kids can't read, I've finally learned, they take the failure personally. Though they might say a book is boring or a teacher is bad, those are just the words they dare to say. What they rarely share is what you finally blurted out that cold winter day: "It's me. I'm just too dumb." George, you showed me that day that becoming a reader shapes who we are, how we see the world, and how we see ourselves in this world. Tragically, failure to become a reader shapes our perceptions as well.

Part 4

Making Reading Matter

Dear George,

I picked up your notebook you left in class one day. A piece of paper fell out. "Hate, hate, hate. Dumb. Stupid. Stupid. Boring." In your tiny print, these words sat in the margin of that page. And what was on that paper? This was a worksheet I had created. It was labeled "New Words!" This was where you were to record new words you noticed as you were reading. Alongside them, you were to write each word's definition. (Why I thought this would be engaging or helpful, I do not know.) Your page was blank. The margin, however, told me all I needed to know.

The next day when you asked if you had left your notebook in class, I showed you the vocabulary page that had fallen on the floor. I didn't care that it was blank. I cared about what you had written. "What is it you hate, George?" I asked.

Quietly, you replied, "Most of the time I hate me."

I wish your answer had been *me*. I could deal with you hating me.

"I hate being the dumb one. I hate, hate, hate it. I *never* know the answers. Do you know how many words I would have to write if I wrote down all the words that are new for anything I read?"

You were going to cry. "Can I go to the nurse's office?" you asked, your voice quiet. I had long realized that you went to the nurse's office when you needed a safe place, when you needed something far more hurtful than a headache to be healed.

"Sure," I told you, wishing you confidence I had yet to provide, willing you to channel that anger onto me.

The Value of Reading More

IF WE CAN'T PRETEACH ENOUGH WORDS TO HELP kids learn all the words that they need to know to comprehend all the texts they read, then what should we do? It's a simple answer: we must increase their volume of reading.

Jim Trelease wrote, "All babies are born equal. Not one can speak, count, read, or write at birth, but by the time they go to kindergarten they are not equal" (2001, 36). What happens in those years between birth and kindergarten that most affects *vocabulary* development? The answer is one we have known for a long time. It's the number of books kids have read to them during those years.

The Million-Word Gap

Some five-year-olds enter kindergarten with a million-word head start when compared with other five-year-olds. How did they get that million-word bonus? The answer isn't too surprising: their parents or caregivers read to them. The better question is How much did they read to them?

Research shows that reading aloud one book a day creates that million-word advantage, 1.4 million to be exact (Logan 2019). Reporting in the study in the *Journal of Developmental and Behavioral Pediatrics*, Logan explained that children who were not read to (or read to only once or twice a month) entered kindergarten having heard about 4,600 words from books. Children who were read to one to two times per week since birth started kindergarten having heard about 63,000 words. And kids who were read

The person reading to children does not have to be a parent. What matters most is if the person reading aloud has a dialogue with kids while reading. "I think this part is funny, don't you?" "Let's read that part again!" "Which word says cat?" "Where is that red balloon?" (That last question is a question of love because by the hundredth time you've read *Goodnight Moon,* you don't really give a damn about that red balloon.)

to daily, one book a day, from birth to age five, started kindergarten having heard 1.4 million words (see Figure 16.1).

That's a million-word advantage some students have from the moment school begins. Why is this an advantage? First, as students learn to decode words, they need to attach each sounded-out word to something. If there's a word with an associated meaning in their long-term memory, then they now know what this word looks like on paper. If there is not, then they have learned to sound out something but have nothing to attach it to. This is like me reading Latin. Latin was my foreign language in high school. I can still decode the words, but I don't know what they mean. That knowledge once stored in long-term memory is now merely long gone.

Second, words in books, including children's books, are oftentimes words that we don't use in everyday language. Take a look at this passage from *Rosie Revere, Engineer*, a book that four- and five-year-olds enjoy as much as seven- and eight-year-olds. Rosie loves to invent things until one day . . .

> *And when it was finished, young Rosie was proud,*
> *But Fred slapped his knee and he chuckled out loud.*
> *He laughed till he wheezed and his eyes filled with tears,*
> *All to the horror of Rosie Revere,*
> *Who stood there embarrassed, perplexed, and dismayed.*
> *(Beaty 2013, 12)*

When parents read this book, they introduce children to some sophisticated words: *chuckled, wheezed, horror, embarrassed, perplexed,* and *dismayed.* Those words, considered to be tier 2 vocabulary words (see page 170 for a discussion of tier 2 words), don't make it into the common conversations most adults have with young children. Parents are more likely to say to four-year-olds, "You seem confused" far more often than "You seem perplexed." While reading *Rosie Revere, Engineer* offers little ones a great story about perseverance and believing in yourself, it also exposes readers to many words they might not otherwise encounter. That's not unique to this one book. Cunningham and Stanovich found that "the words in children's books are considerably rarer than those in speech on prime-time adult television" (1998, 139).

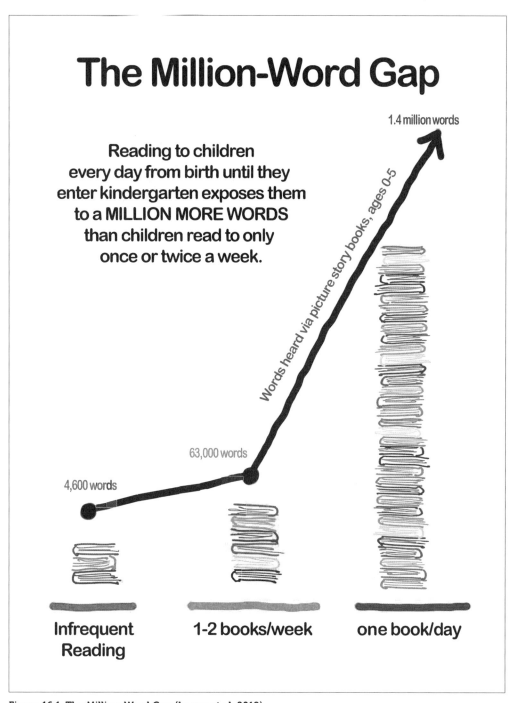

Figure 16.1 The Million-Word Gap (Logan et al. 2019)

This seemed to be the case for George's family. The parents weren't readers and they didn't remember being read to as children. When George was born, no one told them what reading to him would accomplish.

When Time and Access Are the Problems

Why do some kids have more books read to them than others? Perhaps in some families, parents and caregivers do not understand the value of reading aloud to young children. In other families, parents themselves might not have been read to when they were children. Pausing daily routines to read aloud a book isn't something they have considered doing.

And in other families, time and access are critical variables. When the parents are working multiple jobs to make a living wage; when childcare workers do not understand the value of reading aloud to children; when families don't have funds to purchase books; when cities don't offer public libraries in all neighborhoods or when those libraries are open only during parents' working hours; when bookstores are not in all neighborhoods; when food is scarce or less than nourishing and health care is minimal, thereby causing hunger and illness to take time away from other endeavors—when those are the things parents must navigate, we begin to understand why they might forgo daily read-aloud time. But when research shows one book a day can give a child a million-word advantage, then as a nation, we are required to ensure all children have access to books. To do less creates an inequity among children that is more than wrong; it is shameful. This million-word gap, more often than not, is another example of systemic problems we must, as a nation, overcome.

"When research shows one book a day can give a child a million-word advantage, then as a nation, we are required to ensure all children have access to books. To do less creates an inequity among children that is more than wrong; it is shameful."

The Word Gap Widens

When children start school, research reveals a strong positive correlation between those who continue reading and high achievement on reading comprehension tests when compared with those who do not read (Allington and McGill-Franzen 2021; National Center for Education Statistics 2019; Jerrim, Oliver, and Sims 2019; Torppa et al. 2020).

More precisely, once young children acquire basic proficiency in decoding and fluency, they use those skills to continue expanding their knowledge about subjects, resulting in a positive effect on reading comprehension. Early on, achievement affects volume; as kids move through school, volume affects achievement (Mol and Bus 2011; van Bergen et al. 2020). Put another way, the better students can read, the more likely they are to read; the more they read, the more likely their reading skills will keep improving.

Many students, however, report that as they move through school, they read less and less. The 2020 long-term reading assessment published by the National Assessment of Educational Progress showed that nine- and thirteen-year-olds report reading less for fun than in previous years (NAEP 2020). A look at the chart in Figure 16.2 shows that in 2012, the last time the seventeen-year-olds were surveyed, the percentage of students who never or hardly ever read for fun had increased. Seventeen-year-olds,

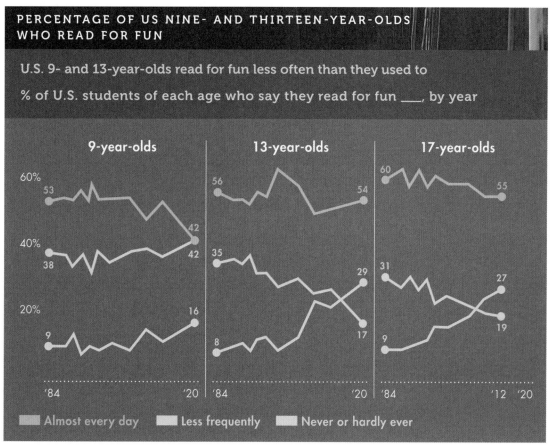

PERCENTAGE OF US NINE- AND THIRTEEN-YEAR-OLDS WHO READ FOR FUN

U.S. 9- and 13-year-olds read for fun less often than they used to

% of U.S. students of each age who say they read for fun ___, by year

Note: 2020 assessment was not fielded to 17-year-olds. Totals may not sum to 100% due to rounding. "Less frequently" combines responses of "once or twice a week," "once or twice a month" and "a few times a year." Source: U.S. Department of Education, Institute of Education Sciences, National Center for Education Statistics, National Assessment of Eduational Progress (NAEP), 2020 Long-Term Reading Assessment. PEW Research Center

Figure 16.2 Percentage of US Nine- and Thirteen-Year-Olds Who Read for Fun

generally a part of this recurring study, were not included in 2020, as school buildings were closed because of COVID-19.

We see that this trend of reading less for pleasure appears across race and ethnicity (see Figure 16.3).

Information such as this would seem to suggest that if we encourage more "reading for fun," reading achievement scores will increase. But is that accurate?

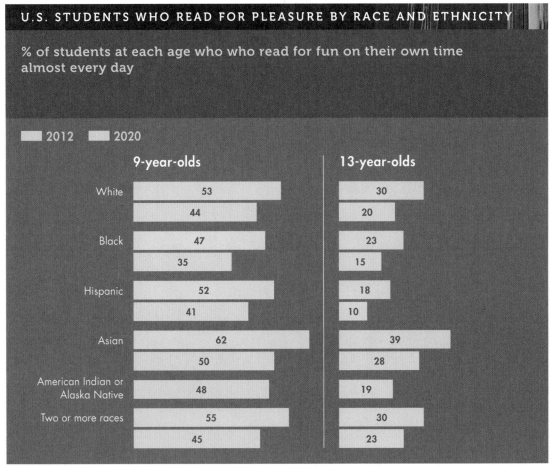

Note: Totals may not sum to 100% due to rounding. When it comes to race, students are single-race and not Hispanic, except for students who chose "two or more races." Hispanics are of any race. For Native Hawaiins or Pacific Islanders, sample sizes were too small to reliably report data and are not shown, as is also the case for 2012 data for American Indians or Alaska Natives. Source: U.S. Department of Education, Institute of Education Sciences, National Center for Education Statistics, National Assessment of Eduational Progress (NAEP), 2020 Long-Term Reading Assessment. PEW Research Center

Figure 16.3 US Students Who Read for Pleasure by Race and Ethnicity

Turning Up the Volume

When we see home-time reading diminishing, it makes sense to want to encourage more of this pleasure reading at school.

The problem is that research about the effectiveness of increasing the volume of reading is not unanimous. Some claim increasing volume won't develop reading skills that affect reading achievement with complex texts (NRP and NICHD 2000). Others claim it will (NEA 2004, 2007).

Taking up the argument of either side of this ongoing debate is not helpful here. What is helpful is for me to agree with the National Reading Panel's finding that programs such as DEAR (Drop Everything and Read) do not improve the reading abilities of great numbers of struggling readers. I'm not saying that an individual teacher here or there doesn't have low-performing students make great gains with those programs. But research studies regarding DEAR can't link that stop, drop, and read program to improved reading comprehension. And rarely have those studies looked at the type of reading students were doing (fiction or nonfiction), the complexity of the text (easily accessible or causing some struggles), or the mode of delivery (digital, print, audio, both). These factors might be what caused the increase in reading ability more than merely increasing the volume (Torppa et al. 2019). When many teachers—including me—have tried such programs for many years and, still, many students struggle with reading, I think we must question the effectiveness of such programs.

> If you are interested in jumping deep into this divide, I suggest starting with Allington and McGill-Franzen's 2021 article "Reading Volume and Reading Achievement: A Review of Recent Research," which you can find online.

The Conundrum

Many teachers recognize that during these minutes of pleasure reading—no matter what you call that time—some students will fake read. Have you noticed this is the time when some will nap and others will get a pass to go back to their locker (as they did yesterday and the day before) to get the book they forgot? It's the time when some will look through the books you have in your classroom, thumbing through this one and then that one. It's the time when phones come out behind raised books and text messages begin flying. We know this, and yet we continue the practice. Perhaps that's because we see those who covet this time and dive happily into their books when sustained reading time begins and hate it when you say time is up. Maybe we don't want to give up this time because that teacher down the hall casts long glances if you don't let your students participate in DEAR time.

At the same time, some teachers know that during these free reading times, too many students turn pages, skip over parts they don't understand, don't pay attention to context clues, become frustrated if they get confused, give up and choose another book, and certainly don't push themselves to read anything beyond the easiest of books. This is not the independent reading we want for kids, and it is certainly not a good use of instructional time.

And yet, we know that reading is important. Reading, more than anything else, will build a robust vocabulary, and a robust vocabulary is important for reading success. It is a conundrum, but perhaps there is a solution.

Perhaps what we need is a better understanding of what should happen during silent reading time. Is this the time for kids to get lost in a good book, or is this the time, when they are in class with you, that you want them thinking about how they are navigating this text—not only finding meaning for themselves but thinking about how they find meaning when they are confused? The very name Drop Everything and Read suggests to kids that they are putting aside anything they have learned about comprehension strategies to go off and enjoy a story. But shouldn't those strategies go with them? When the football coach tells his players before they head off for the Friday night game, "Enjoy the game!" he is not simultaneously encouraging them to forget everything they have been learning in practice. They enjoy the game as they put what they have learned into practice. That's what we need in a classroom: a time in which students both enjoy the game and put their knowledge about reading into practice. Don't drop a thing. Bring it all with you. Bob Probst and I have called this type of independent reading time "directed silent reading" (2016, 2018).

The Solution

Unlike DEAR, a directed silent reading time requires that you teach students something you want them to practice before they begin their reading. Perhaps you remind them,

> *As you read today, I want you think about the signposts you notice. Put a sticky note where you notice one and ask yourself the anchor question. Think about how noticing the Aha Moment or the Tough Question is changing your understanding of the text. After we all read, you'll talk in small groups about what you noticed.*

Or maybe your minilesson focuses on a fix-up strategy:

> *We all can become confused as we read. Perhaps you stopped paying attention. Maybe you lost track of who was doing what. Maybe the sentence was too long and you couldn't remember what was happening at the end by the time you reached the end. Getting lost happens. What shouldn't happen, though, is staying lost. Skilled readers do something once they realize they are confused. They might reread, read a portion aloud, decide to go on a bit further to see if that helps, look up a word, or underline exactly what is confusing. Our chart up here shows more fix-up strategies. As you read today, I want you paying attention to which strategies you use and when you use them. We'll discuss the fix-up strategies you used at the end of our reading time.*

Now students have direction for what they are doing. They are practicing something that you know helps improve reading comprehension. And practice is the key.

The Role of Practice

In 2008 Malcolm Gladwell wrote what became a best-selling book, *Outliers*. In that book, he explained that for someone to achieve mastery of something—playing chess or an instrument or golf—that person needed to practice for ten thousand hours. He cited Ericcson, Krampe, and Tesch-Römer's well-respected research, "The Role of Deliberate Practice in the Acquisition of Expert Performance" (1993). Gladwell's assertion gave way to the idea that with enough practice, any of us could be the next Yo-Yo Ma or Serena Williams. We all liked that idea. The best of the best weren't all that different from us; they simply had practiced more. The problem was that Gladwell's chapter about this magical ten thousand hours of practice omitted the word *deliberate*, and the authors of the 1993 research never mentioned anything about ten thousand hours. That was Gladwell's insertion. His omission, though, has perhaps done the most harm.

Deliberate Practice

In their research report, Ericcson, Krampe, and Tesch-Römer carefully explained that great masters of something practiced *deliberately* (and practiced far more than then thousand hours). Deliberate practice, as the researchers defined it, is a very specific type of practice.

👥 Step Inside a Home

I learned about this type of practice when my husband and I changed our son's piano teacher when Baker was in fifth grade. Baker had always wanted to play the piano. Having done everything wrong a parent could do with piano lessons with our oldest, Meredith, I promised myself when her younger brother began asking for lessons that he would have to ask on bended, bloodied knees before we traveled that path again. By fourth grade, he had asked and cajoled enough that we looked around to find him a teacher. A mom in our neighborhood taught piano lessons. One quick call and she agreed that she would teach Baker on Tuesday afternoons at 5:30. After only a few lessons, she called me and suggested his talents warranted a different type of teacher. I promised her that he was making great progress; he loved jumping on his bike and riding to her house, and during the week he enjoyed playing the pieces she had selected for him. Plus, I still remembered all I had done wrong with Meredith as I pushed too hard for her to succeed. About a year later, though, she and her family moved, and Baker's wonderful neighborhood teacher was gone.

Baker still wanted lessons, so I asked around and discovered that "if we could get him to take Baker, Mr. Harris was the best." I began calling this highly respected and much desired piano teacher. He told me that he interviewed students before agreeing to take them and then explained that he did not fill openings with students already in fifth grade who had studied only one year. First, I was stunned that a piano teacher required students to audition, but if this was what was happening these days, then that was what Baker would do. Second, when did fifth grade become a late entry point? How had I missed that memo? I kept calling, asking him to listen to Baker play. He kept repeating the same comments. Finally, one day, he called me. "If your son can be here in half an hour, I've had a lesson cancellation and

I'm willing to hear him play." Baker grabbed his music; I grabbed my car keys; we were off.

About an hour later, Mr. Harris said he would be very happy for Baker to study with him. That was new language. Study? But Baker was ecstatic, telling me later, "I could tell right away he was a different kind of teacher." Mr. Harris told Baker that he needed to get a spiral notebook to bring to class. "You'll use that to take practice notes." Practice notes? This was new, too. Baker studied with him through twelfth grade and filled dozens of spiral notebooks along the way, notebooks he still has.

In those notebooks, Mr. Harris wrote down exactly how Baker was to practice a particular line or even only a few measures during the week. That week, as Baker would practice, he then would reflect on what he accomplished or what was still giving him trouble. "You can play whatever you want to play," Mr. Harris explained, "But when you practice, you will practice with deliberation and focus." Then, during Baker's lessons, the two of them would review whatever Baker had written.

Years later, I read the Ericcson article and nodded my head, understanding exactly what deliberate practice was. With deliberate practice, Baker's

Figure 16.4 Here, an older Baker, practicing after all those years.

practice time became focused, purposeful, and valuable. And when he would later sit and play, just to play, just to enjoy the music he was creating, he played better than he had ever played because he better understood what he was doing.

The Teacher's Role in Deliberate Practice

Gladwell did all who read his book a disservice by dropping that one word, *deliberate*. Deliberate practice, as defined by Ericcson and colleagues, requires the following:

This criterion alone makes it clear that my first year of teaching, I was not a highly qualified teacher. Being on the dean's list, receiving an Outstanding Student Teacher award, and earning a degree with honors suggested I was highly qualified. But no. I was not. I needed deliberate practice with a mentor who helped me gain expertise.

1. A highly qualified teacher who will work with a student to assess how the student is progressing. Those assessments guide decisions about what to do next.

2. The teacher sets goals for each practice session. The teacher must explain these goals so that the student understands what he is trying to accomplish before attempting the practice. In other words, when Mr. Harris told Baker, "During practice this week, I want you to focus on these measures, playing the bass line softer than the treble line," unless Baker could imagine what that might sound like, then his practice would not help him reach that instructional goal.

3. The teacher provides feedback about the practice. When Baker would arrive each week, the lesson began with Mr. Harris looking back at what Baker was to practice and then discussing what worked well and did not work well.

When I hear teachers say, "I give homework, but we never review it," I want to demand they stop requiring the homework. For the practice to be effective, students need to have their efforts evaluated.

4. The teacher expects ongoing and repeated practice.

Is All Practice Deliberate?

All practice is not deliberate. Since that 1993 research, Ericcson, Krampe, and Tesch-Römer have refined that understanding of deliberate practice to now offer distinct categories:

- *Deliberate Practice*: Individuals practice following the steps previously described.

- *Purposeful Practice*: Individuals try on their own to improve purposefully, but they do not have the input of a teacher.

- *Naïve Practice*: Individuals practice simply because they are doing something: playing baseball with friends, riding a bike on a Saturday afternoon, baking a cake for a party. There is no purposeful thinking about what one is doing so as to improve and there is no teacher guiding the practice.

My husband and I are taking ballroom dance classes. Though we don't have a ballroom and are not invited to many balls (well, none), those grand, sweeping ballroom dances look like such fun. For years we've tried to get better at dances like the waltz or tango, but our practice was mostly naïve practice, though sometimes, after watching *The Sound of Music* or *Take the Lead*, for instance, one might have said it was purposeful. Now, though, with our classes, our patient instructors, and our weekly assignment books with steps drawn out for us, our practice is deliberate, if only in our living room. And someday, Brad might put on a tux and I might find a ballgown, and we just might show off that waltz.

My point is that we don't need to develop a desire; we have that. We don't need someone to talk us into the joys of such dancing; we understand those joys. We need practice that is deliberate and designed to help us improve.

Now, Back to Reading

I think that free reading or DEAR programs could be categorized as naïve practice. Kids sit and read a book. No one has offered direction; the students themselves aren't reflecting on how they used context clues or figured out a tricky bit of syntax. Students enter each reading session knowing that they need to read a certain number of pages or need to be able to answer some basic questions, but they aren't practicing anything. And feedback on their practice is often minimal, as teachers tell them, "Good job! Keep reading." Naïve practice isn't going to create a Serena Williams or a Yo-Yo Ma. And naïve practice isn't going to help our students learn to read complex texts. Deliberate practice used during your directed silent reading program might.

My experience has shown me that I was never consistently effective with moving struggling readers directly from no reading to sustained silent reading. Occasionally, some students would make this jump from aversion to immersion. Mostly though, students who hated to read did not turn to loving to read because I gave them a book, even the right book. Instead, I found that the following progression worked well (see Figure 16.5).

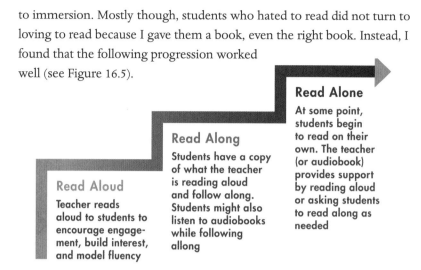

Read Alone

At some point, students begin to read on their own. The teacher (or audiobook) provides support by reading aloud or asking students to read along as needed

Read Along

Students have a copy of what the teacher is reading aloud and follow along. Students might also listen to audiobooks while following allong

Read Aloud

Teacher reads aloud to students to encourage engagement, build interest, and model fluency

Figure 16.5 Progression of Sharing a Text

Earlier in the year, I needed to read aloud to many students. They needed to hear the text to help develop fluency, and I wanted to share various authors and genres with them. We were becoming a community of readers, which meant doing some things in common. But soon I wanted students to follow along as I was reading aloud. This was particularly important for students who lacked word recognition skills or for second language learners who were building a vocabulary. Seeing words while hearing them is always valuable. The goal, though, was to move students to reading alone. Many students are ready to move to this step early in the year; others will need to go through this progression each time you change a genre. For example, students in a book club or literature circle might need you scaffold their move into various books throughout the year. Then, you join the small group to read aloud Chapter 1. The next day, you read aloud Chapter 2 as they follow along. On day three, they might all be ready to begin reading the book on their own.

Read aloud; read along; read alone. No matter where you are in this progression, remember that if you want students' reading time to be highly beneficial, it helps to have some specific lessons you share prior to the reading (see Figure 16.6 for examples).

LESSONS FOR A DIRECTED SILENT READING PROGRAM

Lessons	Example Language for Those Lessons
Using transition words to think about text organization	As you read today, pay attention to transition words authors use to signal what's happening next in the text. When you notice a word or phrase such as *primarily* or *finally* or *in a similar manner*, stop and think about what might happen next in the text. Note where some of these phrases are. We'll talk about what they signaled to you when reading time is complete.
Using Syntax Surgery to untangle long sentences	Today in science class, you will all continue reading the articles you've chosen. Yesterday, several of you mentioned that science is hard to read because the sentences are often long. That's correct. Science writers often compact a lot of information into one sentence. Remember, when a sentence is confusing, don't skip over it. Study it. You have learned how to mark up your sentence to do what we call Syntax Surgery. This will help you link words and ideas. Look at all the links I made for this sentence: *Ecologists are people who study the relationship between living organisms and their habitats (the places organisms live) to learn how they interact with living and nonliving things.* As you are reading today, use Syntax Surgery when you are confused. Think about how linking the words and ideas helps you think about the meaning of the sentence.
Using rereading to clarify confusion	In social studies today, during your reading time, you'll be reading a book you've chosen that tells you more about World War II. While I want you to jot notes about interesting facts you learn, I also want you to notice the places that are confusing. We've discussed how something as simple as backing up a few sentences and rereading that section can help clarify your confusion. Put a sticky note anyplace you did that while reading. Think about how rereading helped you clarify your confusion. We'll discuss how this was helpful at the end of your reading time.
Using paraphrasing to help remember what has happened	Before you begin reading, let's remember that skilled readers often pause to think about what they have read and put that into their own words. That's called paraphrasing. Find a couple of places today to pause, and on your sticky notes, paraphrase what you have just read. When we come back together after you all have read, let's talk about how the paraphrasing helped you remember what you were reading and let's discuss anything that made paraphrasing hard.

Figure 16.6 Examples of Lessons for a Directed Silent Reading Program

Practice Takes Time

Creating a directed silent reading program doesn't matter one whit if there is no time to read. Gladwell came up with ten thousand hours to create deep expertise. Ericcson and colleagues reported closer to twenty-five thousand hours. Let's agree that deep mastery of anything requires thousands of hours of practice. To be generous, we can keep Gladwell's lower estimate of ten thousand hours in mind.

Let's do some math. If kids are in school for an average of 180 days a year for 13 years and if each school day has an average of 5 instructional hours, then after 13 years, they will have been in school for 11,700 hours, or 900 hours per year. We immediately see a problem. Their total hours in school, when students are to master so much, is only slightly over that 10,000-hour threshold. Furthermore, those 11,700 hours are not focused on one single topic. During this time, students are to become skilled in mathematics, history, social studies, literature, various types of writing, science, foreign language, art, music, and physical education. There are two through lines throughout all disciplines: reading and writing. Let's, therefore, look at how much reading students do.

If students spend 40 minutes a day in directed silent reading, then in a year, they will have had 124 hours of directed practice. In 13 years, they will have had 1,612 hours of directed silent reading. That's a far distance from Gladwell's magical number or Ericcson and colleagues' reported number. What's dismaying is that the bulk of these hours will occur in one class (ELA) or perhaps two classes (ELA and social studies). Students can spend entire chunks of their school day using reading to copy or to complete assignments.

Realistically, forty minutes a day is not the norm. When Bob and I surveyed about 1,600 teachers in 2016, we asked them how many minutes students spent in any time of sustained reading. The average answer was twenty minutes a *week*. Many teachers explained that they had too much content to cover to let students do any reading in class. Yet, more than 95 percent of the respondents also said they wanted students to become better readers and the same percentage wanted students to become more skilled readers of their content. Taking time to read is the solution and finding the time is the problem.

You and colleagues might want to discuss these questions:

- What is our goal for all readers?

- Do we need to set aside more time for some directed practice of reading?

- Do we all recognize the importance of volume of reading for improving vocabulary?

- What support do we feel from administrators for implementing a directed sustained silent reading program? What additional support would be helpful?

- How can time spent reading translate into time spent learning?

When a School Values Reading

I want students to be able to read increasingly complex fiction and nonfiction each year; I want them able to pass any tests that any politician might decide is important (so he can tell his base he supports rigorous testing). And I want students to find deep value in reading, value that extends far beyond a test score.

My frustration—perhaps *confusion* is the better word—comes as I watch communities (administrators, parents, grandparents, members of the business community) applaud when kindergartners are reading. Parents want their kids in *that* school, the one where four-year-olds know so, so many words by end of preschool and are reading *Frog and Toad Are Friends* by the end of September of their kindergarten year.

And yet, once these young children learn to break that alphabetic code, rarely do principals demand students have time during school hours to read daily; rarely do superintendents require each school principal to submit how many hours students spent reading that week; rarely do I see extensive classroom libraries in the social studies, science, foreign language, math, or art classrooms; rarely do principals commend teachers for their well-developed directed silent reading programs. Rarely do enough teachers expect students to learn

"In too many places, fear of not getting through a pacing guide reduces instruction to a show-and-tell curriculum: we show kids what they need to know and tell them what to write in their notes."

via reading. We test reading comprehension but do not expect students to comprehend content by reading it. In too many places, fear of not getting through a pacing guide reduces instruction to a show-and-tell curriculum: we show kids what they need to know and tell them what to write in their notes. I know because I have done that.

If reading is valuable—and it is—then we must treat it as the treasure it is. We motivate kids to read by giving them the tools they need so that they can read. Perhaps that is what motivates kids the most. We are all more likely to want to do something we know we can do. That's far more motivating than pieces of pizza. We motivate kids to read by surrounding them with books that reflect who they are and what their interests are, by giving them time to read, and by making sure that time encourages them to think about themselves as readers. We remind them, as Gholdy Muhammed (2020) encourages us to do, that we see the genius inside them and want them to see it, too.

> *"We motivate kids to read by surrounding them with books that reflect who they are and what their interests are, by giving them time to read, and by making sure that time encourages them to think about themselves as readers."*

Those free reading times that do not encourage reflection on how students read are not an effective use of their time. We must offer instruction before they begin and let them talk after they have read—about the book and the comprehension strategies they used while reading. We should allow for some naïve practice from time to time as they read with joy that new book they have wanted, but we must depend on deliberate practice to actually improve comprehension.

If we want to create readers, we must provide time and materials for students to read.

Dear George,

We had "free reading" on Fridays. You loved that day. You would rush in, find a copy of *The Guinness Book of World Records*, open it to any page, look at the pictures of the world's tallest man or world's smallest dog, and then, eventually, close it, look around the room, and put your head down to sleep. I didn't understand why you wouldn't read more. I had shelves of books. I book-talked many books each week. I displayed them, covers out, on my chalkboard holder. I had beanbag chairs to make our classroom feel homey (those chairs were a mistake). I completed this cozy classroom look with plants, lamps, and a small carpet.

One day you asked me what was supposed to be happening while you were reading. "Hmm?" I asked.

"While we read. Are we supposed to be learning something?" you said again.

I mumbled something about discovering the joy of reading. You stared. I added, "And you learn new things from what you are reading. . . ."

You nodded, grinned, and shared, "So, today I learned that a man rolled a ball from New York to California. Good stuff, huh? Think I'll share that tonight when Mom asks me what I learned at school." You left, smiling; I stood there, perplexed.

Dear George,

"Why won't you ever participate?" I asked you quietly as I stood at your desk. You said nothing. "I can't help you if you won't at least try," I said. You picked up your pencil and started drawing on the margin of your paper. "I know you've got things to say about some of the stuff we read," I said.

You finally looked up at me. "You think I'm going to say something so you can tell me it's wrong or the know-it-alls can laugh at what I say? No way."

"George, has anyone in here ever made fun of anything you've said?" I asked.

"No—because I never say anything," you replied.

I smiled at your logic. "George, who's ever laughed at something you said?"

You looked at me with dismay, suddenly far wiser about what happens in schools than I, a first-year teacher. "You don't know nothin' if you think kids don't make fun of you when you're dumb."

I knelt beside your desk. "George, you're not dumb."

You interrupted me. "Yeah? What do you call it when you can't do the work everyone else can? I call it dumb."

"You've got to try, George. Just try," I whispered.

You never even looked up. You just shook your head and whispered back, "No. No, I don't."

CHAPTER 17

The Interdependent Relationship of Skill and Will

In *CONFIDENCE: HOW WINNING STREAKS AND Losing Streaks Begin and End*, Rosabeth Kanter (2004, 97–98) from the Harvard School of Business lists the following self-protective behaviors people turn to when failure is ongoing; the descriptions of each behavior are my own.

- *Communication decreases.* People avoid unpleasant conversations about problems.

- *Criticism and blame increase.* People do anything to avoid self-scrutiny.

- *Respect decreases.* People feel surrounded by mediocrity.

- *Isolation increases.* People don't want to be reminded of failure by others.

- *Focus turns inward.* People look out for their own interests.

- *Rifts widen and inequities grow.* People hoard assets, play favorites, and exhibit rivalries.

- *Initiative decreases.* People are paralyzed by anxiety.

- *Aspirations diminish.* People look for life satisfaction elsewhere.

- *Negativity spreads.* Contagious negativity reduces everyone's mood.

While Kanter was writing about sports teams and large businesses, as I studied her work, I saw overlaps with older students who struggle with reading.

- *Communication decreases.* Struggling readers often avoid discussing reading problems.

- *Criticism and blame increase.* Struggling readers will blame the book, the class, other classmates, or the teacher.

- *Respect decreases.* Struggling readers often share, "I'm in the dumb class. I don't want to be with these people." Sometimes, the frustration spills over into feelings about the entire school.

- *Isolation increases.* Students who struggle with reading rarely participate in discussions about books or voluntarily sit with others who want to talk about books. They often choose desks at the back or toward the edge of the room.

- *Focus turns inward.* Students who struggle often provide excuses for not reading that preserve their dignity: "I forgot my book"; "I didn't do my homework." These are students who would rather get in trouble for not doing something than be embarrassed by efforts that fall short of the goal.

- *Rifts widen and inequities grow.* Struggling readers act negatively toward those who are more successful readers. Their behavior can border on bullying. They also point out that "those kids get special attention" or "that class gets to read the good books."

- *Initiative decreases.* Struggling readers rarely try with full effort. Their heads are on their desks. They sit slumped in their chairs with arms crossed, sweatshirt hoods over their heads.

- *Aspirations diminish.* Struggling readers sometimes appear not to care about anything.

- *Negativity spreads.* Struggling readers will sometimes purposefully make fun of those students who are more skilled readers.

As I consider these behaviors, I easily can name many students who fit one, two, or all of those characteristics. When I told George to try, what was I asking him to try to do? Stop blaming others? Stop blaming himself? Show more initiative? Not be so negative? Look at Figure 17.1, an if-then negative behavior chart that might help you think about these negative behaviors and language you could use to counteract those feelings.

WAYS TO COUNTERACT NEGATIVE BEHAVIORS

If this is the behavior that you notice . . .	**When** students . . .	**Then** you might say . . .
Communication decreases	Avoid discussing reading problems	"I was impressed when today you not only told me you didn't understand something, but you said it was the vocabulary that was hard. Your ability to explain the problem showed a lot of insight. Good for you."
Criticism and blame increase	Blame the book, the class, other classmates, or the teacher	"We can look for other books you might enjoy more. But I also want you to think about one thing you think you can do to help yourself as you are reading. What's one thing you want to work on?"
Respect decreases	Say things like, "I'm in the dumb class. I don't want to be with these people" Indicate that the frustration has spilled over into feelings about the entire school	"Did you know that Bo over there finished another book last night? And Orlando decided to come in during lunch to work on his project. You are surrounded by folks who know if they work hard, they can do hard work."
Isolation increases	Won't participate in discussions about books or voluntarily sit with others who want to talk about books Choose desks at the back or toward the edge of the room	"I'd like you to join this group today. Your sense of humor is something they will all appreciate, and I'm interested in hearing you offer one idea to the conversation."

Figure 17.1 Ways to Counteract Negative Behaviors

continues

WAYS TO COUNTERACT NEGATIVE BEHAVIORS

If this is the behavior that you notice . . .	When students . . .	Then you might say . . .
Focus turns inward	Offer excuses for not reading that preserve their dignity: "I forgot my book" or "I didn't do my homework" Would rather get in trouble for not doing something than be embarrassed by efforts that fall short of the goal	"I know answering questions in front of others is something you don't really like to do. I also believe that you have smart ideas to share. Tomorrow in class, I'm going to ask students what surprised them about what we read today. Why don't you think about that tonight? What was surprising?"
Rifts widen and inequities grow	Act negatively toward those who are more successful readers, sometimes bordering on bullying Point out that "those kids get special attention" or "that class gets to read the good books"	"Everyone struggles with something they read. Some people just have more tools to help them when they struggle. Did you know that with the same tools, you can get through texts faster and understand them better? Let's focus on what you can do to improve your reading."
Initiative decreases	Won't complete work, participate in conversations, or answer your questions Show it through their posture or their unfinished—or never started—work Show it through their tardiness to class and constant refusal to bring their book to class	"I have noticed that when you put some effort, even a little, into your work, you have very smart thoughts to share. That little bit of effort makes a difference. Have you noticed that?"
Aspirations diminish	No longer seem to care about anything	"I saw how you decided to reread that passage. That was when you noticed the Aha Moment. Did you realize that? When you tried once more, you noticed that signpost. Well done."
Negativity spreads	Purposefully make fun of those students who are more skilled readers	"Did you see how Sam smiled when you said you agreed with his statement? I liked the way you encouraged him."

Figure 17.1 Ways to Counteract Negative Behaviors, *continued*

Self-Efficacy, Self-Concept, and Anxiety

George would have been better served if I had known enough to consider his unwillingness to try as related to three constructs: self-efficacy, self-concept, and anxiety.

Self-efficacy is your belief in your abilities to accomplish a specific goal. Self-concept is a more general view of yourself. A student may have a strong self-concept (sense of self) as she describes herself as good in math, easy to get along with, and responsible but have low self-efficacy as an artist ("I just can't draw."). Anxiety refers to students' affective emotions about a task. That affective emotion is what we often notice first in a classroom. Anxiety is the outward and visible sign of inward, invisible feelings. Students slam down books; drop backpacks noisily onto the floor; look upset or sullen; say that reading sucks. Often, teachers attend to the affective emotions ("Don't slam your books, please." "Put your backpack where it belongs." "Don't use that language.") without connecting the behavior, the anxiousness, to the underlying issues of low self-concept and low self-efficacy. Anxious feelings interfere with the ability to learn, and the downward spiral becomes self-perpetuating.

Improving Self-Efficacy

Stopping this downward spiral and creating a more confident reader begins with motivating the student, and the best motivation is the acquisition of needed skills. If you want students to be motivated to do something, make sure they can do it.

Many think reading motivation begins with handing kids a good book. If the book really is a good book that might encourage interest in that one book, but motivation to learn more, to stick with a text when it is difficult, to focus on the task at hand—that happens when skills improve. Improved skills, then, mean students might do something more readily, so their will improves. It's an interdependent relationship: as the skill to read improves, the will improves; as the will improves, skills improve.

Once there is some level of skill, though, *will* becomes the driver. That's why you'll notice that with some students, you simply need to let them find the book they want to read, and they are motivated to read. They have developed enough skills that they enter the task with strong self-efficacy: they believe they can read the book. Students with low skills lack that belief. Improving their skills, therefore, becomes the motivating force. That's why with less skilled students I teach them Somebody Wanted But So early in the year. This scaffold for writing a summary is easy to understand and allows students to experience success. Along with that, I show them one or two signposts. Those are things in the text they can notice and that help them make inferences. If students have a low reading rate, we'll start doing repeated rereadings right away. I'm doing more than building skills; I'm improving their self-efficacy.

If you need to review this, it's discussed on page 137.

"If you want students to be motivated to do something, make sure they can do it."

That then leads to a more positive view of self. The kid who couldn't read is now the kid who is succeeding. And with that success, anxiety lowers. It will reappear during high-stress situations, but day to day, little by little, anxiousness regarding reading can diminish. Eventually, activity will replace apathy and a willingness to try will replace a reluctance to engage. Eventually.

👥 Step Inside a Classroom

In an eighth-grade classroom, the students looked at the assignment chart at the front of the room, which outlined what all the classes were doing that week. The notes revealed that one class was going to begin reading a well-worn classic. This class saw they were expected to begin reading excerpts from that classic. One student asked the teacher if she thought they were too dumb to read hard books. Another laughed and said everyone in the class was too dumb.

Look back at Figure 17.1 on pages 289–90 as you consider these two statements. What characteristics of failure are revealed with these comments?

The teacher thought about this for a moment (and looked at me sitting in the back of the room) and said they too could read the entire book "but [they would] need to work hard." Some students were pleased; others looked bored.

"It's an interdependent relationship: as the skill to read improves, the will improves; as the will improves, skills improve."

The teacher provided an array of supports to help students manage the text. Students read some sections aloud in paired reading; the teacher read aloud other chapters. Some students followed along as they listened to the audiobook. As students read independently, they stopped often to think aloud about their confusion, predictions, or clarifications with peers or the

Figure 17.2 When kids feel dumb, they disengage.

teacher. They used sticky notes to keep up with questions, unusual vocabulary, and comments they wanted to make. They used the *Notice and Note* signposts to think about how characters were changing. The teacher gave them a "cheat sheet" I created to help them use, as one student explained, "smart words" to discuss the plot, characters, and theme (see Figure 17.3 on the following page).

At the end of each chapter, they wrote Somebody Wanted But So statements for several characters. They met daily for about ten minutes in small groups to discuss what they understood, what they didn't understand, and what they were going to do to figure out what they didn't understand (a nice adaptation of the KWL framework). And they finally finished the book. At that point, they said they wanted to take the same test that the

SMART WORDS THAT HELP STUDENTS DISCUSS FICTION

When students lack words for talking about selections they've read, it's hard for them to enter into literary conversations. Let them use this chart to help them find the words they need to move them past the "It was boring" or "I really liked it" stage of conversation.

Words to Describe the Plot

Positive	Negative
Realistic	Unrealistic
Good pace from scene to scene	Plodding
Suspenseful	Predictable
Satisfying ending	Frustrating ending
Subplots tied together well	Confusing subplots

Words to Describe Characters

Positive	Negative
Original	Stereotyped
Believable	Unbelievable
Well-rounded	Flat
Multidimensional—change and grow	Static—remain the same
Well developed	Flawed

Words to Describe the Theme

Positive	Negative
Important message	Unimportant message
Subtle	Overbearing
Unique	Overworked
Powerful	Ineffective

Words to Describe the Author's Writing Style

Positive	Negative
Descriptive, filled with metaphors	Boring, no imagery
Original	Filled with clichés
Lively, full of action	Slow moving

Figure 17.3 Smart Words That Help Students Discuss Fiction

kids in the advanced class took. They did, and all scored between 80 and 94 percent on the test.

As students looked at their tests with incredible pride, one said, "I guess now we're just as smart at those other kids."

Another said, "Yeah, maybe we're even smarter."

A third remarked, "Being smart is hard work, but it sure feels good once you've done it."

After a moment of silence, another said, "I guess now we've got to keep it up. What's the next book they're going to read?"

By the end of the year, these students had read all the same texts as the students in the advanced language arts class had read. At that point, one asked, "So, should our report card say Adv LA (advanced language arts) instead of just language arts?" The teacher agreed and talked with the principal. He agreed, and these students suddenly found themselves in an advanced language arts class.

> These comments reflect a strong sense of self and strong self-efficacy.

When Confidence Emerges

The students' comments were the outward expression of the confidence they gained while doing this work. The success these students had with these texts was tied to the work the teacher was willing to do in providing the necessary scaffolds.

For those who needed it, the teacher continued to send some students to see the reading specialist, who worked with a few on word recognition. The teacher didn't expect word recognition, automaticity, and fluency to improve with a reading of this classic. She helped these students gain access to this text by taking away the word recognition constraints, and the few who needed help with some decoding skills got that practice in another class.

Once all students had finished the novel, she wrote:

> I don't think I've ever worked this hard. I've always just given
> the students in this class easier books to read. But this was
> incredible. In spite of working harder than I've ever worked, I
> feel more excited to go into this class than ever before. These kids
> can do this work. I think I've never expected that they could

really do hard work, so I never pushed. But it's really not just pushing. It's about using all those strategies we've been talking about. It's that self-fulfilling prophecy: kids will do what we tell them they can—or cannot—do. Our next stop: Shakespeare!

As we connect less skilled readers to texts, we are helping them build the confidence they need to fully enter into the community of readers. This level of connection requires patience and tenacity on our part. Struggling readers don't only lack skills but lack the confidence to believe they can succeed. They don't believe they have anything to offer. You must believe for them.

Dear George,

You brought me a present one day, a well-worn copy of *The Little Engine That Could*. After class, you stood at my desk and said that you knew how much I liked books, and you had been at a garage sale with your mother, where you saw this book for a dime. You thought I might like it.

You handed it to me and said, "And besides, it's about always trying." You grinned. "And you know how you are with trying." I smiled. "And anyway, I thought you might like it."

Nope. I loved it.

Dear George,

I remember with such clarity the day you came into class early, looking quite proud of yourself. As you sat down and began going through your backpack, you looked up and said, "Before you ask, the main character's name was Paul."

"That's great, George. How do you know?"

"His name is in the title," you explained.

"Right. But that isn't what I was going to ask."

"Oh. OK. What are you going to ask?"

"What in this story changed your mind about something?" I asked.

"What do you mean?"

"I mean, what in this story changed your mind about something?"

You were silent and then you answered my question with a question: "Can't you just ask what the names of the other characters are?"

Monologic and Dialogic Talk

TALKING ABOUT A SUBJECT HELPS IMPROVE THE understanding of that topic—especially when the talk is dialogic (Nystrand and Gamoran 1991; Boyd and Markarian 2015; Kim and Wilkinson 2019). Monologic talk is authoritative, like a lecture. The listener's job is to listen and learn. The speaker's job is to impart. Sermons are monologic; TED talks are monologic. Minilessons are often monologic.

In classrooms, monologic talk is often labeled a discussion even when there is no actual discussion. The teacher asks a question; the students respond; the teacher assesses the response and then either asks Johnny to help Billy with his answer or moves on. These monologic questions don't encourage exploration; they aren't asked to help students *create* understanding; instead, they are questions to *check* for understanding. Monologic questions are easy to spot: the person asking the question already knows the answer. If you ask students what motivated the character's actions, students know you aren't actually confused about this. You know the answer; now you are checking to see if they know.

By contrast, dialogic talk expects that listener and speaker will exchange roles throughout the conversation. I talk and you listen; then you talk and I listen. There is a give-and-take of ideas, and new thoughts emerge. Neither party is privileged as they work together to understand something. Both share the responsibility for discernment and discovery. Dialogic questions, the questions that spur such talk, are questions in which the person asking the question does not know the answer. See Figure 18.1 on the following page for details of some differences between monologic and dialogic talk.

Courtney Cazden wrote about this "discussion" protocol, labeling it IRE: initiate, respond, evaluate. The teacher initiates the discussion with a question; the student responds; the teacher evaluates. (Manke 1990)

When I would ask a student, "Did you read last night?" I knew the answer and the student recognized that. She would shrug or mumble, "Not really." Asking, "What's hard about reading after school?" opened up dialogue. Together the student and I could work to discover a solution.

CHARACTERISTICS OF MONOLOGIC AND DIALOGIC TALK

Monologic	Dialogic
Teachers usually instigate the talk as they check to see if students have understood what they previously read.	Students usually instigate the talk, often in small groups or Socratic circles, as they ask questions that they need to explore to better understand the text.
Teacher asks questions for which answers are already determined.	Teacher or student asks questions for which answers are not predetermined.
The teacher usually evaluates answers as correct or incorrect, right or wrong, sufficient or insufficient.	Teachers and students rarely identify an answer as right or wrong but instead say things like, "That's so interesting," or "Oh, that helps me understand why . . . ," or "Now I get it."
Students usually direct their answers to the teacher, so often other students do not listen.	Students direct their answers to other students or, more generally, the room, and others often want to respond to them.
Students often provide answers in the fewest words possible.	Students often speak in long sentences as they work to express themselves to others.

Figure 18.1 Differences in Monologic and Dialogic Talk

Asking Real Questions

Read the following passage and answer the questions at the end of it:

> *Corandic is an emurient grof with many fribs; it granks from corite, an olg which cargs like lange. Corite grinkles several other tarances, which garkers excarp by glarcking the corite and starping it in tranker-clarped storbs. The tarances starp a chark which is exparged with worters, branking a slorp. This*

*slorp is garped through several other coruscers, finally frasting
a pragety, blickant crankle: coranda. Coranda is a cargurt,
grinkling corandic and borigen. The corandic is nacerated from
the borigen by means of loracity. Thus garkers finally ghrap a
glick, bracht, glupous grapant, corandic, which granks in many
starps. (Weaver 2002, 39)*

1. What is a corandic?

2. Where does it grank from?

3. How do garkers excarp tarances?

4. What is coranda?

These are monologic
questions because they
simply check students'
understanding.

This short quiz has four questions, so each item is worth twenty-five
points. I suspect you made 100. You might want to say to me, "But I would
never ask only these recall kinds of questions." I agree. I would not either,
so let me add one additional question:

5. Do you want any corandic in your home?

That's a better question. To answer it, you must know what corandic
is. You don't; consequently, your quiz score has dropped to 80, but that's
still passing. You still have a passing grade even though you still don't know
what corandic is.

This is one way our struggling readers progress from year to year. We
ask questions they can answer without truly understanding what the text
is about. These monologic questions—questions that have an answer that
we already know—do not encourage conversation, discussion, or meaning
making. Monologic questions do not help students work through the
process of understanding.

Now let's look at this passage:

*The blonke was maily, like all the others. Unlike the other
blonkes, however, it had spiss crinet completely covering
its fairney cloots and concealing, just below one of them, a
small wam.*

*This particular blonke was quite drumly—lennow, in fact,
and almost samded. When yerden, it did not quetch like the
other blonkes or even blore. The others blored very readily.*

In one tenth-grade class, one student who was not at all interested in this passage as I was reading aloud did interrupt the reading when I said, "The bellytimber was quite kexy."

"Hey, read that part again about a kexy bellytimber. I think I like that part." More students were suddenly interested in this text.

This is a dialogic question as it helps students create understanding.

It was probably his bellytimber that had made the one blonke so drumly. The bellytimber was quite kexy, had a strong shawk, and was apparently venenated. There was only one thing to do with the venenated bellytimber: grivel it in the flosh. This would be much better than to sparple it in the wong, since the blonkes that were not drumly could icchen in the wong but not in the flosh. (Weaver 2002, 32)

Now answer the following question:

1. What three words do you most need to know to determine the gist of this passage?

When I have shared the corandic and *blonke* passages with teachers and students, I've found that teachers and students spend more time answering that one blonke question than they spend answering the questions for the corandic passage. I've also always seen that teachers and students want to work collaboratively with others to answer the question about the blonke passage. They want to hear what others thought and they want to share their own thinking. This passage becomes relevant—at least for a moment—because they are interacting with the text to figure out what they most need to know.

I suspect that you decided you want to know what a *blonke* is. After all, that's the subject of the passage. Understanding the subject helps you access all your prior knowledge on that topic. If a blonke is a goldfish, then you begin thinking about round fishbowls, clear water, fish food, and perhaps a toilet for Freddy the goldfish once he floats in his fishbowl rather than swims. You also probably decided that you needed the definition of *drumly* because that's what made the blonke unique when compared with others. We always need to know the words that distinguish one thing from others. Finally, you might have chosen *bellytimber* because that was a word that caused something. Focusing on words that explain causes or illustrate effects is also important. Notice that I did more than tell you the definition of those three words (well, I haven't yet told you the definitions); I told you why you wanted to know those words. One provided a context; one offered a distinguishing characteristic; one was a cause of something.

This one question—What words do you need to know?—is a dialogic question. If you think you most need to know *venenated*, then that's what I'll tell you. Dialogic questions encourage a conversation, which in turn encourages thinking, rereading, speculating, explaining, and looking for evidence. In one sixth-grade classroom, one student told me, "Mostly teachers ask questions that aren't real questions. You know, with a real question, you don't already know the answer. But when teachers ask questions, they always know the answer. It's not a real question. It's a question to see if you know the right stuff."

"This [blonke passage] was harder [than the corandic passage], but I liked it more," a tenth grader told me once.

Another added, "I like this kind of thinking."

George preferred monologic questions because they did not require him to do much more than match the question to something in the text. George liked that type of question. But the question for the blonke passage? He would have disliked that one. That would have required too much interaction with the text.

And those definitions? A *blonke* is a large, powerful horse; *drumly* means ill; and *bellytimber* is grain. Read the final paragraph again and then in your own words, explain what must happen to venenated bellytimber.

> "Dialogic questions encourage a conversation, which in turn encourages thinking, rereading, speculating, explaining, and looking for evidence."

I use the blonke passage with students to level the playing field because no one knows what a blonke is. I read it aloud, students follow along, and then they work in small groups. Often, students who typically don't try to answer join in. This isn't about knowing words; this is about thinking. Don't confuse a limited academic vocabulary with limited thinking skills.

Dialogic Talk in a Classroom

Classrooms have long used monologic talk as the primary way of encouraging students to share what they know about a text in spite of research that tells us that dialogic talk improves understanding of a text and test performance (Cotton 1988). When moving to dialogic talk, you might try the following:

1. Begin by asking one of the Three Big Questions (see page 149).

2. As you are teaching a lesson, remember to pause every five to ten minutes and ask students to turn and talk with one or two other students. They can discuss one of the Big Questions, ask someone to clarify something you said, use their ABC chart (see page 156) to capture what was most important to them, or make a connection between something you've said and something they have read.

3. Ask students to respond to something they have read or you have said. As they talk in small groups, walk around the room. When you hear a comment you want the whole group to hear, ask that student to jot it down and then share it with the class when you return to a large-group discussion. This is particularly effective for your students who are reluctant to speak up in a bigger group. You have already shown them you see value in their comment.

Perhaps, though, the most important thing you can do to encourage dialogic talk is to make sure students read with an aesthetic stance.

Aesthetic and Efferent Stances Toward Reading

Louise lived to be a little more than one hundred years old. Her last book was published shortly before she died in 2005. Bob Probst first was a student of Louise's—by studying her work, not by studying with her—and then became a trusted friend of hers. She once told him that she wrote *Literature as Exploration* in defense of democracy. She thought all people needed to know how to do more than extract from a text; they needed to know how to combine their thoughts with the author's thoughts to create their own meaning.

Louise Rosenblatt (1938/1983) explained the difference between an aesthetic stance toward reading and an efferent stance in her ground-breaking book, *Literature as Exploration*. In this book, she explained that readers might take an efferent stance toward reading when their goal is to carry information away *from* the text. You might read, efferently, a recipe, or the directions for putting together that furniture from IKEA, or the information for getting a refund. You want information so that you can do something. You might read this information carefully, but you are not reading it closely.

By contrast, readers assume a more aesthetic stance when the goal is to live *through* the text. You want to walk over the bridge into a make-believe land in *Bridge to Terabithia* or walk down the road with Cassie Logan in *Roll of Thunder, Hear My Cry* or jump aboard the moving train with Lydia as she and her son try to escape a Mexican cartel in *American Dirt*. You read those texts closely, analyzing what is in them that caused your response, understanding what the text means and means in your life. Your goal is not to extract details to answer a ten-item multiple-choice test; you don't hold the content at arm's length (unless the teacher redirects your stance by asking monologic questions). Your goal is to pull the text in close to your life, to interact with that text so that it serves as a sliding glass door, one you walk through and return a slightly different person. When we read with that stance, an aesthetic stance, we become close readers, passionate readers, and perhaps even lifelong readers.

But rarely do we read wholly with one stance or another. Rather than thinking of these stances as an either-or situation, think of them as two points on a single continuum. Sometimes we read with a stance more toward the efferent; other times we lean toward the aesthetic.

Stance Versatility

Skilled readers show an ability to move easily along this continuum, something I've identified as stance versatility (Beers 1990). This stance versatility allows readers to begin reading their history assignment with an efferent purpose (to be able to answer the questions on the review sheet) but then, getting caught up in the battle being described, shift to a more aesthetic stance (living through the danger, the hunger, the fear, the cold), only to finish and, as they answer questions, reread the text with an efferent stance (Where exactly did the battle take place?).

"Your goal is to pull the text in close to your life, to interact with that text so that it serves as a sliding glass door, one you walk through and return a slightly different person."

Likewise, skilled readers begin the short story or novel in their literature class with an aesthetic stance and then, when needed for assignments, shift to an efferent stance. Even if certain students don't like reading about battles and read the entire chapter in their history book with an efferent stance, they recognize their distance from the text as distaste for history, not a dislike of reading. Then, when they pick up a text they *do* like—whether that is the science book or a poem by Nikki Giovanni—they switch easily to that aesthetic stance.

By contrast, struggling readers often lack this stance versatility. They read everything with one dominant stance, an efferent stance. These students see the purpose of all reading, whether a great work of literature or a recipe in a cookbook, as a time to gather information. This more detached stance distances the reader from the text. Such a stance limits a student's chance of discovering the vicarious experiences a text can offer. At times, we must own responsibility for this. The questions we ask affect the stance students adopt as they read. Programs that require students to read a text and then take a test to answer efferent-type questions suggest to students that the reason we read is to extract information.

Many children enter school with years of experience in listening to stories as parents and caregivers have read aloud to them for years. Those experiences help those kids develop an aesthetic stance toward reading as their primary stance. Then, as teachers ask students questions to check what information they have extracted from the text, they develop a secondary stance, an efferent stance. But reading with an aesthetic stance remains their primary stance. Other students, however, enter school without those read-aloud experiences. They have not developed a primary stance, aesthetic or efferent. And while many kindergarten, first-, and second-grade teachers share books with children to encourage a love of reading, those one or two read-aloud sessions each day cannot substitute for the five years of daily reading some children experience. Children who have not been read to at home often develop an efferent stance as their primary stance for reading.

"And while many kindergarten, first-, and second-grade teachers share books with children to encourage a love of reading, those one or two read-aloud sessions each day cannot substitute for the five years of daily reading some children experience."

As efferent-focused readers finish reading Jerry Craft's *New Kid* or Benjamin Alire Sáenz's *Aristotle and Dante Discover the Secrets of the Universe* or Patricia McKissack's and Frederick L. McKissack's *Black Hands, White Sails*, and we ask them, "What would you like to ask the author?" they stare at us and reply, "Ask about what?" or "Do we have to know this for the test?" We read with them *At Her Majesty's Request*, by Walter Dean Myers, and ask, "What surprises you about this child's life?" and they ask if that's a true-or-false question. We are living through the moment of the text, feeling the excitement, the pain, the fear, the joy of the characters, and they are perhaps preparing half-heartedly for the quiz they anticipate and waiting for the bell to ring. The reading of the book is less than satisfying as the experience was an efferent one, one designed to encourage the reader to carry away information rather than encourage the reader to live through the text.

Encouraging an Aesthetic Stance

For students who primarily read with an efferent stance, we need to reposition their stance to reading with an aesthetic purpose. Too often, though, many students define reading as something they do to answer questions, get ready for a test, find the information the teacher told them to find. Until they are willing to bring the text closer, let the ideas and issues, conflicts and contests, triumphs and tragedies of the text become a part of who they are, they'll never discover what that text means to them. Close reading is not about digging deeper into the author's style; it is about digging deeper into their own lives.

"Close reading is not about digging deeper into the author's style; it is about digging deeper into their own lives."

That isn't to suggest that we should ask students to forget the text and think only about their own feelings and thoughts. Dialogic questions, those questions that encourage students to think deeply about a text, questions that encourage that lived-through experience, do not encourage students to ignore or avoid the text. So, if students have read an article about students texting while driving, for instance, don't ask, "Should drivers lose their license if they text while driving?" That is an opinion question that does not require the student to have read the text. Do ask, "What surprised you about the information the author provided?" That is a dialogic question that values the students' thinking while simultaneously requiring that they think about the text.

If your goal is to create lifelong readers, not just school-time readers, then you must use dialogic talk and encourage aesthetic stances. As students read with an aesthetic stance and answer dialogic questions about the text, they will turn to the text time and again, looking closely for evidence that supports their thinking. See Figure 18.2 on pages 308–10 for a range of dialogic questions that encourage a more aesthetic stance in reading.

Dialogic Questions

Dialogic Questions That Encourage a General Response to the Text

1. What are your first thoughts about this text? What in the text caused those thoughts?

2. What emotions or feelings did you have while reading? Identify the parts that caused those feelings.

3. Did anything in this text remind you of anything in your own life?

4. Did this text remind you of any other books? Movies? Plays? Why?

5. If you could talk to the author, what would you ask about or comment on?

6. If you were going to recommend this text to someone, who would it be? What in the text would that person like?

7. What confused you or surprised you in this text?

8. Describe how you felt as you read this text. For example, were you bored, caught up, thinking about characters, thinking about how you might react if in the same situation, enjoying the author's writing style, or enjoying the humor or suspense?

9. Did you like the cover of the book? Why or why not? If not, how would you change it?

10. Did you like the title of the book? Why or why not? If not, how would you change it?

Dialogic Questions to Encourage Reflection About the Plot

1. What went on in this story?

2. What parts of the plot did you find to be the most significant? Why?

3. What were the turning points in this plot for you? Why?

4. What was the most important word in this text? Why?

5. What idea or image or situation meant the most to you as you read this text? Why?

6. What did the author of this text do that helped you enjoy the story? That made you not enjoy the story?

7. If this story were to continue, what do you think would happen next? Why?

8. If you could change the ending, would you? How would you change it?

9. If you were to draw a picture that represented what you found to be important in this text, what would you draw? Why?

10. Evaluate this plot on a scale of 1 to 4, with 1 being "Not worth recommending" and 4 being "Everyone should read this" and tell why you gave it the rating you did.

Figure 18.2 Dialogic Questions to Ask Students

continues

Dialogic Questions

Dialogic Questions to Encourage Reflection on the Characters

1. Which character or characters did you most enjoy? Why?

2. Which character or characters did you least enjoy? Why?

3. Do any of the characters remind you of yourself? Which ones? Why?

4. Did you think the characters were believable? Why or why not?

5. Which character or characters did you think learned the hardest or most important lessons in this text? Why did you choose that character?

6. What surprised you most about any of the characters?

7. If you could take on the qualities of any of the characters in this text, what qualities would those be?

8. Which character changed the most in this text? How did that character change? What did you learn about that character in watching that change? What did you learn about yourself?

9. If this text were to be made into a movie, which movie stars would you cast in which roles? Why?

10. If you were to eliminate a character from this text, which character would you choose? Why? How would eliminating that character change the text?

Dialogic Questions to Encourage Reflection About the Setting

1. Was the setting important to the text?

2. Would changing the place change the outcome?

3. Would changing the time change the outcome?

4. Which scene most depends on the setting (time or place)?

5. Does this setting remind you of a place you know?

6. Which events in the text are most connected to the setting?

7. How did the author let you know what the setting was?

8. Did the setting affect what the characters did or didn't do?

9. If you could talk to the author about the setting of this book, what would you ask?

10. If you were to write a story, would you choose the setting first or think about characters and the conflicts they would face and let that dictate the choice of setting?

Figure 18.2 Dialogic Questions to Ask Students

continues

Dialogic Questions

Dialogic Questions to Encourage Reflection About the Theme

1. What message did you take away from reading this text? Why?

2. Which passage in the text would you consider most significant or most important? Why? Did that passage help shape what you considered to be the message of this text?

3. If you were talking with the author, can you speculate what the author might say the theme is? What is in the text that gives hints to that?

4. How do the title, chapter titles, and cover illustration help you determine a theme for the text?

5. How do the changes the main character undergoes help you make a decision about the message of this text?

6. Talk with someone else who has read the same text. What does that person see as the message? If you see different messages, discuss what caused those differences.

7. The plot (the series of events in the text) and the theme (the lesson or message you take away from text) are not the same. Think of the text you just read. What is the plot? What is the theme? How does the plot relate to or affect the theme?

8. What affected your interpretation of the theme the most: the plot, the characters, or the setting?

9. If you were to draw the theme symbolically, what would you draw?

10. Think about several texts you've enjoyed. Do they share similar themes? Different themes? If they share similar themes, what does that tell you about what you are looking for in a book or story?

Dialogic Questions to Encourage Reflection on the Point of View, Author's Style, and Author

1. Who told the story in the text you just read? Was the narrator a character in the story or an omniscient narrator? How did the narrator affect your reading of this story?

2. How would the text have changed if a different character had told the story?

3. Can you speculate on why the author chose the narrator they did to tell this story?

4. How did the author make the story come alive in your mind? What specific words or phrases did the author use to help you see events, characters, and the setting vividly?

5. Find a section of the text that you particularly liked. What did the author do to help you like that section?

6. Look at the beginnings of chapters. What did the author do there to make you want to read the rest of the chapter? Also look at the endings. Did the author do something special to make you want to read on to the next chapter?

7. Is there a particular phrase or sentence in the text that you thought was particularly well said? What is there about that passage that makes it stand out in your mind?

8. Did you like how this author wrote this text? What did you like or not like? Consider things like setting description, use of dialogue, characterization, explanation of conflict, foreshadowing, and symbolism as well as length of chapters, length of sentences, choice of chapter titles, and use of illustrations.

9. Would you want to read another book by this author? Why or why not?

10. What other writer or writers does this author remind you of? Why?

Figure 18.2 Dialogic Questions to Ask Students, *continued*

Dear George,

I kept saying that I wanted you to love reading and then I would ask you to list traits of the main character or explain how one text was similar to another or find a passage that would support a point I wanted you to explain. Often my goals for you and the questions I asked gave you conflicting information.

One day, after reading "All Summer in a Day," all in the class were talking about what the children in the story did, how those characters treated their classmate. For a moment, we were a community of readers as we all struggled with the idea of such cruelty. My only question was "What surprised you?" and none of you would stop talking. After class you mentioned, "I'm not saying I liked the story or anything, but it was good how we all talked about what it meant. That part was good." It was the talk that mattered, and it mattered because you and your classmates were not answering my questions; you were creating your own. You weren't figuring out what I thought you needed to know; you were discovering what you thought. That day, literature was, as Rosenblatt explained it should be, an exploration.

Dear George,

You told me on more than one occasion how much you disliked reading: "It's boring and I hate it," you'd say.

"Oh come on, George. You don't really hate it," I'd say.

"No? I'd rather clean bathtubs than read a book," you explained.

I looked at you, stunned. "OK, so you hate it," I agreed. "But you shouldn't. What don't you like about it?" I asked.

"It's boring. Nothing happens," you replied.

"That just means you haven't found the right book," I countered.

"I just read the ones you teachers hand me," you said. You started to walk away, then turned and said, "So do you really think if I had the right book, I'd like to read?" Then you grinned, flashing your new braces, and finished your question: "Or at least like it better than cleaning bathtubs?"

CHAPTER 19

The Power of a Book

IN MY THIRD YEAR OF TEACHING, I SPENT SPRING break chaperoning a group of seventh graders on a weeklong field trip to Washington, DC. Students had to pay a fee to go on the trip. All year long as I talked about this trip with my students, Gary, one of my students, talked a lot about going. Gary was a funny kid, one who could keep any group laughing, and was liked by many. I was excited he wanted to go.

On the last day to pay for the trip, he came to class early. He sat beside my desk and quietly told me he wouldn't be going because his family didn't have the money. He explained, "My mom said we don't have enough money for one of us kids to get to take this trip when others can't take a trip. So, I can't go." He worked hard to hold back tears. I sat still, trying to figure out how to pay for this one child without suddenly finding myself needing to pay for all of the students. After a moment Gary continued, "But it's OK. Mom says that if you'll give us a copy of the itinerary, she'll take me to the library. We'll check out books of the places you'll be seeing. Mom says that on the day you're at the Smithsonian, we'll read about it, and on the day you're at the Lincoln Memorial, we'll read about that. Then, Mom says, when you get back, you can come over for dinner and you can show us your pictures and I can show you my books because Mom says the only difference is that you'll take a trip on a plane and I'll take a trip in my mind. So, can I have a copy of the itinerary?" At that point, I'd have given that child anything.

Eventually spring break arrived, and I headed to Washington with sixty seventh graders while Gary headed to the library. When I returned, his mom invited me over for dinner. Those of you from the South will recognize dinner: meatloaf, mashed potatoes with cream gravy, carrots with peas, and a peach slice atop a lettuce leaf with a dollop of mayonnaise on top. It was perfect.

"But kids come to school to people like you, teachers who know the value of reading, who understand that reading opens doors that otherwise might forever remain locked."

After dinner, we sat in their living room and shared our trips. (I think Gary had a better trip than I did.) As I would pass around a photograph, he would turn to a book to show me the same sight. Eventually it was time for me to leave. I stood at the door and after thanking Gary's mom for a wonderful dinner, I told her that she was the best mom I could imagine. She turned to a small table by that front door, picked up her purse, rummaged through it, and removed a small, blue, well-used library card. She held it up for me to see and said, "There are many things in this life I'll never be able to buy my children, but there is nothing they will ever lack because I have a library card."

I left there wanting the world to be filled with people like Gary's mom.

I thought about how this mom didn't simply tell her son, "You know we can't afford such a trip," and then dismiss his plea to go. No. She gave him an option that showed him a world he would have otherwise missed. Too many of our students don't go home to parents like Gary's mom. But kids come to school to people like you, teachers who know the value of reading, who understand that reading opens doors that otherwise might forever remain locked. You are, for so many children, their only chance at ever experiencing a person like Gary's mom. Like her, find the time to share books with your students. Show them the power of a book.

Helping Kids Find a Book

Because of Gary's mom, I became a strong advocate for taking my students to the school library as often as possible and for filling my classroom with books. Surrounding kids with books, though, did not mean all chose books to read.

When we would go to the library, some students would go immediately to the shelves to select books they wanted to read. Other students headed straight to the couches to sit. A third group of students wandered aimlessly through the library, walking through the stacks, looking at covers, sometimes selecting a book, most often not. One day, I asked a seventh grader from that group of wanderers why she hadn't checked out a book.

"Are you going to tell me what all the other teachers say?" she asked.

"I don't know. What do other teachers say?" I replied.

"They all say the library is filled with good books."

"Well, what's wrong with that?" I asked.

"Where are they?" she said.

"Where are what?"

"The good books. I sure don't see them. Just where are they?"

"Tell me what you mean," I said.

"It's like shopping. You go to Foley's [a very large department store in Houston at the time] and you can shop all day and never find anything. It's why I shop at the Limited now," she said.

I wasn't quite following her line of thinking. "I don't get it; why do you shop at the Limited?"

"Because it's *limited*. There's not as much to choose from. You can actually find things."

"And tell me just how this connects to finding a good book in the library," I said.

She was clearly frustrated at my inability to follow her reasoning. "The library is like Foley's. You can't find anything," she said.

She left me standing there, looking around at this middle school library. Suddenly I thought of all the times I had gone into a large department store to buy one white blouse. I could emerge hours later with no blouse, not because there weren't any but because there were too many. This student was telling me she didn't know the library, didn't know authors, didn't know genres, and, therefore, like when she went shopping in a department store that was too large, she couldn't find what she wanted.

The Good Books Box

I asked the librarian to help me with an experiment. I asked her to take a small box—the type that reams of paper come in—and write "Good Books" on the side, and then fill it with eight or ten great books. I wanted her to put the box on a table the next time this class visited the library. She did just that. When we returned, some kids went directly to the shelves and chose the books they wanted. Others found their spot on the couch. The wanderers kept on wandering. Finally, a boy spotted the Good Books box. He stood staring at it, not touching any books inside. After a while, he asked the librarian what those books were. "Good books," she replied.

"You're kidding," he said, as if he had looked for them for years and suddenly there they were, in a box. Another kid walked by and asked him what he was looking at. "Good books," he answered.

"Really?" the second kid said.

They both stood there. Finally, one asked, "So can you, like, check them out?" The librarian nodded. Eventually, about five students checked out a book from the Good Books box.

On their next visit, the librarian and I waited to see what would happen. As students returned their books, she asked, "Did you read the book?" Each student nodded yes. "What'd you think?" she asked.

"It was a good book," each student answered, somewhat amazed. They all stood there, saying nothing. The librarian and I stood there, waiting.

Finally, one student asked, "We were wondering, do you have any more good books?"

And then, this dear, amazing librarian surprised us all when she pointed to another box on a different table and said, "Sure do." We all turned to look at this second box, labeled "More Good Books."

"Cool," one kid said as they moved to look through that box.

Narrow the Choices

I've told the Good Books box story for many years in many places because the lesson is powerful. Until students are comfortable with authors, genres, and interests, it's hard for them to find a good book. We need to narrow that choice for students. Stand up a few books on your desk, put a few along windowsills, talk about some you want kids to read, or place some in a box labeled "Good Books." But remember, your goal is to move the students from the box to the stacks, so study what types of books your students choose. I watched this librarian point out to one student, who was reading from the Good Books box, that she always chose mysteries. Then the librarian pointed out that there was an entire section in the library devoted to mysteries.

"Until students are comfortable with authors, genres, and interests, it's hard for them to find a good book."

"Where?" the girl asked.

"Under that five-foot sign that says, 'Mysteries.' That one right there, hanging from the ceiling," the librarian explained.

"That is so awesome," the student answered as she finally saw meaning in that sign for the very first time.

Figure 19.1 Teachers work hard to make books available in the classroom only to have to deny access due to ridiculous rules. In this case, a teacher had to put tape across the classroom bookshelf until kids finished their state test.

Offering a Variety of Books

In the first edition, I offered many lists of books and several online sources to find more books. I've chosen not to include such lists in this edition. Finding book recommendations online is easy now and any sites that I might recommend as I write this might not be valuable or available three years from now. Instead, I would remind you to look for books that fill gaps in your classroom library. If you don't have many books with boys as main characters, look for those. If you don't like science fiction, make sure you haven't mistakenly avoided that genre in your selections. Students like graphic novels, even if you do not. Are those in your collections? Do your books represent the diversity of this nation and this world? Racial, religious, economic, and geographic diversity? Are different types of families shown in the books in your classroom? If you are straight, have you included books with characters who are members of

"Any parent can talk with their own child about what that child does and does not read. All parents should do that. No parent, however, has a right to impose his or her standards on other children."

the queer community? If not, why not? There are books with gay characters appropriate for elementary, middle, and high school. Find the ones that fit your students' developmental interests. If you fear backlash from parents who want their children to read only about straight characters, then consider this: kids in the queer community who are hurt at home often turn to teachers. What does it mean to those kids when schools—when teachers—hurt them, too?

Any parent can talk with their own child about what that child does and does not read. All parents should do that. No parent, however, has a right to impose his or her standards on other children. Should you find yourself with those parents who have decided that they do have that right, be sure to go online to https://ncte.org. The National Council of Teachers of English maintains a staff ready to help you deal with book challenges.

My dear friend and longtime colleague Teri Lesesne always said, "When we hand the right book to the right kid at the right time, then we're taking the right steps toward creating lifetime readers." Teri lived her professional life connecting kids to books. How lucky we would each be for others to say the same of us.

Figure 19.2 A happy moment with dear friend Teri Lesesne (1954–2021). Teri helped so many teachers connect kids to books with her wit, her passion, and her laughter.

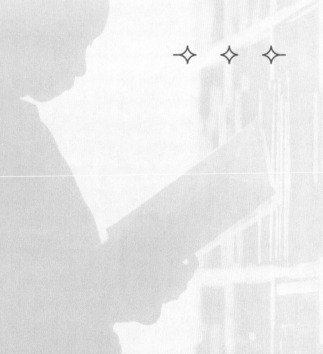

Dear George,

Sometimes you frustrated me; often you worried me. But many times you entertained me with your honesty, your wit, and your willingness to make fun of yourself. After telling me you'd be happy with a book that was more interesting than cleaning the bathtub, that became our measure of success. I'd give you a book; you'd read through and return it. I'd ask, "So, did it beat bathtub cleaning?" You'd grin and shake your head no. But one day, as our class walked back from the library, you walked alongside of me and said, "You know, that book, that one I just turned in, it was definitely better than cleaning the bathtub."

"You're kidding!" I said, wanting to run back to the library, claim it, and never lose it. "What was it?"

You shrugged. "I don't know. But it was really pretty good." You grinned, walked off, turned around, and said, "I think it was called *How to Clean Your Bathtub in Ten Easy Steps.*"

✦　✦　✦

Dear George,

I asked you once if you saw yourself as a learner. You asked me what I meant. I tried again and asked if you saw yourself as someone who liked to discover new things, understand what things mean. You asked if I meant things that were going to be on a test. I paused and tried again, explaining that I meant someone who liked to learn things for learning's sake. You looked at me and said, "But it's not on the test?"

The Role of Relevance

RELEVANCE. WE ALL KNOW THAT RELEVANCE IS what motivates, and what motivates is what engages. And we know what classrooms look like when kids are not engaged. Kids express their desire for a relevant, engaging curriculum in many ways. They ask, "Why does this matter?" and "Why do I need to learn this?" or they announce, "I don't care," or "This is dumb." Sometimes they simply sit or sleep or stare.

These comments don't come from all kids and they don't even come from some kids all the time. But this undercurrent of, "Why learn this?" is there from enough students enough of the time that most any teacher wonders how to make something relevant. Relevance is personal; it is idiosyncratic. That alone makes the admonition "keep your lessons relevant" difficult at best when thirty students sit in the classroom. Hell, it's hard when only ten sit there.

The Relevance Continuum

Most of us define relevance as *something with personal meaning*. Priniski, Hecht, and Harackiewicz (2018) offer a more detailed explanation. They suggest that relevance exists along a continuum, moving from something that is relevant due to a personal association, to something that is relevant due to personal usefulness, to something that is relevant due to our identity (see Figure 20.1).

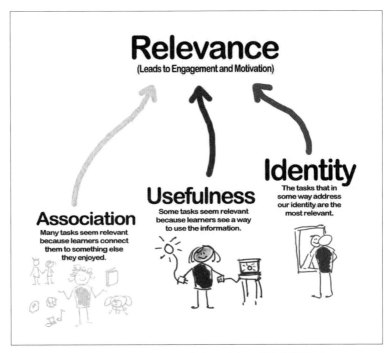

Figure 20.1 Continuum of Relevance (adapted from Priniski, Hecht, and Harackiewicz 2018)

Maurice Ashley, a Jamaican-American chess player, earned the title of Grandmaster in 1999. He was the first Black person to earn this title. In 2016 he was inducted into the US Chess Hall of Fame. If you didn't recognize his name, think about the second of the Three Big Questions discussed on page 149.

Personal association is relevance that is the least connected to the individual because it is relevant only through an association. Students who like to play chess might find an article about Maurice Ashley somewhat relevant because the article is associated with something they like to do. A slightly stronger type of relevance is relevance based on usefulness. Students who need to pass a reading test might find an article about Ashley relevant because reading it will help them develop skills needed to pass the test. The most meaningful type of relevance is connected to identity. Students who see themselves as chess players might say reading that article is very relevant to their lives because it helped them understand more about themselves as chess players.

This means that the lesson you work hard to craft might be relevant to some, only because it reminds them of something else. That relevance is fleeting, perhaps not lasting the entire class period. For others, the relevance might be somewhat stronger as they know they must pass an upcoming test. But once the test is completed, reading any article loses relevance. Many of us know this level of relevance as we stay on a diet until a particular special event has passed. Finally, some of your students might dig into the article, excited to examine every step of Ashley's career, because they see themselves one day being named a Grand Champion.

Step Inside a Classroom

Consider these scenarios.

1. Student A is trying to get a summer job. One opening close to her house is to help with a project her city is doing to look at the health of pond water around the city. The job says the right applicant is one who enjoys being outside, can carefully collect water samples from the assigned lakes, label the samples, bring them back to the lab, create slides, and after studying them under a microscope, categorize them by what was seen in the sample. The right applicant also has a driver's license. The job pays $17.00 per hour and that's the best pay she's seen for any summer job in her area. Student A decides to pay more attention during biology class to learn how to make a slide, how to differentiate organisms found in pond water, and how to use a microscope.

2. Student B is taking Biology I. She does not enjoy biology. She's an artist and doesn't see any reason to learn anything about biology. One day, her teacher tells her that her drawings of amoebas are particularly detailed and very well done, "really professional." A few days later, Student B points out to the teacher that she noticed that organisms she saw through the microscope did not all look the same. She explains that some are round, colorful, and look like opals and others are longer—like a hair—and green and are constantly twitching. She shows the teacher a new drawing she has made. The teacher tells this student she is impressed and liked how she differentiated diatoms and spirogyra. The student added those labels to her drawings in her

notebook. The teacher tells Student B that with her ability to see such detail, she could be an environmentalist or could be an illustrator for an environmental publication. The student writes, "environmental illustrator" in her notebook.

3. Student C thinks her biology class is OK. She likes learning how to use a microscope and examining pond water with it because her grandfather bought her one when she was eight. They used the microscope to study blades of grass, a strand of hair, and water from puddles. She loved doing that with him. She remembered how proud of her he was when she noticed important details. She enjoys those memories as she looks through the microscope now. She sent him some texts about what they were doing in class hoping he would remember those days together.

Each of these students could say that they see relevance in what they are doing in their biology class; yet, the relevance is not the same. Can you label each type of relevance? Don't read on until you've given this some thought.

· · · · ·

As I consider these students, I think that the relevance Student A feels comes from usefulness. Learning to use a microscope is relevant to her because she wants this particular summer job as the pay is good. The relevance that Student B feels comes from identity. She sees herself as an artist and now, learning to use the microscope and learning about different types of organisms might enhance that identity. Student C finds the lessons relevant because of association; they remind her of enjoyable times with her grandfather.

"What we often forget to do, though, is connect relevance to identity."

Relevance isn't only critical, but some types of relevance are actually more important than others. Yet, teachers often spend the most time pointing out to students how learning something is useful to them ("This will help you get into college.") or is related to something a student said they enjoyed ("You said you enjoyed the project you did in fourth grade about the solar system. This is a book about planets."). What we often forget to do, though, is connect relevance to identity.

Identity and Relevance

Letters to George are throughout this book because it was my relation-ship with George that helped create my identity as a teacher. Ironically, what I failed to see when I looked at George that year was who he was. I think I saw him as a student who worked very hard but often had little success. I sometimes saw him as a funny kid. Only years later, through the lens of hindsight, did I see him as a kid who was brutally honest with me, who was tenacious, who was often frustrated, and who did the bravest thing I think struggling readers can do: he kept showing up. He could not read and yet every day he walked into my classroom with some remnant of hope that I might help him. Yes, George was hopeful.

> "Letters to George are throughout this book because it was my relationship with George that helped create my identity as a teacher."

George, however, did not see himself as a learner. That was not a part of his identity and I, sadly, did not encour-age that. Too many times the relevance I encouraged was relevance related to usefulness. But once George did not believe that he was going to college, then doing something because it would help him achieve that goal did not matter. Once George did not think he could improve his grades, then doing homework or classwork was meaning-less and certainly not motivating. I had not tapped into his identity.

By the time I met Darien, years later, I understood the importance of identity. He is one of the most amazing students I've had the privilege of teaching. I met him when he, too, was in seventh grade. By the end of eighth grade, he announced to the high school football coach that he was not going to play football in ninth grade. "I have discovered I'm pretty good at reading and I think maybe what I want to be someday is a lawyer and not a football player. So, thank you for coming to watch some of my games, but I'm going to focus on my classes."

Darien's seventh- and then eighth-grade teachers in his Ohio middle school began to ask him to tell them "What surprised you?" as he read anything—articles in science, his textbook in social studies, short stories or novels in language arts. His physical education teacher asked him what sur-prised him as they did pull-ups or ran sprints. His football coach asked the same question after practices or games. "What's changing your thinking?" or "What was most important to you?" I always thought it was important that the entire faculty embraced this idea and each teacher, in his or her own way, began to show all students their thinking was valued.

For a long time, Darien answered with "nothing" or "I don't know." Eventually he began to offer tentative responses. And when he did, his teachers responded with enthusiasm. "Wow! I had not considered that!" "Me, too! I was surprised by that, too!" "What a great observation. Tell me more!" And slowly, very slowly, Darien began to develop some confidence and with that confidence eventually came improved *competence*. Remember, you don't improve competence without first improving confidence.

> *"Choice is what gives us each a voice, and when a voice is silenced, an identity is silenced. Choice means voice."*

Eventually Darien saw himself as a learner, as a curious person, as a person who had interesting insights to offer to others.

As I watched Darien, I realized that all my years of giving interest surveys to students might have given me entry points for conversations and certainly helped me expand my classroom library, but those interest surveys could not help me encourage the deepest level of relevance. What can help? Two things: first, when possible, give kids choice in what they read; give kids choice in how they respond. Give kids choice. Choice is what gives us each a voice, and when a voice is silenced, an identity is silenced. Choice means voice. That's one reason that choice is such a powerful tool. Second, begin your conversations with kids by using questions that center them.

Questions That Center Each Student

Bob and I use the Three Big Questions to center students. (These questions are discussed on page 149.) Each of those questions asks the student to consider something about herself:

- What surprised *you?*
- What did the author think *you* already knew?
- What changed, challenged, or confirmed *your* thinking?

Figure 20.2 Going through books with Bob is always a pleasure.

Relevance is always about the individual, and at its most intimate and powerful level, relevance is tied to what we think, what we believe, what we hope for, and what dream about. Now compare those big questions with these:

- Why do you think the character did what she did?

- What is the evidence you found that explains the character's actions?

Those questions have the word *you* in them, too. The answers, however, don't depend on you. The questions could have just as easily asked, "Why did the character do what she did?" and "What evidence explains the character's actions?" *You* cannot be gratuitously inserted into the question. The students' thinking must be integral to the answer and answers will be unique to the student.

And then we are back to where we started. Relevance is personal; it is idiosyncratic. It is not only about us providing articles about glaciers to one kid and articles about volcanoes to another. That might help with interest and if you can do that, then you should do that. Attending to interests is always a good start; this type of associative relevance is not

"Relevance is always about the individual, and at its most intimate and powerful level, relevance is tied to what we think, what we believe, what we hope for, and what dream about."

unimportant. But if relevance that is about associations and usefulness has not created classrooms that are intellectual communities, classrooms filled with passionate, engaged students, then perhaps it is time to consider encouraging relevance that is connected to each student's identity and not merely interests.

When relevance is tied to identity, students realize that you want to know what they think, that you want to learn from their thoughts, that you believe they have something important to offer. When they know that you value them, that you value their responses and their ideas, their creativity and their spunk, then topics of study are relevant because students count first—not a test score; not a standard; not a grade that moves them ahead or a skill that gets them a job. Those kids might not fall in love with all you hand them to read, but they do come to love that you want to hear what they have to say. And sometimes, yes sometimes, dear teacher, they also come to love you. They are your kids; but more importantly, you are their teacher. *You* are their teacher.

Dear George,

I loved teaching you, George. I don't mean I enjoyed every day. No, not at all. Does any teacher enjoy every day of any school year? I think not. George, you are an adult now—for a long time now— and perhaps you do something that you mostly enjoy but don't love every day. I think that's the truth for most of us.

Even with all the days when I went home in tears, I can still say I loved teaching you. And all the Georges I've had since you. I loved being your teacher. Thank you, George.

✧   ✧   ✧

EPILOGUE

A Final Letter
to George

Dear George,

  In so many ways, this book is for you.

  I've often wondered what my life as a teacher would have been like had I not taught you that first year, not met your caring parents, not seen your struggles and defeats, not watched your cautious optimism from your occasional successes. When I identify defining moments in my life, that year with you was certainly one. I think it was you who first helped me understand the intense relationship that exists between teacher and student. Thank you.

  I still see you as that child you were in seventh grade. Short, freckled, braces, an amazing smile that was shared generously with friends and hesitantly with me. I know that year you questioned why you struggled so with reading. The question you never voiced, though, was why no one seemed able to help you. But I heard that unasked question, George, and other teachers throughout this nation teaching other students just like you have heard it as well. Since I met you, I've discovered a network of teachers, teacher educators, and researchers who willingly share their knowledge and expertise. I turn to them hungrily. With all the books that so many have written, I wonder what I can add.

I can add you.

You are the critical element, George. We must, at all times, remember that we don't teach a subject, we don't teach to a test, we teach you—specific kids with specific needs. And there's not a teacher out there who doesn't know you.

> *"We must, at all times, remember that we don't teach a subject, we don't teach to a test, we teach you—specific kids with specific needs."*

You walk into classrooms with a swagger that's a pretense or a shove that's a defense. You might be athletic or clumsy, artistic or musical, quiet and shy or bold and outgoing. You come in wearing your Gay Pride or Black Lives Matter T-shirt or wish you were in a school that honored those voices. You wait and wonder who will berate you for all the challenges you have faced. You can be Black or white, Latino or Asian, rich or poor, Muslim or Jewish or Christian or Hindu or atheist. You saunter into classrooms late or always arrive on time. And no matter the circumstance, in public schools, teachers take you as you are, respect you as you are, and promise to teach you, as you are. As I have said before, George, it might be the plaque on the Statue of Liberty that says, "Give me your tired, your poor / Your huddled masses yearning to breathe free," but it's public schools that live that message daily.

Teachers want each student to pass whatever new hurdle policy makers place before them. We want that for all kids, but we want so much more, and that is when teaching becomes hard. Teaching to that one damned test is about checking off lessons that address particular standards and that, most certainly, can be done. But such instruction too often offers students a diminished educational experience. If answering correctly becomes the goal, then somewhere along the way we will lose that chance to create lifelong learners who embrace curiosity, who enjoy analyzing ambiguity, and who value the thoughtful question over the correct answer. We want students who are willing to try one more day because the effort they gave yesterday was valuable to them. And, always, we want to know what to do when kids can't read.

Never doubt that teachers constantly look to research, to practice, to experience to know how best to help students who struggle. Never doubt that we see you. And never doubt that you make a difference in our lives. Many years after you left my classroom, an eighth grader named Derek gave me this note:

> *I read Basher Five-Two. It was a good book. It was about how this fighter pilot got shot down behind enemy lines and had to survive by using survival skills like eating bugs and digging a hole he could stay in at night and he has ants all over him but couldn't move or make any noises because the enemy soldiers where everywhere. He had to have faith that his troop would come back in to get him and save him. I would like to have the same faith that he has got because I am down behind enemy lines to. I got things that make me want to cry but if I cry I get puntched and told I'm a crybaby sissy. He has alot of courage because in the tough times he kept on going. I keep on going alot of times to. But how long would his courage have lasted if noone had come to get him? That's what I want to no. How long does you're courage last when the troops don't come?*

Because of you, George, and the journey you started me on, I was ready to help Derek. Teachers across this nation have learned from students like you so they can help others, like Derek. Teachers must know that for so many of the Dereks of this nation, teachers are the troops. These children sit in classrooms behind the enemy lines of poverty, hunger, pain, and uncertainty. Policy makers demand teachers close the achievement gap. That gap, George, is nursed and nurtured in the arms of so many other gaps. Close those gaps, address those inequities, and then and only then should policy makers talk about closing an achievement gap. The very fact that so many students dress and come to school at all is a testament to their courage and belief that this day might indeed be a better day. That they look to adults in the schools for guidance and perhaps survival is a tribute to each teacher, each administrator, of this nation.

"To be called "teacher" might indeed be one of the greatest compliments one could ever receive."

George, I must tell you that though I am amazed at the strength and resilience of students, I am continually humbled by the professionalism, dedication, and ability of this nation's teachers. Teachers everywhere should know that as a teacher, I can stand beside them in all that they do; but as a parent, I stand in awe of all that they do. Teachers are, for so many children, Gary's mom, George's hope, and Derek's rescue. To be called "teacher" might indeed be one of the greatest compliments one could ever receive.

I don't know what the next decades will hold for me as I consider teaching, George. I suppose none of us really know what's next. But I know that as I look at this next generation of teachers, I see resolve, dedication, and excitement. Some of our newest teachers began their career during a pandemic, and that couldn't drive them away. I suspect they will be able to face all that comes their way. When teachers tell me they are tired at the end of a school year (or end of a week), I know that's because they have never given up. Teachers are exhausted because no matter the challenge, they muster the courage to face it.

Grandma, I need to know if I can come live with you. maybe if I was in a diferant school things wuld be diferant. Its just to hard here. If I culd come live with you I culd help you with stuff and I wuld be real good. I think I just need a place to start over.

Dear George, as you and your classmates rushed out of class that last day of school, I stood there, telling you each to have a great summer. I didn't understand how many of you would linger in my heart for so long after you were gone. I didn't know what a privilege it was to have been a part of your childhood for those brief months. And that's what it was, George, a privilege.

Sometimes when I remember you, I am saddened at all we did not accomplish; other times, I am inspired by your courage. But much of the time, I am heartened as I remember that slow nod of your head as that shy grin would emerge. I remain ever hopeful that you found your way in this world, guided by parents who adored you, by friends who admired you, and by teachers who encouraged you. I hold fast to that note you wrote your grandmother, remembering the lesson it taught: endings are indeed beginnings.

ACKNOWLEDGMENTS

ONE QUIET EVENING IN 2021, AS CONVERSATION
about inconsequential things waned, my husband, Brad, turned to a new topic and asked if I had considered writing a new edition of *When Kids Can't Read—What Teachers Can Do* to celebrate the twentieth anniversary of the book's publication. "That will be in 2022. That's still about a year away. It might be fun," he said. I was stunned. Twenty years? When had *that* happened? And writing a book is many things, but I don't think I've ever said it was *fun*. I glanced over at some bookshelves. There it was, sitting on a shelf, doing just fine. It was not demanding my time or my attention.

I finally answered him, "Nope. I haven't given that any thought."

But then I began giving it some thought, a lot of thought.

I decided to pose the question to Roderick Spelman, senior vice president and publisher of professional books at Heinemann. Surely Roderick would say, "Oh, I think not." Then I could put Brad's idea to rest. I could stop taking that book off the shelf, rereading chapters, and jotting notes.

But no. I had barely finished asking Roderick what he thought about a second edition to celebrate the book's twentieth anniversary when he said, "I *love* this idea. Yes." Suddenly, we began having lots of conversations: What had I learned? How did I feel about writing a book without my long-time coauthor? How would I handle the letters to George? So many conversations. Thank you, Roderick. You are smart and savvy about education and publishing and you know the value of a well-placed question.

When Anita Gildea, a powerhouse name in the world of educational publishing, agreed to be editor of this book, I knew this book was going into the perfect hands. I've known Anita a long time, since the night many years ago when she handed me a lemon drop martini at a hotel entrance after I had flown across the country late at night to give a keynote speech the next day. She understands teachers, students, and the demands of literacy instruction; plus, she knows how to work with authors, or at least *this* author. Somehow, she could encourage me to revise a chapter, or a section, one more time, while still making me believe I was the best author she had ever read. I was so willing to believe that lie, but it's a helpful lie that kept me from reminding Brad often that this process certainly was not fun. The best parts of this book are a result of her questions, prods, and encouragement. Thank you, Anita. Just thank you.

We eventually handed the manuscript over to others at Heinemann, a hard part of the writing process because this is when all those words on a page begin belonging to others. Melissa Inglis, senior production editor, and Sarah Fournier, managing editor, along with Elizabeth Tripp, copy editor, held this book gently as they took a very complicated manuscript, one filled with sidebars, figures, transcripts, anchor charts, infographics, appendices, photographs, hundreds of references to be checked, and put all into ready-to-print condition. Any mistakes that still exist in this book have everything to do with my stubbornness and nothing to do with their talent.

While they were doing their magic, Suzanne Heiser, design manager, was probably wishing Roderick had not asked her to step into this particular project. She worked with me from early in the process until I truly had to stop changing my mind. When I saw the book in the first pour (the first time the manuscript is set the way it will look in the book), I decided I did not like the font. Suzanne stayed calm as she listened to my concerns and then found me a font I liked. She understood my long-held belief that content and design must go together. She recognized that as a handbook, navigation is critical, but as a recollection of me and one student, heart was as important. If patience and talent each had another name, that name would be *Suzanne*.

While she was doing her work, Josh Evans, director of product marketing, was meeting with me along with others to discuss getting this book into your hands. What impressed me most about Josh was he wanted to know the book before he ever discussed how to tell teachers, principals, and parents about it. Josh is a marketing director who reads the books he is going to market. That alone sets him apart from others.

Then another team stepped forward: Brett Whitmarsh, vice president of digital content and communications; Ashley Montgomery, audiobook producer; and Adam Scharff, lead audio engineer. These folks emerged as it was time to create the audiobook. They are a fabulous team who make a complex process easy—and dare I say *fun?*—for the author.

Special thanks go to Dr. Meredith Beers, my daughter, who is the reader for the audiobook. I was concerned about making the recording because ongoing chemotherapy has left me with vocal cords damaged, so hoarseness can arrive on any day for almost any reason. I could not figure out how to get through recording a book of this length. Then Meredith offered to do this. As an emergency manager, she is often the voice that helps others. This time, that help was for me. You are a never-ending joy in my life, Mer. Thank you.

Many others shared their time and expertise with me in creating this book. Teachers in the greater Houston area, Waco, New York City, Miami, Los Angeles, Omaha, Charleston, Milwaukee, El Paso, Brownsville, Phoenix, and Little Rock shared lessons in this book with their students, offered feedback to me, invited me into their classrooms, and met me on Zoom when meeting in person was no longer an option. Thank you. I can never say thank you enough to Cornelius Minor, Jeff Williams, Linda Rief, Penny Kittle, Kwame Alexander, and Chris Crutcher for always being willing to discuss issues with me. Brent Gilson, Cheryl Bair, Buffy Hamilton, Lindsey Eliis, Jennifer Wolf, Melanie Unser, Jessica Barlow, and Tara Smith stepped in with student work. Kate Roberts, Lester Laminack, Tonya Perry, and Jen Ochoa have long been the people I turn to and they have never been too busy to offer their help. In particular, Jen is willing to talk late, listen hard, and laugh loudly almost any time.

And though Bob Probst's name is not on this book, he read chapters, offered critiques, searched for research, checked references, thought through issues with me, and always offered his support. In other words, he did the work a colleague does and he did it the way a longtime friend does. Thank you, Bob.

Dearest friends Suzanne and Michael Alexander lived through another book project doing what dear friends do: they understood when I was distracted; they listened to me discuss chapters on spelling or making an inference even though these were not their topics of choice; and they were willing to change evening plans when, again, I didn't want to stop what I was doing. I hope each of you have a Suzanne and Michael in your life.

My son, Baker, has often been an early reader of my writing. A brilliant young lawyer who could have easily become a novelist or an editor, Baker has always offered helpful ideas and revisions. Plus, whenever I say to him, "Do you want to come to the ranch and help me move some furniture?" he understood that was code for "I'm stuck and rearranging couches, carpets, and chairs will help me rearrange words on the page." He would always show up.

Of course, a thank-you to Brad, my husband. I think I'm a writer until I try to find words to say thank you for all that he does for all of us all the time. The words disappear. But my smile when I think of you never does. For all the smiles we have shared and for those that are still to come, thank you. And, Brad, you were right: this *was* fun.

Appendices

Instructional Plan

Student Name _____ **Date** _____

	Reading Behaviors	Rarely Sometimes Often	Instructional Practices
Engagement	Enjoys listening to stories		
	Has a favorite genre/author		
	Has stamina to stick with a text		
	Enters conversations about texts		
Vocabulary	Understands and uses a range of Tier 1 words		
	Understands and uses a range of Tier 2 words		
	Can use the context to understand Tier 3 words		
	Can use roots and affixes to help determine meaning of unknown words		
	Can identify which words in a text are problematic		
Decoding/ Fluency/ Spelling	Decodes accurately single syllable words		

Instructional Plan *continued*

Student Name _____ **Date** _____

	Reading Behaviors	Rarely Sometimes Often	Instructional Practices
	Decodes accurately multiple syllable words		
	Can accurately recognize sight words		
	Reads with appropriate expression		
	Reads at an appropriate rate		
	Spells words using knowledge of letters and sounds		
Comprehension	Recalls information, makes connections, and summarizes text easily		
	Uses prior knowledge		
	Makes appropriate inferences		
	Uses close reading to understand theme		
	Uses close reading to understand author's purpose or bias		
	Uses fix-up strategies to solve confusions		

Signal Words

Words that signal . . .	Examples
Category	classes, divisions, kinds, part, sets, species, type
Cause or effect	accordingly, because, consequently, due to, given that, so, thus
Comparison	also, alike, both, comparable, furthermore, related to, too
Conclusion	as a result, conclusively, finally, last of all, thus
Continuation	additionally, also, furthermore, likewise, moreover
Contrasts	although, conversely, even though, in spite of, still, then again
Emphasis	above all, important to note, most of all, most significantly, namely
Exception	even though, instead of, otherwise, the opposite, though
Example	for example, to illustrate, particularly, specifically, such as
Main idea	a major development, the critical point, remember that
Qualifying thinking	alleged, almost, except, looks like, mostly, purported, seems like
Restatement	also called, in other words, sometimes called, that is to say
Sequence/ chronology	after, at last, during, later, next, prior to, since, today, while
Spatial proximity	across, adjacent, between, bordering, contiguous, flanking, near

Words with Multiple Meanings

Back	Draft	Loom	Produce	Stamp
Bank	Face	Mean	Prune	Staple
Bear	Fence	Mine	Pupil	Star
Bend	Fork	Minor	Race	Steer
Bill	Game	Mint	Range	Stern
Blue	Glasses	Mold	Refrain	Stick
Box	Grave	Monitor	Reservation	Stoop
Boxes	Green	Note	Right	Store
Brush	Ground	Novel	Ring	Stories
Buckle	Gum	Order	Riot	Story
Can	Hamper	Organ	Rose	Tie
Certain	Handle	Park	Ruler	Tissue
Chair	Harbor	Paste	Run	Trace
Change	Hide	Patient	Sanction	Train
Channel	Interest	Pet	Saw	Trip
Check	Jam	Pipe	Scales	Trunk
Clear	Kid	Pitcher	Second	Volume
Clip	Kind	Plain	Shed	Watch
Club	Lash	Plane	Ship	Wave
Coach	Late	Plate	Sole	Well
Cold	Leaves	Play	Spare	Yard
Count	Light	Point	Spell	
Current	Log	Pool	Spot	
Date	Look	Pound	Squash	

Anticipation Guide

Part 1: Before you begin reading the selection, consider each of the following statements in the center column. Do you mostly agree or mostly disagree with the statement? Write your answer in the "Before Reading" column. Then, after you finish reading the selection, reconsider each statement and write your answer in the "After Reading" column.

Before Reading	What do you think?	After Reading

Part 2: If any of your answers changed after you read the selection, explain what you read that encouraged you to change your mind.

KWL 2.0 Think Sheet

Name _____ Date _____ Period _____

What do I know?	What do I want to know?	What answers did I learn?	What did I learn that's new?

Probable Passage

Title of Selection _____

Characters

Setting

Problem

Gist Statement . . .

_____

_____

_____

_____

Outcomes

Unknown Words

To discover . . .

1.

2.

3.

Possible Sentences

Name _____ **Date** _____

Key Vocabulary_____

Making Predictions: Write up to five sentences using the words above. You may use more than one word or phrase in a sentence.

1.

2.

3.

4.

5.

Modifying Predictions: After reading the selection, review the sentences you wrote. If the way you used the word or phrase fits with the text, simply write, "No change needed." If not, revise your possible sentence to fit the text.

1.

2.

3.

4.

5.

Poem for Tea Party

Grandmother Grace

I didn't give her a good-bye kiss
as I went off in the bus for the last time,
away from her house in Williamsburg, Iowa,
away from her empty house with Jesus
on all of the walls, with clawfoot tub and sink
with the angular rooms that trapped all my
    summers.

I remember going there every summer—
every day beginning with that lavender kiss,
that face sprayed and powdered at the
    upstairs sink,
then mornings of fragile teacups and
    old times,
afternoons of spit-moistened hankies
    and Jesus,
keeping me clean in Williamsburg, Iowa.

Cast off, abandoned, in Williamsburg, Iowa,
I sat in that angular house with summer
dragging me onward, hearing how Jesus
loved Judas despite his last kiss,
how he turned his other cheek time after time,
how God wouldn't let the good person sink.

Months later, at Christmas, my heart
    would sink
when that flowery letter from Williamsburg,
    Iowa,
arrived, insistent, always on time,
stiff and perfumed as summer.
She always sealed it with a kiss,
a taped-over dime, and the words of Jesus.

I could have done without the words of Jesus;
the dime was there to make the message sink
in, I thought; and the violet kiss,
quavering and frail, all the way from
    Williamsburg, Iowa,
sealed some agreement we had for the next
    summer
as certain and relentless as time.

I didn't know this would be the last time.
If I had, I might even have prayed to Jesus
to let me see her once again next summer.
But how could I know she would sink,
her feet fat boats of cancer, in Williamsburg,
    Iowa,
alone, forsaken, without my last kiss?

I was ten, Jesus, and the idea of a kiss
at that time made my young stomach sink.
Let it be summer. Let it be Williamsburg, Iowa.

                    —Ronald Wallace

Knowledge Rating Chart

How Well Do I know These Words?

Vocabulary Word	I have never heard this!	I have heard it but couldn't explain it. (Describe where you have heard it.)	I have an idea what it means. (Explain what you think it might mean.)	I know what this means and could explain it. (Provide your explanation.)
1.				
2.				
3.				
4.				
5.				
6.				
7.				

Before, During, and After Reading

Name _____ Section _____ Pages _____

What the text tells me *before I read*	My thoughts and questions *as I read*	My ideas *after I read*
☐ Who is the author? What do I know about this person? ☐ When was it written? Is that important? ☐ What is the title? What does that suggest? ☐ Are there certain vocabulary words that are associated with this topic I already know?	☐ What parts are confusing? ☐ What parts remind me of another text or something in my own life? ☐ What parts surprised me? ☐ What questions do I have? ☐ What inferences can I make?	☐ My SWBS statement(s) ☐ What do I think about what I just read? ☐ My thinking changed because . . . . ☐ The most interesting part was . . . . ? ☐ The author thought I knew . . . . ☐ The names/dates/events I most need to remember are . . . . ☐ The signposts I noticed . . . .
Vocabulary		

Sketch to Stretch

Name _____

Text _____

Draw your sketch here:

Explain your sketch:

Somebody Wanted But So

Name _____ **Date** _____

Text _____ **Class** _____

Somebody	Wanted	But	So

Retelling Rubric

Name _____ **Date** _____

Text _____ **Class** _____

Directions: Use the following checklist to rate the retelling. For each item below, circle a number from 0–3 in the appropriate column. On this scale, 0 means the retelling didn't include the item at all, and 3 means the retelling completely and successfully included the item.

Does this retelling

1. have an introduction that includes the story's title and setting?	0	1	2	3
2. give the characters' names and explain how the characters are related to one another?	0	1	2	3
3. identify the antagonists and protagonists?	0	1	2	3
4. include the main events?	0	1	2	3
5. keep the main events in the correct sequence?	0	1	2	3
6. provide supporting details?	0	1	2	3
7. make sense?	0	1	2	3
8. sound organized?	0	1	2	3
9. discuss the main conflict?	0	1	2	3
10. explain how the main conflict problem was resolved?	0	1	2	3
11. connect the story to another story or to the reader's life?	0	1	2	3
12. include the reader's personal response to the story?	0	1	2	3

Total Score _____

Comments from listener about the retelling:

Suggestions for the next retelling:

Retellings Progress Chart

Name _____   Class _____

	Sept.	Oct.	Nov.	Dec.	Jan.	Feb.	Mar.	Apr.	May
R13									
R12									
R11									
R10									
R9									
R8									
R7									
R6									
R5									
R4									
R3									
R2									
R1									

Three Big Questions Think Sheet

Name _____   **Topic** _____

Summary: In two or more sentences, explain what this text is about:

_____

_____

_____

_____

_____

What surprised you?	What did the author think you already knew?	What challenged, changed, or confirmed your thinking?

Semantic Differential Scales

Directions: Rate each character twice, once for the beginning of the story and once for the end by writing *B* (for beginning) and *E* (for end) on the scale. Then, explain which character has changed the most.

1. _____

honest -- dishonest

2. _____

unselfish --- selfish

3. _____

wise --foolish

4. _____

forgiving -- vindictive

_____

_____

_____

ABC Boxes

A–B	C–D	E–F

G–H	I–J	K–L

M–N	O–P	Q–R

S–T	U–V	WXYX

It Says, I Say, And So

Question	It Says	I Say	And So
1. Read the question.	2. Find information from the text that will help you answer the question.	3. Think about what you know about that information.	4. Combine what the text says with what you know to come up with the answer.

Book Head Heart (BHH)

Name _____ **Text** _____

What's in the book? Think about these types of things:	What's in your head? Think about these types of things:	What did you take to heart? Think about these types of things:
☐ Who is telling the story? ☐ What happened? ☐ What signposts did you notice? ☐ When/where did this take place? ☐ What were main events? ☐ What was the author's purpose?	☐ What surprised you? ☐ What changed, challenged, or confirmed your thinking? ☐ What did the signposts you noticed make you wonder about? ☐ What would you like to ask the author or someone else?	☐ What did this text make you think about? ☐ What lessons did you take to heart? ☐ What do you now know about yourself or others you did not know before reading this text?

Words Across Contexts

Name _____   **Date** _____

1. What would the word _____ mean to	a. b. c.
2. What would the word _____ mean to	a. b. c.
3. What would the word _____ mean to	a. b. c.
4. What would the word _____ mean to	a. b. c.

Academic Word List

The following three groups of words were compiled by Averil Coxhead (1998). She studied hundreds of academic texts from all subject areas and then compiled a list of words that occurred in all the texts. She then arranged the words in ten sublists with words in Sublist 1 occurring more often than words in Sublist 3. The first three sublists are provided below. This list of words is not to be distributed to students with the directions, "Learn these." Instead, use this as a discussion starter for you and your colleagues. Study the words and look through your own curriculum materials. Which words appear most often in the texts you use? What words might appear on state tests? What academic words do you use as you give students. directions? Then, create an academic word list that is helpful for your students.

Sublist 1

analysis	consistent	established	individual	period	significant
approach	constitutional	estimate	interpretation	policy	similar
area	context	evidence	involved	principle	source
assessment	contract	export	issues	procedure	specific
assume	create	factors	labor	process	structure
authority	data	financial	legal	required	theory
available	definition	formula	legislation	research	variables
benefit	derived	function	major	response	
concept	distribution	identified	method	role	
	economic	income	occur	section	
	environment	indicate	percent	sector	

Sublist 2

achieve	commission	design	investment	primary	select
acquisition	community	distinction	items	purchase	site
administration	complex	elements	journal	range	strategies
affect	computer	equation	maintenance	region	survey
appropriate	conclusion	evaluation	normal	regulations	text
aspects	conduct	features	obtained	relevant	traditional
assistance	consequences	final	participation	resident	transfer
categories	construction	focus	perceived	resources	
chapter	consumer	impact	positive	restricted	
	credit	injury	potential	security	
	cultural	institute	previous	sought	

Sublist 3

alternative	contribution	emphasis	justification	proportion	sufficient
circumstances	convention	ensure	layer	published	task
comments	coordination	excluded	link	reaction	technical
compensation	core	framework	location	registered	techniques
components	corporate	funds	maximum	reliance	technology
consent	corresponding	illustrated	minorities	removed	validity
considerable	criteria	immigration	negative	scheme	volume
constant	deduction	implies	outcomes	sequence	
constraints	demonstrate	initial	partnership	sex	
	document	instance	philosophy	shift	
	dominant	interaction	physical	specified	

Semantic Map

Name _____ **Date** _____

Synonyms _____ Antonyms

My sentence

_____

_____

Examples

Word Axis

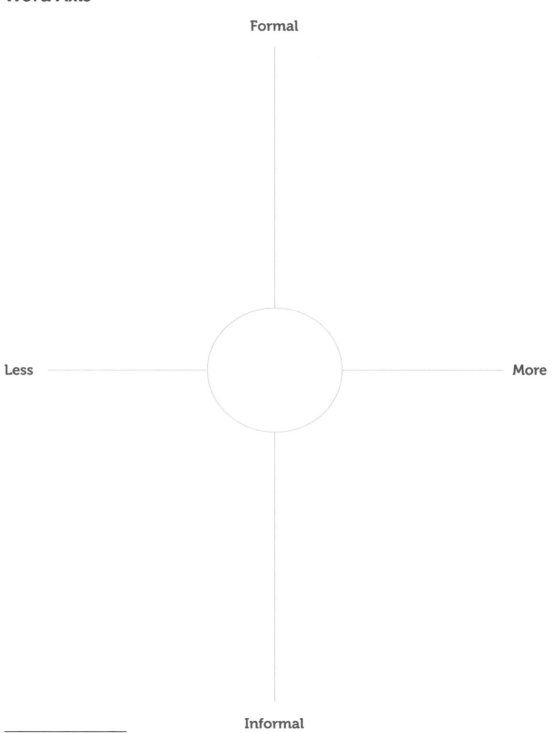

Formal

Less ———————————— **More**

Informal

Common Roots, Prefixes, and Suffixes

Root	Meaning	Examples
act	do	action, actor, react, transact, enact
aud	hear	audience, auditorium, audible, audition
cred	believe	credit, discredit, incredible, credulous
dic	speak	dictate, predict, contradict, verdict, diction
graph	write	autograph, paragraph, phonograph, photograph, telegraph
loc	place	allocate, dislocate, locate, location
man	hand	manual, manufacture, manuscript, manipulate
mot	move	demote, motion, motor, promote
ped	foot	pedal, pedestrian, pedestal
pop	people	population, popular, populace
port	carry	import, export, portable, porter, transport
sign	mark	insignia, signal, significant, signature
spec	see	inspect, respect, spectacle, spectator, suspect
tract	pull, drag	attract, detract, contract, subtract, traction, tractor

continues

Common Roots, Prefixes, and Suffixes *continued*

Prefix	Meaning	Examples
ad-	to	adapt, addict, adhere, admit
amphi-	both, around	amphibian, amphitheater
an-	not	anarchy, anesthesia, anorexia, anonymous
auto-	self	automobile, automatic, autograph, autobiography
co-	together	coauthor, cognate, coincide, cooperate, coordinate
de-	opposite	deactivate, deform, degrade, deplete, descend
dis-	opposite	disagree, disarm, discontinue, disgust, dishonest
for-	not	forbid, forget, forego
il-	not	illegal, illegible, illegitimate, illiterate, illogical
im-	into	immediate, immerse, immigrate, implant, import
im-	not	imbalance, immaculate, immature, immobilize, impossible
in-	not	inaccurate, inactive, inadvertent, incognito, indecisive
ir-	not	irregular, irreconcilable, irredeemable, irresponsible
mal-	bad	maladjusted, malaise, malevolent, malfunction, malice
pro-	before	prognosis, progeny, program, prologue, prophet
pro-	forward	proceed, produce, proficient, progress, project
re-	again	redo, rewrite, reappear, repaint, relive
re-	back	recall, recede, reflect, repay, retract
sub-	under	subcontract, subject, submarine, submerge, subordinate, subterranean
trans-	across	transatlantic, transcend, transcribe, transfer, translate
un-	not	unable, uncomfortable, uncertain, unhappy

continues

Common Roots, Prefixes, and Suffixes *continued*

Suffix	Meaning	Examples
-ade	action or process	blockade, escapade, parade
-age	action or process	marriage, pilgrimage, voyage
-ant	one who	assistant, immigrant, merchant, servant
-cle	small	corpuscle, cubicle, particle
-dom	state or quality of	boredom, freedom, martyrdom, wisdom
-ent	one who	resident, regent, superintendent
-ful	full of	careful, fearful, joyful, thoughtful
-ic	relating to	comic, historic, poetic, public
-less	without	ageless, careless, thoughtless, tireless
-let	small	islet, leaflet, owlet, rivulet, starlet
-ly	resembling	fatherly, motherly, scholarly
-ly	every	daily, weekly, monthly, yearly
-ment	action or process	development, embezzlement, government
-ment	action or quality of	amusement, amazement, predicament
-ment	product or thing	fragment, instrument, ornament
-or	one who	actor, auditor, doctor, donor

Content-Specific Roots and Affixes

Root	Meaning	Examples
aero	air	aerobics, aerodynamics, aeronautics, aerate
agr	field	agriculture, agrarian, agronomy
alt	high	altitude, altimeter, alto
alter	other	alternate, alternative, altercation
ambul	walk, go	ambulance, amble, ambulatory, preamble
amo, ami	love	amiable, amorous, amity
ang	bend	angle, angular, rectangle, triangle
anim	life, spirit	animate, animosity, animal
ann, enn	year	annual, anniversary, annuity, biennial
anthro	man	anthropology, anthropoid, misanthrope, philanthropist
apt, ept	suitable	adept, apt, aptitude, inept
ast	star	astronaut, astronomy, disaster, asterisk
belli	war	bellicose, belligerent, rebellion
biblio	book	Bible, bibliography, bibliophile
bio	life	biology, biography, biopsy
brev	shorten	abbreviate, abbreviation, brevity
cad, cas	fall	cadaver, cadence, cascade, decadence
cam	field	camp, campus, campaign, encamp
cap	head	cap, captain, capital, decapitate
cardi	heart	cardiac, cardiology
cede, ceed	go, yield	concede, exceed, proceed, succeed
ceive, cept	take, receive	accept, conception, exception, receive, reception
centr	center	central, eccentric, egocentric
cert	sure	ascertain, certain, certify, certificate
chron	time	chronic, chronicle, chronological, synchronize
cip	take, receive	incipient, participate, recipe, recipient
claim, clam	shout	acclaim, clamor, exclaim, proclaim
clar	clear	clarify, clarity, declaration, declare
cline	lean	decline, inclination, incline, recline
clud	shut	conclude, exclude, include, preclude, seclude

continues

Content-Specific Roots and Affixes *continued*

Root	Meaning	Examples
cogn	know	cognate, cognition, incognito, recognize
cord	heart	accord, concord, cordial, discord
cosm	universe	cosmonaut, cosmos, cosmopolitan, microcosm
crat	rule	aristocrat, autocratic, bureaucracy, democrat
cred	believe	credit, credulous, discredit, incredible
cur	care	curable, cure, manicure, pedicure
cur	run	concur, current, excursion, occur, recur
cycle	circle	cycle, cyclone, bicycle, recycle
dem	people	democrat, demagogy, epidemic
div	divide, part	divide, dividend, division, divorce
doc	teach	docile, doctor, doctrine, document
don	give	donate, donation, donor, predominate
duc	lead, carry	aquaduct, conduct, deduct, duct, educate, induct
fac	do, make	benefactor, factory, facsimile, manufacture
fer	bear, carry	conifer, ferry, infer, refer, transfer
fic	make	efficient, proficient, sufficient
fig	form	configuration, disfigure, effigy, figment, figure
firm	tightly fixed	affirm, confirm, firmly, firmament, reaffirm
flect	bend	deflect, inflection, reflection
form	shape	deform, form, reform, transformation, uniformity
fug	flee	centrifuge, fugitive, refuge, refugee
gen	birth	generate, generation, geneology
grad	step	grade, gradual, graduation
gram	letter	diagram, epigram, grammar, monogram
grat	pleasing	congratulations, grateful, gratitude, ungrateful
greg	gather	aggregate, congregation, gregarious, segregation
hab, hib	hold	exhibit, habit, habitat, habitual, prohibit
hosp, host	host	hospice, hospital, hospitality, hostess, host
hydr	water	dehydrate, hydrant, hydrogen
imag	like, likeness	image, imagine, imaginary, imagery, imagination

continues

Content-Specific Roots and Affixes *continued*

Root	Meaning	Examples
init	beginning	initial, initiate, initiative
junct	join	adjunct, conjunction, injunction, juncture
jud, jur, jus	law	judge, jury, justice
lab	work	collaborate, elaborate, labor, laboratory
lat	carry	collate, relate, translate
log	word	apology, dialogue, eulogy, monologue, prologue
luc, lum	light	elucidate, lucid, translucent, illuminate, luminescent
lust	shine	illustrate, illustrious, luster
mar	sea	marine, maritime, mariner, submarine
mem	mindful of	commemorate, memory, memorial, remember
merge, mers	dip	emerge, merge, merger, submerge, immerse
meter	measure	barometer, centimeter, diameter, thermometer
migr	move	emigrate, immigrate, immigrant, migrate
mim	same	mime, mimic, mimeograph, pantomime
min	small	mini, minimize, minor, minute
miss, mit	send	dismiss, missile, mission, remit, submit
mob	move	automobile, mobile, mobilize, mobility
mort	death	immortal, mortal, mortician
mut	change	commute, immutable, mutual, mutuation
narr	tell	narrate, narrative, narrator
neo	new	neonatal, neophyte, neoclassic
not	mark	denote, notable, notation, notice
noun, nun	declare, state	announce, denounce, enunciate, pronounce
nov	new	innovate, nova, novel, novelty, novice
onym	name	antonym, homonym, pseudonym, synonymn
opt	eye	optic, optician, optical, optometrist
opt	best	optimal, optimist, optimize, optimum
ord	row, lined up	extraordinary, order, ordinary, ordinal, ordinance
path	feeling	antipathy, empathy, pathology, sympathy
pel	drive	compel, expel, propel, repel

continues

Content-Specific Roots and Affixes *continued*

Root	Meaning	Examples
pend	hang	append, appendix, pendulum, suspend
phon	sound	microphone, phonics, phonograph, symphony
phys	nature	physical, physician, physique
plex, plic	fold	complex, duplex, perplex, complicate, duplicate, implicate
plur	more	plural, pluralism, plurality, pluralistic
pod	foot	podiatrist, podium, tripod
poli	city	cosmopolitan, metropolis, police, political
pon, pos	plac	exponent, opponent, postpone, proponent, compose, depose, deposit, position
pug	fight	impugn, pugnacious, pugilist, repugnant
pul	urge	compulsion, compulsory, expulsion, repulse
quer, ques, quir	ask	query, inquiry, inquest, quest, question, request
ras	scrape	abrasive, erase, rasp, razor
rect	straight	correct, direct, direction, director, erect, rectify
reg	guide	regal, regent, regulate, regulatory
rid	laugh	deride, derisive, ridicule, ridiculous
rupt	break	abrupt, bankrupt, erupt, interrupt, rupture
san	health	insane, insanity, sane, sanitary, sanitarium
scend	climb	ascend, descend, descendent, transcend
sci	know	conscience, conscious, omniscient, science
scop	see	microscope, periscope, scope, stethoscope, telescope
scribe, script	write	describe, inscribe, prescribe, scribe, descript, script, transcript
sect	cut	dissect, intersect, sect, section
sed	settle	sedate, sedative, sedentary, sediment
sens, sent	feel	sensation, sense, sensitive, sensible, sensory, assent, consent, dissent, sentimental
serv	save	conserve, preserve, reserve, reservoir
sim	like	similar, simile, simulate, simultaneous
sist	stand	assist, consist, resist, subsist

continues

Content-Specific Roots and Affixes *continued*

Root	Meaning	Examples
sol	alone	desolate, solitary, soliloquy, solo
solve	loosen	absolve, dissolve, resolve, solve, solvent
soph	wise	philosopher, sophisticated, sophomore
spir	breathe	conspire, conspirator, inspire, perspire, respiration
sta	stand	stagnate, station, stationary, statue, status
strict	make tight	constrict, restrict, strict
struct	build	construct, destruct, destruction, instruct, instruction, structure
sum	highest	sum, summary, summit, summons
surg, surr	rise	insurgent, resurgent, surge, insurrection, resurrect
tact	touch	contact, intact, tact, tactile
tain	hold	attain, contain, detain, retain
ten	stretch	tendency, tense, tension, tent
term	end	determine, exterminate, term, terminal, terminate
tex	weave	context, text, textile, texture
the	god	atheism, monotheism, polytheism, theology
therm	heat	thermal, thermometer, thermos
tort	twist	contort, retort, tort, torture
trib	give	attribute, contribute, tribute
trud, trus	push	intrude, intruder, protrude, abstruse, intrusive
turb	confusion	disturb, perturb, turbulent
urb	city	urban, suburb, suburban
vac	empty	evacuate, vacate, vacant, vacation, vacuum
var	different	invariable, variant, variety, vary
ven	come	advent, convent, convene, convention, invent, venue
ver	truth	aver, veracity, verdict, verify
voc	voice	advocate, convocation, evocation, vocal
vol	will	benevolent, malevolent, volition, voluntary, volunteer
vor	eat	carnivorous, herbivore, omnivore, voracious

Dolch Basic Sight Vocabulary

a	clean	green	many	run	together
about	cold	grow	may	said	too
after	come	had	me	saw	try
again	could	has	much	say	two
all	cut	have	must	see	under
always	did	he	my	seven	up
am	do	help	myself	shall	upon
an	does	her	never	she	us
and	done	here	new	show	use
any	don't	him	no	sing	very
are	down	his	not	sit	walk
around	draw	hold	now	six	want
as	drink	hot	of	sleep	warm
ask	eat	how	off	small	was
at	eight	hurt	old	so	wash
ate	every	I	on	some	we
away	fall	if	once	soon	well
be	far	in	one	start	went
because	fast	into	only	stop	were
been	find	is	open	take	what
before	first	it	or	tell	when
best	five	its	our	ten	where
better	fly	jump	out	thank	which
big	for	just	over	that	white
black	found	keep	own	the	who
blue	four	kind	pick	their	why
both	from	know	play	them	will
bring	full	laugh	please	then	wish
brown	funny	let	pretty	there	with
but	gave	light	pull	these	work
buy	get	like	put	they	would
by	give	little	ran	think	write
call	go	live	read	this	yellow
came	goes	long	red	those	yes
can	going	look	ride	three	you
carry	good	made	right	to	your
	got	make	round	today	

Fry's Instant Words

The following words are the most common words in the English language (Fry, Kress, and Fountoukidis, 1993, 23). Fry et al. remind us that "the first twenty-five words make up about a third of all printed material," while the first hundred "make up about half of all written material" and the first three hundred "make up about 65 percent of all written material."

First Hundred

the	at	there	some	my
of	be	use	her	than
and	this	an	would	first
a	have	each	make	water
to	from	which	like	been
in	or	she	him	call
is	one	do	into	who
you	had	how	time	oil
that	by	their	has	its
it	word	if	look	now
he	but	will	two	find
was	not	up	more	long
for	what	other	write	down
on	all	about	go	day
are	were	out	see	did
as	we	many	number	get
with	when	then	no	come
his	your	them	way	made
they	can	these	could	may
I	said	so	people	part

Second Hundred

over	name	boy	such	change
new	good	follow	because	off
sound	sentence	came	turn	play
take	man	went	here	spell
only	think	show	why	air
little	say	also	ask	away
work	great	around	went	animal
know	where	form	men	house

continues

Fry's Instant Words *continued*

Second Hundred *continued*

place	help	three	read	point
year	through	small	need	page
live	much	set	land	letter
me	before	put	different	mother
back	line	end	home	answer
give	right	does	us	found
most	too	another	move	study
very	mean	well	try	still
after	old	large	kind	learn
thing	any	must	hand	should
our	same	big	picture	America
just	tell	even	again	world

Third Hundred

high	never	along	together	sea
every	start	might	got	began
near	city	close	group	grow
add	earth	something	often	took
food	eye	seem	run	river
between	light	next	important	four
own	thought	hard	until	carry
below	head	open	children	state
country	under	example	side	once
plant	story	begin	feet	book
last	saw	life	car	hear
school	left	always	mile	stop
father	don't	those	night	without
keep	few	both	walk	second
tree	while	paper	white	later
miss	watch	let	cut	song
idea	far	above	young	being
enough	Indian	girl	talk	leave
eat	really	sometimes	soon	family
face	almost	mountain	list	it's

continues

Fry's Instant Words *continued*

Fourth Hundred

body	usually	hours	five	cold
music	didn't	black	step	cried
color	friends	products	morning	plan
stand	easy	happened	passed	notice
sun	heard	whole	vowel	south
questions	order	measure	true	sing
fish	red	remember	hundred	war
area	door	early	against	ground
mark	sure	waves	pattern	fall
dog	become	reached	numeral	king
horse	top	listen	table	town
birds	ship	wind	north	I'll
problem	across	rock	slowly	unit
complete	today	space	money	figure
room	during	covered	map	certain
knew	short	fast	farm	field
since	better	several	pulled	travel
ever	best	hold	draw	wood
piece	however	himself	voice	fire
told	low	toward	seen	upon

Fifth Hundred

done	fly	correct	minutes	machine
English	gave	oh	strong	fact
road	box	quickly	verb	base
halt	class	person	stars	inches
surface	finally	became	front	street
ten	wait	shown	feel	decided
contain	stay	round	deep	noun
course	green	boat	thousands	power
ran	known	game	yes	cannot
produce	island	rule	pair	able
building	week	brought	circle	six
ocean	less	understand	yet	size
force	clear	warm	government	dark

continues

Fry's Instant Words *continued*

Fifth Hundred *continued*

note	equation	common	filled	ball
nothing	ago	bring	heat	material
rest	stood	explain	full	special
carefully	plane	dry	check	heavy
scientists	system	though	object	fine
inside	behind	language	am	include
wheels	hot	shape	among	built

Sixth Hundred

can't	region	window	arms	west
matter	return	difference	brother	lay
square	believe	distance	race	weather
syllables	dance	heart	present	root
perhaps	members	sit	beautiful	instruments
bill	picked	sum	store	meet
felt	simple	summer	job	third
suddenly	cells	wall	edge	months
test	paint	forest	past	paragraph
direction	mind	probably	sign	raised
center	love	legs	record	represent
farmers	cause	sat	finished	soft
ready	rain	main	discovered	whether
anything	exercise	winter	wild	clothes
divided	eggs	wide	happy	flowers
general	train	written	beside	shall
energy	blue	length	gone	teacher
subject	wish	reason	sky	held
Europe	drop	kept	glass	describe
moon	developed	interest	million	drive

continues

Fry's Instant Words *continued*

Seventh Hundred

cross	buy	temperature	possible	fraction
speak	century	bright	gold	Africa
solve	outside	lead	milk	killed
appear	everything	everyone	quiet	melody
metal	tall	method	natural	bottom
son	already	section	lot	trip
either	instead	lake	stone	hole
ice	phrase	consonant	act	poor
sleep	soil	within	build	let's
village	bed	dictionary	middle	fight
factors	copy	hair	speed	surprise
result	free	age	count	French
jumped	hope	amount	cat	died
snow	spring	scale	someone	beat
ride	case	pounds	sail	exactly
care	laughed	although	rolled	remain
floor	nation	per	bear	dress
hill	quite	broken	wonder	iron
pushed	type	moment	smiled	couldn't
baby	themselves	tiny	angle	fingers

Eighth Hundred

row	joined	cool	single	statement
least	foot	cloud	touch	stick
catch	law	lost	information	party
climbed	ears	sent	express	seeds
wrote	grass	symbols	mouth	suppose
shouted	you're	wear	yard	woman
continued	grew	bad	equal	coast
itself	skin	save	decimal	bank
else	valley	experiment	yourself	period
plains	cents	engine	control	wire
gas	key	alone	practice	choose
England	president	drawing	report	clean
burning	brown	east	straight	visit

continues

Fry's Instant Words *continued*

Eighth Hundred *continued*

design	trouble	pay	rise	bit
whose	fell	serve	maybe	flow
received	team	child	business	lady
garden	God	desert	separate	students
please	captain	increase	break	human
strange	direct	history	uncle	art
caught	ring	cost	hunting	feelings

Ninth Hundred

supply	fit	sense	position	meat
corner	addition	string	entered	lifted
electric	belong	blow	fruit	process
insects	safe	famous	tied	army
crops	soldiers	value	rich	hat
tone	guess	wing	dollars	property
hit	silent	movement	send	particular
sand	trade	pole	sight	swim
doctor	rather	exciting	chief	terms
provide	compare	branches	Japanese	current
thus	crowd	thick	stream	park
won't	poem	blood	plants	sell
cook	enjoy	lie	rhythm	shoulder
bones	elements	spot	eight	industry
tail	indicate	bell	science	wash
board	except	fun	major	block
modern	expect	loud	observe	spread
compound	flat	consider	tube	cattle
mine	seven	suggested	necessary	wife
wasn't	interesting	thin	weight	sharp

continues

Fry's Instant Words *continued*

Tenth Hundred

company	factories	truck	chance	France
radio	settled	fair	born	repeated
we'll	yellow	printed	level	column
action	isn't	wouldn't	triangle	western
capital	southern	ahead	molecules	church
sister	shoes	stretched	difficult	corn
oxygen	actually	experience	match	substances
plural	nose	rose	win	smell
various	afraid	allow	doesn't	tools
agreed	dead	fear	steel	conditions
opposite	sugar	workers	total	cows
wrong	adjective	Washington	deal	track
chart	fig	Greek	determine	arrived
prepared	office	women	evening	located
pretty	huge	bought	nor	sir
solution	gun	led	rope	seat
fresh	similar	march	cotton	division
shop	death	northern	apple	effect
suffix	score	create	details	underline
especially	forward	British	entire	view

Common Spelling Rules

1. Rules for Adding Prefixes

a. When a prefix is added to a word, do not drop a letter from either the prefix or the base word (*dis-* + *approve* = *disapprove*; *ir-* + *regular* = *irregular*, *mis-* + *spell* = *misspell*, *il-* + *legal* = *illegal*).

b. The exception to the prefix rule is for *ad-*, *com-*, and *in-*, which can be "absorbed" by the base word so that the last letter in the prefix changes to match the beginning consonant of the base word. This is done to make the word easier to say. For example, instead of *inlegal* (meaning not legal), we write *illegal*. Instead of *adsemble* (meaning toward moving together), we write *assemble*. Instead of *conmit* (meaning to send together), we write *commit*. Other examples of words with absorbed prefixes include *allot, affair, arrange, acclaim, colleague, correlate, irresponsible, immature, irrational, immortal*.

2. Rules for Plurals

Nouns

a. For most nouns, add s (*boy/boys, table/tables*).

b. For nouns ending in *s, x, z, ch*, or *sh*, add es (*glasses, foxes, arches, wishes*).

c. For nouns ending in *y* when the *y* is preceded by a vowel, add s (*turkeys, attorneys*).

d. For nouns ending in *y* when the *y* is preceded by a consonant, change the *y* to *i* and then add es (*cities, spies*).

e. For some nouns ending in *f* or *fe*, add s; others change the *f* or *fe* to *v* and add es (*roofs, beliefs, scarves, leaves*).

f. For nouns ending in *o* when the *o* is preceded by a consonant, add es (*tomatoes, heroes*).

g. For nouns ending in *o* when the *o* is preceded by a vowel, add s (*patios, rodeos*).

h. For some nouns that end in *o* when the *o* is preceded by a vowel, just add an s. This is particularly true of words that are connected to music (*solos, altos, sopranos*).

i. For some nouns, the plural form is a new word: *teeth, mice, oxen*.

Verbs

a. While verbs are not plural like nouns, they take the plural form to be in agreement with the subject: He *does*; they *do*. Verbs that end in *o*, add es; verbs that end in a consonant, add s (*go/goes; win/wins*).

continues

Common Spelling Rules *continued*

3. Rules for Suffixes

a. If adding the suffix *-ly* or *-ness*, do not change the spelling of the base word unless the base word ends in *y* (*careful/carefully; usual/usually; fond/fondness; happy/happily*).

Rules for adding a suffix to words that end in silent **e**

a. If adding a suffix that begins with a vowel to a word that ends in a silent *e*, drop the final silent *e* (*give/giving; safe/safest; take/taking; admire/admirable, create/creative*).

b. If adding a suffix that begins with the letter *a* or *o* to a word that ends in *ce* or *ge*, keep the final *e* (*manage/manageable; notice/noticeable; outrage/outrageous*).[1]

c. If adding a suffix that begins with a consonant to a word that ends with a silent *e*, keep the silent *e* (*measure/measurement; use/useful; creative/creatively*).

Rules for adding a suffix to words that end in **y**

a. If adding a suffix to a word that ends in *y* when the *y* is preceded by a consonant, change the *y* to *i* to add any suffix that does not begin with *i* (*cry/cried /crying; terrify/terrified/terrifying*).

b. If adding a suffix to a word that ends in *y* when the *y* is preceded by a vowel, do not change the *y* to *i*; instead, just add the suffix (*annoy/ annoyed; delay/delayed/delaying*). Exceptions include *say/said, pay/paid, lay/laid.*

Rules for doubling the final consonant in a word before adding the suffix

a. If the word is a one-syllable word that has only one vowel and only one consonant after the vowel, then double the final consonant before adding a suffix that begins with a vowel (*sit/sitting; run/running; pit/pitted; wrap/wrapper*). This is sometimes called the 1-1-1 Doubling Rule (one syllable-one vowel-one consonant after the vowel).

b. If the word has two or more syllables and the last syllable is a CVC pattern (consonant-vowel-consonant) and is the accented syllable, then follow the 1-1-1 Doubling Rule (*permit/permitted; refer/referring; forbid/forbidden; occur/occurred; forget/forgetting*).

c. If the word has two or more syllables and the last syllable follows the CVC pattern but is unaccented, do not double the last consonant (*barrel/barreling; gallop/galloping; blanket/blanketing; trumpet/trumpeting*).

continues

---

[1] The *e* must be kept at the ends of the words to keep the *c* and *g* making their "soft" sounds of /s/ and /j/. Usually *c* makes the /k/ sound except when followed by the letters *e, i,* and *y. G* usually makes the /g/ sound except when followed by *e, i,* and *y.*

Common Spelling Rules *continued*

Rules for adding the suffixes -ible *or* -able

a. If the root is not a complete word (technically called a *bound morpheme*), add -ible. Examples: *visible, horrible, terrible, possible, edible, eligible, incredible, permissible, suitable, invisible, illegible.*

b. If the root is a complete word without the suffix (technically called an *unbound morpheme*), then add -able. Examples: *fashionable, laughable, suitable, dependable, comfortable.*

c. If the root is a complete word that ends in silent *e*, drop the silent *e* and then add -able. Examples: *excuse/excusable, advise/advisable, desire/desirable, value/valuable, debate/debatable.*

d. Exceptions to the -ible/-able rule occur when the final sound is the hard *g* or hard *c* sound; then the suffix is -able: *navigable, applicable.* Other exceptions include *digestible, contemptible, inevitable, flexible, responsible, irritable.*

Rules for adding -ion

a. If the root ends in *ct*, add -ion (*selects/election; subtract/subtraction*).

b. If the root ends in *ss*, add -ion (*discuss/discussion; impress/impression*).

c. If the root ends in *te*, drop the *e* and add -ion (*educate/education; create/creation*).

d. If the root ends in *it*, change the *t* to *s* and add -sion (*permit/permission; omit/omission*).

e. If the root ends Vde (vowel, letter *d*, letter *e*), drop the *e*, change the *d* to *s*, and add -ion (*explode/explosion; persuade/persuasion*).

f. If the root ends in Vre, Vne, or Vze, drop the *e* and add -ation (*declare/declaration; combine/combination; organize/organization*).

4. Other Helpful Rules

a. Use the word *a* before words that begin with a consonant sound; use *an* before words that begin with a vowel sound (*a car; an apple; an hour*—the *h* is silent; *a one-dollar bill*—the *o* makes a /w/ sound).

b. Use an apostrophe to take the place of omitted letters in contractions. Examples: *let's, that's, don't, doesn't, it's, can't, won't, wouldn't, shouldn't, couldn't, I'm, I've, I'd, I'll, they're, they've, they'd, they'll, you're, you've, you'd, you'll, we're, we'll, we've, we'd, she'd, she'll, could've, would've, should've.*

continues

Common Spelling Rules *continued*

c.   Long vowel sounds will not precede a doubled consonant. Exceptions include *toll, roll, droll,* and *troll.*

d.   Do not end words in the letter *v* or *z.* Add a silent *e* to words that end in those sounds (*give,* not *giv; breeze,* not *breez; have,* not *hav; love,* not *lov; snooze,* not *snooz; above,* not *abov*).

e.   Only one English word ends in *-sede: supersede.* Three words end in *-ceed: exceed, proceed,* and *succeed*; all other verbs ending in the /sed/ sound are spelled with *-cede: intercede, precede; concede.*

f.   Spelling the wrong word the correct way is still a spelling error. So, using *right* for *write* isn't right. Help students to spell homophones correctly by making sure they know the meaning of each word.

Interesting Sorts

Directions: For each sort, put one word on an index card. Do not keep words separated as they are here. Give students the words and ask them to sort to figure out what the rule is that would help them understand whatever is the target of that sort. As students figure out rules for sorts, they should be able to state that rule. Have them look through books for other words that would either confirm the rule they've generated or be an exception to the rule. You can also do this with the whole class by writing each word on a transparency, cutting out the words, and sorting on the overhead projector. Finally, put the rules on large pieces of chart paper with the words underneath. As students find additional words that fit the rule or don't, they should add those words to the chart paper.

For Plurals of Words Ending in *y*

babies	boys
ponies	toys
carries	monkeys
funnies	keys
tummies	enjoys
lobbies	days
flies	plays

Sort Rule: When the word ends in a *y* that is immediately preceded by a consonant, change the *y* to *i* and add *es*. When it ends in a *y* that is immediately preceded by a vowel, just add *s*.

For Adding *-ing*

running	riding	boating
hopping	hiding	floating
sitting	biking	sweeping
batting	faking	fighting
swapping	poking	painting
tanning	making	doing
tapping	smiling	treating
bragging	shaving	docking

continues

Interesting Sorts *continued*

Sort Rule: When the word ends in the VC pattern and the vowel makes its short sound, double the final consonant before adding -*ing*. This keeps the vowel sound short. If the word ends in a VCe pattern, drop the *e* and add -*ing*. This preserves the VCV pattern that makes the vowel long. If the word ends in a VVC pattern or just a V, just add -*ing*.

For Choosing Between *ch* and *tch* at the End of a Word

				exceptions
each	fetch	bench	couch	
bleach	witch	wench	pouch	rich
coach	patch	clench	vouch	which
peach	pitch	trench	crouch	such
screech	sketch	French	grouch	much
speech	hitch	drench	slouch	
roach	switch	quench		

Sort Rule: If the vowel sound in the word is long, as in *each*, is followed by the letter *n* as in *bench*, or makes the sound as in *cow*, just add *ch*. If the vowel sound is short but not followed by the letter *n*, add *tch*. Exceptions to this include *rich, which, such, much*.

For Adding -*tion* Versus -*sion*

selection	profession
extinction	procession
subtraction	discussion
prediction	succession
traction	depression
contraction	repression

Sort Rule: If the base word ends in *ct*, add -*ion*. If the base word ends in *ss*, add -*ion*.

creation	repulsion
imitation	convulsion
congratulation	expulsion
reproduction	introduction
seduction	deduction

continues

Interesting Sorts *continued*

Sort Rule: If the base word ends in *te*, drop the *e* and add *-ion*. If the base word ends in *se*, drop the *e* and add *-ion*. If the base word ends in *ce*, drop the *e*, change the *c* to *t* and add *-ion*.

transmission   omission   permission   emission   commission

Sort Rule: If the base word ends in Vt, change the *t* to *s* and add *-sion*.

explosion   inclusion
conclusion   persuasion   erosion

Sort Rule: If the base word ends in *de*, drop the *e* and change the *d* to *s*, then add *-ion*.

For Adding *-able* Versus *-ible*

dependable	horrible	usable	changeable	amicable
breakable	visible	desirable	manageable	applicable
agreeable	terrible	excusable	noticeable	despicable
profitable	legible	lovable	peaceable	impeccable
remarkable	possible	comparable	serviceable	
doable	feasible	trainable		

Sort Rule: If the base word can stand alone, add *-able*. If the base word cannot stand alone, add *-ible*. If the base word can stand alone but ends in *e*, drop the *e* and then add *-able*. If the base word ends in *ce* or *ge* and the *c* or the *g* makes its soft sound, then add *-able*. If the *c* makes its hard sound, add *-able*.

Common Phonics Generalizations

Clymer (1963) looked at phonics rules to determine how often the rule stood and how often there was an exception to the rule. Most of the rules had exceptions. What follows are the rules Clymer examined, an example of the rule, and when needed, an exception to the rule.

*Generalization	Example	Exception	Percent of utility
1. When there are two vowels side by side, the long sound of the first one is heard and the second is usually silent.	bead	chief	45
2. When a vowel is in the middle of a one-syllable word, the vowel is short.			62
middle letter	dress	scold	69
one of the middle two letters in a word of four letters	rest	told	59
one vowel *within* a word of more than four letters	splash	fight	46
3. If the only vowel letter is at the end of a word, the letter usually stands for a long sound.	he	to	74
4. When there are two vowels, one of which is final *e*, the first vowel is long and the *e* is silent.	bone	done	63
* 5. The *r* gives the preceding vowel a sound that is neither long nor short.	horn	wire	78
6. The first vowel is usually long and the second silent in the digraphs *ai, ea, oa,* and *ui*.			66
ai	nail	said	64
ea	bead	head	66
oa	boat	cupboard	97
ui	suit	build	6

continues

Common Phonics Generalizations *continued*

*Generalization	Example	Exception	Percent of utility
7. In the phonogram *ie*, the *i* is silent and the *e* has a long sound.	field	friend	17
*8. Words having double *e* usually have the long *e* sound.	seem	been	98
9. When words end with silent *e*, the preceding *a* or *i* is long.	cake	have	60
10. In *ay* the *y* is silent and gives *a* its long sound.	play	always	78
11. When the letter *i* is followed by the letters *gh*, the *i* usually stands for its long sound and the *gh* is silent.	high	neighbor	71
12. When *a* follows *w* in a word, it usually has the sound *a* as in *was*.	watch	swan	32
13. When *e* is followed by *w*, the vowel sound is the same as represented by *oo*.	blew	sew	35
14. The two letters *ow* make the long *o* sound.	own	down	59
15. *W* is sometimes a vowel and follows the vowel digraph rule.	crow	threw	40
*16. When *y* is the final letter in a word, it usually has a vowel sound.	dry	tray	84
17. When *y* is used as a vowel in words, it sometimes has the sound of long *i*.	fly	funny	15
18. The letter *a* has the same sound (ô) when followed by *i*, *w*, and *u*.	all	canal	48
19. When *a* is followed by *r* and final *e*, we expect to hear the sound heard in *care*.	dare	are	90
*20. When *c* and *h* are next to each other, they make only one sound.	peach		100
*21. *Ch* is usually pronounced as it is in *kitchen*, *catch*, and *chair*, not like *sh*.	catch	machine	95

continues

Common Phonics Generalizations *continued*

*Generalization	Example	Exception	Percent of utility
* 22. When *c* is followed by *e* or *i*, the sound of *s* is likely to be heard.	cent	ocean	96
* 23. When the letter *c* is followed by *o* or *a* the sound of *k* is likely to be heard.	camp		100
24. The letter *g* often has a sound similar to that of *j* in *jump* when it precedes the letter *i* or *e*.	engine	give	64
* 25. When *ght* is seen in a word, *gh* is silent.	fight		100
26. When a word begins *kn*, the *k* is silent.	knife		100
27. When a word begins with *wr*, the *w* is silent.	write		100
* 28. When two of the same consonants are side by side only one is heard.	carry	suggest	99
* 29. When a word ends in *ck*, it has the same last sound as in *look*.	brick		100
* 30. In most two-syllable words, the first syllable is accented.	famous	polite	85
* 31. If *a, in, re, ex, de*, or *be* is the first syllable in a word, it is usually unaccented.	belong	insect	87
* 32. In most two-syllable words that end in a consonant followed by *y*, the first syllable is accented and the last is unaccented.	baby	supply	96
33. One vowel letter in an accented syllable has its short sound.	city	lady	61
34. When *y* or *ey* is seen in the last syllable that is not accented, the long sound of *e* is heard.	baby		100
35. When *ture* is the final syllable in a word, it is unaccented.	picture		100

continues

Common Phonics Generalizations *continued*

*Generalization	Example	Exception	Percent of utility
36. When *tion* is the final syllable in a word, it is unaccented.	station		100
37. In many two- and three-syllable words, the final *e* lengthens the vowel in the last syllable.	invite	gasoline	46
38. If the first vowel sound in a word is followed by two consonants, the first syllable usually ends with the first of the two consonants.	bullet	singer	72
39. If the first vowel sound in a word is followed by a single consonant, that consonant usually begins the second syllable.	over	oven	44
*40. If the last syllable of a word ends in *ie*, the consonant preceding the *ie* usually begins the last syllable.	tumble	buckle	97
* 41. When the first vowel in a word is followed by *th*, *ch*, or *sh*, these letters are not broken when the word is divided into syllables and may go with either the first or second syllable.	dishes		100
42. In a word of more than one syllable, the letter *v* usually goes with the preceding vowel to form a syllable.	cover	clover	73
43. When a word has only one vowel letter, the vowel sound is likely to be short.	hid	kind	57
*44. When there is one *e* in a word that ends in a consonant, the *e* usually has a short sound.	leg	blew	76
*45. When the last syllable is the sound *r*, it is unaccented.	butter	appear	95

*Generalizations marked with an asterisk were found "useful" according to the criteria.

175 Most Common Syllables (Including Prefixes and Suffixes) in the 5,000 Most Frequent English Words

1. ing	26. ti	51. po	76. tle	101. fac	126. li	151. ern
2. er	27. ri	52. sion	77. day	102. fer	127. lo	152. eve
3. a	28. be	53. vi	78. ny	103. gen	128. men	153. hap
4. ly	29. per	54. el	79. pen	104. ic	129. min	154. ies
5. ed	30. to	55. est	80. pre	105. land	130. mon	155. ket
6. i	31. pro	56. la	81. tive	106. light	131. op	156. lec
7. es	32. ac	57. lar	82. car	107. ob	132. out	157. main
8. re	33. ad	58. pa	83. ci	108. of	133. rec	158. mar
9. tion	34. ar	59. ture	84. mo	109. pos	134. ro	159. mis
10. in	35. ers	60. for	85. an	110. tain	135. sen	160. my
11. e	36. ment	61. is	86. aus	111. den	136. side	161. nal
12. con	37. or	62. mer	87. pi	112. ings	137. tal	162. ness
13. y	38. tions	63. pe	88. se	113. mag	138. tic	163. ning
14. ter	39. ble	64. ra	89. ten	114. ments	139. ties	164. n't
15. ex	40. der	65. so	90. tor	115. set	140. ward	165. nu
16. al	41. ma	66. ta	91. ver	116. some	141. age	166. oc
17. de	42. na	67. as	92. ber	117. sub	142. ba	167. pres
18. com	43. si	68. col	93. can	118. sur	143. but	168. sup
19. o	44. un	69. fi	94. dy	119. ters	144. cit	169. te
20. di	45. at	70. ful	95. et	120. tu	145. cle	170. ted
21. en	46. dis	71. get	96. it	121. af	146. co	171. tem
22. an	47. ca	72. low	97. mu	122. au	147. cov	172. tin
23. ty	48. cal	73. ni	98. no	123. cy	148. da	173. tri
24. ry	49. man	74. par	99. ple	124. fa	149. dif	174. tro
25. u	50. ap	75. son	100. cu	125. im	150. ence	175. up

For a longer list of common syllables, see Blevins, 2001. *Teaching Phonics and Word Study in the Intermediate Grades*. New York: Scholastic, p. 196.

REFERENCES

Adams, Marilyn J. 1990. *Beginning to Read: Thinking and Learning About Print*. Cambridge, MA: Harvard University Press.

Adecco. 2022. "Top 7 Resume Mistakes to Avoid." https://www.adeccousa.com /resources/top-resume-mistakes/.

Ahmadi, Belquis, and Asma Ebadi. 2022. "Taliban's Ban on Girls' Education in Afghanistan." United States Institute on Peace. April 1. https://www.usip.org/publications/2022/04 /talibans-ban-girls-education-afghanistan.

Allan, Keith. 2010. *The Western Classical Tradition in Linguistics*. 2nd ed. Sheffield, UK: Equinox.

Allington, Richard L., and Anne M. McGill-Franzen. 2021. "Reading Volume and Reading Achievement: A Review of Recent Research." *Reading Research Quarterly* 56 (1): S231–38. https://www.researchgate.net/publication/351040351_Reading_Volume _and_Reading_Achievement_A_Review_of_Recent_Research.

Anderson, T. H. 1980. "Study Strategies and Adjunct Aids." In *Theoretical Issues in Comprehension: Perspectives from Cognitive Psychology, Artificial Intelligence, Linguistics, and Education*, edited by R. I. Spiro, B. C. Bruce, and W. F. Brewer, 483–502. Hillsdale, NJ: Lawrence Erlbaum Associates.

Applebee, Arthur N., and Judith A. Langer. 2009. "What Is Happening in the Teaching of Writing?" *English Journal* 98 (5): 18–28.

Associated Press. 2022. "Money Spat Resolved over LGBTQ Books at Mississippi Library." *AP News*, January 27. https://apnews.com/article/entertainment-business-mississippi -arts-and-libraries-89afff1f56a1ef79d5d3f533005b0e79.

Baekgaard, Martin, and Søren Serritzlew. 2015. "Interpreting Performance Information: Motivated Reasoning or Unbiased Comprehension." *Public Administration Review* 76 (1): 73–82. https://onlinelibrary.wiley.com/doi/epdf/10.1111/puar.12406.

Baldwin, James. 1960. "They Can't Turn Back." History Is a Weapon. https://www
.historyisaweapon.com/defcon1/baldwincantturnback.html.

———. 2007. *No Name in the Street*. 1st vintage international ed. New York: Random
House.

Barnett, Jerrold E., and Richard W. Seefeldt. 1989. "Read Something Once, Why Read
It Again? Repetitive Reading and Recall." *Journal of Reading Behavior* 21 (4): 351–60.
https://journals.sagepub.com/doi/pdf/10.1080/10862968909547684.

Barr, Rebecca, Camille Blachowicz, Ann Bates, Claudia Katz, and Barbara Kaufman. 2007.
Reading Diagnosis for Teachers: An Instructional Approach. 5th ed. Boston: Allyn and Bacon.

Baumann, J. F., and E. J. Kameenui. 1991. "Research on Vocabulary Instruction: Ode to
Voltaire." In *Handbook on Teaching the English Language Arts*, edited by James Flood, Julie
M. Jensen, Diane Lapp, and James R. Squire, 604–32. Newark, DE, and Urbana, IL:
International Reading Association and the National Council of Teachers of English.

Bear, Donald R., Marcia Invernizzi, Shane Templeton, and Francine Johnston. 2019. *Words
Their Way: Word Study for Phonics, Vocabulary, and Spelling Instruction*. 7th ed. Hoboken,
NJ: Pearson.

Beaty, Andrea. 2013. *Rosie Revere, Engineer*. New York: Abrams Books for Young Readers.

Beauchamp, Zack. 2022. "Why Book Banning Is Back." Vox. February 10. https://www
.vox.com/policy-and-politics/22914767/book-banning-crt-school-boards-republicans.

Beers, James. 1980. "Developmental Strategies of Spelling Competence in Primary
School Children." In *Cognitive and Developmental Aspects of Learning to Spell: A Reflection
of Word Knowledge*, edited by Edmund H. Henderson and James W. Beers, 36–45.
Newark, DE: International Reading Association.

Beers, James, and Edmund Henderson. 1977. "A Study of Developing Orthographic
Concepts Among First Graders." *Research in the Teaching of English* 11 (2): 133–48.

Beers, Kylene. 1990. "Choosing Not to Read: An Ethnographic Study of Seventh-Grade
Aliterate Students." Unpublished doctoral diss., University of Houston.

———. 2002. "Editor's Message: When Spelling Is a Challenge." *Voices from the Middle* 9
(3): 4–5.

———. 2006. "Editor's Message: The Challenge of Change." *Voices from the Middle* 13 (3):
4–5.

Beers, Kylene, and Robert E. Probst. 2013. *Notice and Note: Strategies for Close Reading*.
Portsmouth, NH: Heinemann.

———. 2016. *Reading Nonfiction: Stances, Signposts, and Strategies*. Portsmouth, NH:
Heinemann.

———. 2018. *Disrupting Thinking: Why How We Read Matters*. New York: Scholastic.

———. 2020. *Forged by Reading: The Power of a Literate Life*. New York: Scholastic.

Bernecker, Sven, and Kourken Michaelian, eds. 2017. *The Routledge Handbook of Philosophy
of Memory*. New York: Routledge.

Berns, Gregory S., Kristina Blaine, Michael J. Prietula, and Brandon E. Pye. 2013.
"Shortand Long-Term Effects of a Novel on Connectivity in the Brain." *Brain
Connectivity* 3 (6): 590–600.

Bishop, Rudine Sims. 1990. "Mirrors, Windows, and Sliding Glass Doors." *Perspectives: Choosing and Using Books for the Classroom* 6 (3): ix–xi.

Bittman, Mark. 2013. "How to Feed the World." *New York Times*, October 14. https://www.nytimes.com/2013/10/15/opinion/how-to-feed-the-world.html.

Blachowicz, Camille L. Z. 1986. "Making Connections: Alternatives to the Vocabulary Notebook." *Journal of Reading* 29 (7): 643–49.

Blevins, Wiley. 2001. *Teaching Phonics and Word Study in the Intermediate Grades.* New York: Scholastic.

Bojowald, Martin. 2008. "Big Bang or Big Bounce? New Theory on the Universe's Birth." *Scientific American*, October 1. https://www.scientificamerican.com/article/big-bang-or-big-bounce/.

Bond, Guy L., and Robert Dykstra. 1967. "The Cooperative Research Program in First-Grade Reading Instruction." *Reading Research Quarterly* 2 (4): 5–142.

Boyd, Maureen P., and William C. Markarian. 2015. "Dialogic Teaching and Dialogic Stance: Moving Beyond Interactional Form." *Research in the Teaching of English* 49 (3): 272–96.

Braddock, Richard, Richard Lloyd-Jones, and Lowell Schoer. *Research in Written Composition.* Urbana, IL: NCTE, 1963.

Callender, Aimee A., and Mark A. Mcdaniel. 2009. "The Limited Benefits of Rereading Educational Texts." *Contemporary Educational Psychology* 34 (1): 30–41.

Carroll, John B., Peter Davies, and Barry Richman. 1971. *Word Frequency Book.* Boston: Houghton Mifflin.

Cazden, Courtney. 1988. *Classroom Discourse: The Language of Teaching and Learning.* Portsmouth, NH: Heinemann.

Centers for Disease Control and Prevention. 2022. COVID Data Tracker. Atlanta, GA: US Department of Health and Human Services, CDC. https://covid.cdc.gov/covid-data-tracker.

Clay, Marie M., and Robert H. Imlach. 1971. "Juncture, Pitch, and Stress as Reading Behavior Variables." *Journal of Verbal Learning and Verbal Behavior* 10 (2): 133–39.

Clinton, Virginia. 2019. "Reading from Paper Compared to Screens: A Systematic Review and Meta-analysis." *Journal of Research in Reading* 42 (2): 288–325. https://onlinelibrary.wiley.com/doi/abs/10.1111/1467-9817.12269.

Clymer, T. 1963. "Utility of Phonics Generalizations in the Primary Grades." *The Reading Teacher* 16: 252–58.

Coleman, David, and Susan Pimentel. 2012. "Revised Publishers' Criteria for the Common Core State Standards in English Language Arts and Literacy, Grades 3–12." Common Core State Standards Initiative (website). Revised April 12. http://www.corestandards.org/assets/Publishers_Criteria_for_3-12.pdf.

Consumer Reports. 2012. "How to Not Get Phished: Our Tips on How to Identify Phishing Scams Will Keep You from Falling for Them." https://www.consumerreports.org/cro/2012/10/how-to-not-get-phished/index.htm.

Cooperative Children's Book Center (CCBC), School of Education, University of Wisconsin-Madison. 2022. "Children's Books by and/or About Black, Indigenous and People of Color 2018-." Cooperative Children's Book Center (website). Last updated September 1. https://ccbc.education.wisc.edu/literature-resources/ccbc-diversity-statistics/books-by-and-or-about-poc-2018/.

Cotton, Kathleen. 1988. *Instructional Reinforcement.* Portland, OR: Northwest Regional Educational Laboratory.

Coxhead, Averil. 1998. *An Academic Word List.* Wellington, NZ: Victoria University of Wellington.

Cunningham, Anne E., and Keith E. Stanovich. 1998. "What Reading Does for the Mind." *American Educator* 22 (1–2): 8–15.

Cunningham, Patricia. 1995. *Phonics They Use: Words for Reading and Writing.* New York: HarperCollins.

Davey, Beth. 1983. "Think-Aloud: Modeling the Cognitive Processes of Reading Comprehension." *Journal of Reading* 27 (1): 44–47.

Delgado, Pablo, Cristina Vargas, Rakefet Ackerman, and Ladislao Salmerón. 2018. "Don't Throw Away Your Printed Books: A Meta-analysis on the Effects of Reading Media on Reading Comprehension." *Educational Research Review* 25: 23–38. https://www.sciencedirect.com/science/article/pii/S1747938X18300101.

Dewar, James A. 1998. "The Information Age and the Printing Press: Looking Backward to See Ahead." RAND Corporation. https://www.rand.org/pubs/papers/P8014.html.

Doheny, Kathleen. 2007. "Sex Education Works, Study Shows." WebMD. December 20. https://www.webmd.com/sex-relationships/news/20071220/sex-education-works-study-shows.

Dong, Anmei, Morris Siu-Yung Jong, and Ronnel B. King. 2020. "How Does Prior Knowledge Influence Learning Engagement? The Mediating Roles of Cognitive Load and Help-Seeking." *Frontiers in Psychology.* October 29. https://www.frontiersin.org/articles/10.3389/fpsyg.2020.591203/full.

Duke, Nell K., and P. David Pearson. 2017. "Effective Practices for Developing Reading Comprehension." *Journal of Education* 189 (1–2): 107–22. https://journals.sagepub.com/doi/abs/10.1177/0022057409189001-208.

Duncan, Charles. 2021. "Wake County Libraries Pull LGBTQ Book from Shelves After Complaint." Spectrum News 1 (website). December 15. https://spectrumlocalnews.com/nc/charlotte/politics/2021/12/15/wake-county-libraries-pull-lgbtq-book-from-shelves-after-complaint.

Durkin, Dolores. 1993. *Teaching Them to Read.* 6th ed. Boston: Allyn and Bacon.

Ehri, Linnea. 1986. "Sources of Difficulty in Learning to Spell and Read." In *Advances in Developmental and Behavioral Pediatrics,* edited by Mark Wolraich and Donald Routh, 121–95. Greenwich, CT: Jai Press.

Ehri, Linnea, Simone Nunes, Steven Stahl, and Dale Willows. 2001. "Systematic Phonics Instruction Helps Students to Read: Evidence from the National Reading Panel's Meta-Analysis." *Review of Education Research* 71 (3): 393–447.

Ehri, Linnea, and Steven Stahl. 2001. "Beyond Smoke and Mirrors: Putting Out the Fire." *Phi Delta Kappan* 83 (1): 17–20.

Eisenstein, Elizabeth L. 1980. *The Printing Press as an Agent of Change: Communications and Cultural Transformations in Early-Modern Europe, Complete in One Volume.* Cambridge: Cambridge University Press.

Ericsson, K. Anders, Ralf T. Krampe, and Clemens Tesch-Römer. 1993. "The Role of Deliberate Practice in the Acquisition of Expert Performance." *Psychological Review* 100 (3): 363–406.

Feathers, Karen. 1993. *Infotext: Reading and Learning.* Portsmouth, NH: Heinemann.

Fletcher, Jack M., Robert Savage, and Sharon Vaughn. 2020. "A Commentary on Bowers (2020) and the Role of Phonics Instruction in Reading." *Educational Psychology Review* 33: 1–26.

Fox, Barbara J. 1996. *Strategies for Word Identification: Phonics from a New Perspective.* Englewood Cliffs, NJ: Prentice Hall.

Fry, Edward B., Jacqueline E. Kress, and Dona Lee Fountoukidis. 1993. *The Reading Teacher's Book of Lists.* 3d ed. Englewood Cliffs, NJ: Prentice Hall.

Garan, Elaine M. 2001a. "Beyond Smoke and Mirrors: A Critique of the National Reading Panel Report on Phonics." *Phi Delta Kappan* 82 (7): 500–506.

———. 2001b. "More Smoking Guns: A Response to Linnea Ehri and Steven Stahl." *Phi Delta Kappan* 83 (1): 21–24.

———. 2001c. "What Does the Report of the National Reading Panel Really Tell Us About Teaching Phonics?" *Language Arts* 79 (1): 61–70.

Gardner, Dee, and Mark Davies. 2014. "A New Academic Vocabulary List." *Applied Linguistics* 35 (3): 305–27. https://doi.org/10.1093/applin/amt015.

Garner, Ruth, and Ron Reis. 1981. "Monitoring and Resolving Comprehension Obstacles: An Investigation of Spontaneous Text Lookbacks Among Upper-Grade Good and Poor Comprehenders." *Reading Research Quarterly* 16: 569–82.

Gaskins, Irene, and Thorne T. Elliot. 1991. *The Benchmark Model for Teaching Thinking Strategies: A Manual for Teachers.* Cambridge, MA: Brookline Books.

Gennari, Silvia P., Maryellen C. MacDonald, Bradley R. Postle, and Mark S. Seidenberg. 2007. "Context-Dependent Interpretation of Words: Evidence for Interactive Neural Processes." *NeuroImage* 35 (3): 1278–86.

Gerber, Alan, Gregory Huber, and Ebonya Washington. 2010. "Understanding the Connection Between Party Affiliation, Partisanship, and Political Beliefs in the United States." J-PAL (website). https://www.povertyactionlab.org/evaluation/understanding-connection-between-party-affiliation-partisanship-and-political-beliefs.

Germán, Lorena E. 2021. *Textured Teaching: A Framework for Culturally Sustaining Practices.* Portsmouth, NH: Heinemann.

Gladwell, Michael. 2008. *Outliers: The Story of Success.* New York: Little, Brown.

Graham, Steve, and Dolores Perin. 2007. "A Meta-Analysis of Writing Instruction for Adolescent Students." *Journal of Educational Psychology* 99 (3): 445–76.

Graham, Steve, and Tanya Santangelo. 2014. "Does Spelling Instruction Make Students Better Spellers, Readers, and Writers? A Meta-Analytic Review." *Reading and Writing* 27: 1703–43.

Gruver, Mead. 2021. "Wyoming Librarians Under Fire for Books About Sex, LGBTQ." *The San Diego Union-Tribune*, October 1. https://www.sandiegouniontribune.com/business/nation/story/2021-10-01/wyoming-librarians-under-fire-for-books-about-sex-lgbtq.

Hall, Leigh A. 2005. "Teachers and Content Area Reading: Attitudes, Beliefs and Change." *Teaching and Teacher Education* 21 (4): 403–14. https://www.sciencedirect.com/science/article/abs/pii/S0742051X05000235.

Harper's Weekly staff. 2006. "Education in the Southern States." American Antiquarian Society (website). Curated by Lucia Z. Knoles. Originally published November 9, 1867. https://www.americanantiquarian.org/Manuscripts/edinsouthern.html.

Harris, Albert J., and Edward R. Sipay. 1990. *How to Increase Reading Ability: A Guide to Developmental and Remedial Methods.* 8th ed. White Plains, NY: Longman.

Harris, Elizabeth A., and Alexandra Alter. 2022. "Book Ban Efforts Spread Across the U.S." *New York Times*, January 30. Updated February 8, 2022. https://www.nytimes.com/2022/01/30/books/book-ban-us-schools.html.

Harste, Jerome C., Kathy G. Short, and Carolyn Burke. 1988. *Creating Classrooms for Authors: The Reading-Writing Connection.* Portsmouth, NH: Heinemann.

Henry, O. 1997. *The Gift of the Magi.* New York: Simon & Schuster.

Herrell, Adrienne L. 2000. *Fifty Strategies for Teaching English Language Learners.* New York: Merrill.

Hillocks, George, Jr. 1986. *Research on Written Composition: New Directions for Teaching.* Urbana, IL: NCTE.

Holland, Jennifer S. 2013. "Can Dung Beetles Battle Global Warming?" *National Geographic*, September 6. https://www.nationalgeographic.com/animals/article/130904-dung-beetles-global-warming-animals-science.

Hoover, Wesley A., and Philip B. Gough. 1990. "The Simple View of Reading." *Reading and Writing* 2: 127–60.

Huey, Edmund. 1908. *The Psychology and Pedagogy of Reading.* New York: Macmillan.

Hughes, Langston. 1986. "Thank You, M'am." In *Impact Fifty Short Stories*, edited by Fannie Safier. New York: Harcourt Brace Jovanovich.

Jerrim, John, Mary Oliver, and Sam Sims. 2019. "The Relationship Between Inquiry-Based Teaching and Students' Achievement. New Evidence from a Longitudinal PISA Study in England." *Learning and Instruction* 61: 35–44.

Johns, Jerry L. 1980. "First Graders' Concepts About Print." *Reading Research Quarterly* 15 (4): 529–49.

Joseph, Laurice M., Sheila Alber-Morgan, Jennifer Cullen, and Christina Rouse. 2015. "The Effects of Self-Questioning on Reading Comprehension: A Literature Review." *Reading and Writing Quarterly* 32 (2): 152–73. https://www.tandfonline.com/doi/abs/10.1080/10573569.2014.891449.

Kafka, Franz. 1958/1977. *Letters to Friends, Family, and Editors.* New York: Schocken Books.

Kanter, Rosabeth Moss. 2004. *Confidence: How Winning Streaks and Losing Streaks Begin and End*. New York: Penguin Random House.

Kavanagh, Jennifer, and Michael D. Rich. 2018. *Truth Decay: An Initial Exploration of the Diminishing Role of Facts and Analysis in American Public Life*. Santa Monica, CA: Rand. https://www.rand.org/content/dam/rand/pubs/research_reports/RR2300/RR2314/RAND_RR2314.pdf.

Kilmeade, Brian, and Don Yeager. 2013. *George Washington's Secret Six*. New York: Penguin Random House/Sentinel.

Kim, Min-Young, and Ian A. G. Wilkinson. 2019. "What Is Dialogic Teaching? Constructing, Deconstructing, and Reconstructing a Pedagogy of Classroom Talk." *Learning, Culture and Social Interaction* 21: 70–86. https://www.sciencedirect.com/science/article/abs/pii/S2210656118301764.

Kweldju, Siusana. 2015. "Neurobiology Research Findings: How the Brain Works During Reading." *Journal of Language Teaching and Learning in Thailand* 50 (Jul–Dec): 125–42.

Langenberg, Donald N., Gloria Correro, Linnea Ehri, Gwenette Ferguson, Norma Garza, Michael L. Kamil, Cora Bagley Marrett, S. J. Samuels, Timothy Shanahan, Sally E. Shaywitz, Thomas Trabasso, Joanna Williams, Dale Willows, and Joanne Yatvin. 2000. *Report of the National Reading Panel: Teaching Children to Read, an Evidence-Based Assessment of the Scientific Research Literature on Reading and Its Implications for Reading Instruction*. Washington, DC: National Institute of Child Health and Human Development, National Institutes of Health.

Le Guin, Ursula K. 1985. "She Unnames Them." *The New Yorker*, January 21: 27.

Lehr, Fran, Jean Osborn, and Elfrieda H. Hiebert. 2004. *A Focus on Vocabulary*. Honolulu: Pacific Resources for Education and Learning.

Logan, Jessica A. R., Laura M. Justice, Melike Yumuş, and Leydi Johana Chaparro-Moreno. 2019. "When Children Are Not Read to at Home: The Million Word Gap." *Journal of Developmental and Behavioral Pediatrics* 40 (5): 383–86.

Lubell, Sam. 2017. "The Science of Teaching Reading." *National Council on Teacher Quality Blog*, February 9. https://www.nctq.org/blog/The-Science-of-Teaching-Reading.

Lyons, Jonathan. 2009. *The House of Wisdom: How the Arabs Transformed Western Civilization*. New York: Bloomsbury Press.

MacOn, James, Diane Bewell, and MaryEllen Vogt. 1991. *Responses to Literature*. Newark, DE: International Reading Association.

MacPhee, Deborah, Lara J. Handsfield, and Patricia Paugh. 2021. "Conflict or Conversation? Media Portrayals of the Science of Reading." *Reading Research Quarterly* 56 (S1): S145–55.

Manke, Mary 1990. "Courtney Cazden, Classroom discourse: The language of teaching and learning. Portsmouth, NH: Heinemann, 1988. Pp. vii–230." *Language in Society* 19: 436–439. doi:10.1017/S0047404500014676.

Martin-Lacroux, Christelle, and Alain Lacroux. 2017. "Do Employers Forgive Applicants' Bad Spelling in Résumés?" *Business and Professional Communication Quarterly* 80 (3): 321–35.

McQuillan, Jeffrey Lawrence. 2019. "The Inefficiency of Vocabulary Instruction." *International Electronic Journal of Elementary Education* 11 (4): 309–18.

Millis, Keith K., and Anne King. 2010. "Rereading Strategically: The Influences of Comprehension Ability and a Prior Reading on the Memory for Expository Text." *Reading Psychology* 22 (1): 41–65. https://doi.org/10.1080/02702710117227.

Minor, Cornelius. 2018. *We Got This. Equity, Access, and the Quest to Be Who Our Students Need Us to Be.* Portsmouth, NH: Heinemann.

Minty, Judith. 1980. *Letter to My Daughters.* Ann Arbor, MI: Mayapple Press.

Moats, Louisa. C. 2005. "How Spelling Supports Reading: And Why It Is More Regular and Predictable Than You Think." *American Educator* 4: 12–43.

Moats, Louisa Cook. 2020. *Speech to Print: Language Essentials for Teachers.* 3d ed. Baltimore, MD: Paul H. Brookes.

Mol, Suzanne E., and Adriana G. Bus. 2011. "To Read or Not to Read: A Meta-Analysis of Print Exposure from Infancy to Early Adulthood." *Psychological Bulletin* 137 (2): 267–96.

Moore, David W., and Sharon A. Moore. 1986. "Possible Sentences." In *Reading in the Content Areas*, 2d ed., edited by Ernest K. Dishner, Thomas W. Bean, John E. Readence, and David W. Moore, 174–79. Dubuque, IA: Kendall/Hunt.

Moorman, Amanda, Richard T. Boon, Yolanda Keller-Bell, Christina Stagliano, and Tara Jeffs. 2010. "Effects of Text-to-Speech Software on the Reading Rate and Comprehension Skills of High School Students with Specific Learning Disabilities." *Learning Disabilities: A Multidisciplinary Journal* 16 (1): 41–49. https://eric.ed.gov/?id=EJ874470.

Mora, Pat. 1966. "Sonrisas." *Borders.* Houston: Arté Publico Press.

Mueller, Trisha E., Lorrie E. Gavin, and Aniket Kulkarni. 2008. "The Association Between Sex Education and Youth's Engagement in Sexual Intercourse, Age at First Intercourse, and Birth Control Use at First Sex." *Journal of Adolescent Health* 42 (1): 89–96.

Muhammed, Gholdy. 2020. *Cultivating Genius: An Equity Framework for Culturally and Historically Responsive Literacy.* New York: Scholastic.

Nabokov, Vladimir. 1997. *Lolita.* 2d vintage international ed. New York: Random House.

Nagy, William E. 1988. *Teaching Vocabulary to Improve Reading Comprehension.* Newark, DE: International Reading Association.

Nagy, William E., and Patricia A. Herman. 1987. "Breadth and Depth of Vocabulary Knowledge: Implications for Acquisition and Instruction." In *The Nature of Vocabulary Instruction*, edited by Margaret G. McKeown and Mary E. Curtis, 19–36. New York: Psychology Press.

Nagy, William E., and Dianna Townsend. 2012. "Words as Tools: Learning Academic Vocabulary as Language Acquisition." *Reading Research Quarterly* 47: 91–108.

National Assessment of Educational Progress (NAEP). 2020. "NAEP Long-Term Trend Assessment Results." The Nation's Report Card. https://www.nationsreportcard.gov/ltt/?age=9.

National Center for Education Statistics. 2019. The Nation's Report Card. Washington, DC: US Department of Education and the Institute of Education Sciences.

National Council of Teachers of English (NCTE). 2022. "NCTE Intellectual Freedom Center." NCTE (website). https://ncte.org/resources/ncte-intellectual-freedom-center/.

National Endowment for the Arts. 2004. "Reading at Risk: A Survey of Literary Reading in America (Research Division Report No. 46)."

———. 2007. "To Read or Not to Read: A Question of National Consequence (Research Report No. 47)."

National Reading Panel and National Institute of Child Health and Human Development. 2000. "Teaching Children to Read: An Evidence-Based Assessment of the Scientific Research Literature on Reading and Its Implications for Reading Instruction."

Neufeld, Paul. 2005/2006. "Comprehension Instruction in Content Area Classes." *The Reading Teacher* 59 (4): 302–12.

Nystrand, Martin, and Adam Gamoran. 1991. "Instructional Discourse, Student Engagement, and Literature Achievement." *Research in the Teaching of English* 25 (3): 261–90.

Ogle, Donna. 1986. "K-W-L: A Teaching Model That Develops Active Reading of Expository Text." *The Reading Teacher* 39 (6): 564–70.

Olshavsky, Jill Edwards. 1976–77. "Reading as Problem-Solving: An Investigation of Strategies." *Reading Research Quarterly* 12 (4): 654–74.

O'Reilly, Tenaha, Zouwei Wang, and John Sabatini. 2019. "How Much Knowledge Is Too Little? When Knowledge Becomes a Barrier to Comprehension." *Psychological Science* 30 (9): 1344–1351.

Page, Kent. 2002. "Garana's Story." *National Geographic Explorer*, September 1, 18–23.

Palacio, R. J. 2012. *Wonder.* New York: Alfred A. Knopf.

Pan, Steven C., Timothy C. Rickard, and Robert A. Bjork. 2021. "Does Spelling Still Matter—and If So, How Should It Be Taught? Perspectives from Contemporary and Historical Research." Educational Psychology Review 33: 1523–52.

Perry, Tonya B., Steven Zemelman, and Katy Smith. 2022. *Teaching for Racial Equity: Becoming Disrupters.* Portsmouth, NH: Stenhouse.

Pink, Randi. 2021. *The Angel of Greenwood.* New York: Feiwel and Friends.

Pound, Pandora, Sarah Denford, Janet Shucksmith, Clare Tanton, Anne M. Johnson, Jenny Owen, Rebecca Hutten, Leanne Mohan, Chris Bonell, Charles Abraham, and Rona Campbell. 2017. "What Is Best Practice in Sex and Relationship Education? A Synthesis of Evidence, Including Stakeholders' Views." *BMJ Open* 7 (5). https://bmjopen.bmj.com/content/7/5/e014791.

Priniski, Stacy J., Cameron A. Hecht, and Judith M. Harackiewicz. 2018. "Making Learning Personally Meaningful: A New Framework for Relevance Research." *Journal of Experimental Education* 86 (1):11–29. doi:10.1080/00220973.2017.1380589.

Rasinski, Timothy V. 2004. *Assessing Reading Fluency.* Honolulu: Pacific Resources for Education and Learning.

Rawson, Katherine A., John Dunlosky, and Keith W. Thiede. 2000. "The Rereading Effect: Metacomprehension Accuracy Improves Across Reading Trials." *Memory and Cognition* 28: 1004–10. https://doi.org/10.3758/BF03209348.

Read, Charles. 1971. "Pre-school Children's Knowledge of English Phonology." *Harvard Educational Review* 41 (1): 150–79.

Reading Rockets. 2014. "Students Take Charge: Reciprocal Teaching." YouTube. April 15. Video, 2:15. https://www.youtube.com/watch?v=My68SDGeTHI.

Recht, Donna R., and Lauren Leslie. 1988. "Effect of Prior Knowledge on Good and Poor Readers' Memory of Text." *Journal of Educational Psychology* 80 (1): 16–20.

Rohrer, Doug. 2015. "Student Instruction Should Be Distributed over Long Time Periods." *Educational Psychology Review* 27 (4): 635–43.

Rosenblatt, Louise M. 1938/1983. *Literature as Exploration.* New York: Modern Language Association.

Samuels, S. Jay. 1979. "The Method of Repeated Readings." *The Reading Teacher* 32 (4): 403–8.

Scarborough, Hollis S. 2001. "Connecting Early Language and Literacy to Later Reading (Dis)abilities: Evidence, Theory, and Practice. In *Handbook of Early Literacy Research,* edited by Susan B. Neuman and David K. Dickinson, 97–110. New York: Guilford.

Schlagal, Robert C. 1989. "Constancy and Change in Spelling Development." *Reading Psychology* 10 (3): 207–29.

Seidenberg, Mark S., Matt Cooper Borkenhagen, and Devin M. Kearns. 2020. "Lost in Translation? Challenges in Connecting Reading Science and Educational Practice." *Reading Research Quarterly* 55 (S1): S119–30.

Shanahan, Timothy. 2001. "Response to Elaine Garan." *Language Arts* 79 (1): 70–71.

Smith, Deborah D. 1979. "The Improvement of Children's Oral Reading Through the Use of Teacher Modeling." *Journal of Learning Disabilities* 12 (3): 39–42.

Stahl, Steven. 1997. "Teaching Children with Reading Problems to Recognize Words." In *Readings on Language and Literacy: Essays in Honor of Jeanne S. Chall,* edited by Lillian R. Putnam. Cambridge, MA: Brookline Books.

Stahl, Steven A., and Marilyn M. Fairbanks. 1986. "The Effects of Vocabulary Instruction: A Model-Based Meta-Analysis. *Review of Educational Research* 56 (1): 72–110.

Stechyson, Natalie. 2019. "Kids Books Still Have a Lack-of-Diversity Problem, Powerful Image Shows." *HuffPost,* June 21. Updated July 3, 2019. https://www.huffpost.com/entry/diversity-kids-books-statistics_l_61087501e4b0497e67026f1c.

Stiff, Chris. 2012. "Watch What You Write: How Errors in Feedback Influence Consumer Attitudes and Behavior." *Journal of Internet Commerce* 11 (1): 41–67.

Stodden, Robert A., Kelly D. Roberts, Kiriko Takahashi, Hye Jin Park, Norma Jean Stodden. 2012. "Use of Text-to-Speech Software to Improve Reading Skills of High School Struggling Readers." *Procedia Computer Science* 14: 359–62. https://www.sciencedirect.com/science/article/pii/S1877050912008034.

Sweller, John, Jeroen J. G. van Merrienboer, and Fred G. W. C. Paas. 1998. "Cognitive Architecture and Instructional Design." *Educational Psychology Review* 10 (3): 251–96.

Taboada, Ana, and John T. Guthrie. 2006. "Contributions of Student Questioning and Prior Knowledge to Construction of Knowledge from Reading Information Text." *Journal of Literacy Research* 38 (1): 1–35. https://journals.sagepub.com/doi/abs/10.1207/s15548430jlr3801_1.

Taylor, Edward. "Huswifery." N.p.: ca. 1685.

Templeton, Shane. 1983. "Using the Spelling/Meaning Connection to Develop Word Knowledge in Older Students." *Journal of Reading* 27 (1): 8–14.

———. 2002. "Effective Spelling Instruction in the Middle Grades: It's a Lot More Than Memorization." *Voices from the Middle* 9 (3): 8–14.

Tierney, Robert J., John E. Readence, and Ernest K. Dishner. 1995. *Reading Strategies and Practices: A Compendium.* 4th ed. Boston: Allyn and Bacon.

Tinkham, Thomas. 1997. "The Effects of Semantic and Thematic Clustering on the Learning of Second Language Vocabulary." *Second Language Research* 13 (2): 138–63.

Tonatiuh, Duncan. 2014. *Separate Is Never Equal: Sylvia Mendez and Her Family's Fight for Desegregation.* New York: Abrams Books for Young Readers.

Torppa, Minna, Pekka Niemi, Kati Vasalampi, Marja-Kristiina Lerkkanen, Asko Tolvanen, and Anna-Maija Poikkeus. 2019. "Leisure Reading (But Not Any Kind) and Reading Comprehension Support Each Other—A Longitudinal Study Across Grades 1 and 9." *Child Development.* Advance online publication. https://doi.org/10.1111/cdev.13241.

Torppa, Minna, Pekka Niemi, Kati Vasalampi, Marja-Kristiina Lerkkanen, Asko Tolvanen, and Anna-Maija. 2020. "Leisure Reading (But Not Any Kind) and Reading Comprehension Support Each Other: A Longitudinal Study Across Grades 1 and 9." *Child Development* 91 (3): 876–900.

Trelease, Jim. 2001. *The Read-Aloud Handbook.* New York: Penguin.

Vacca, Jo Anne, Richard T. Vacca, and Mary K. Gove. 2000. *Reading and Learning to Read.* 4th ed. New York: Longman.

Van Bergen, Elsje, Kati Vasalampi, and Minna Torppa. 2020. "How Are Practice and Performance Related? Development of Reading From Age 5 to 15." *Reading Research Quarterly.* https://doi.org/10.1002/rrq.309.

Van Bergen, Elsje, Sara A. Hart, Antti Latvala, Eero Vuoksimaa, and Minna Torppa. 2022. "Literacy Skills Seem to Fuel Literacy Enjoyment, Rather Than Vice Versa." *Developmental Science* e13325. https://onlinelibrary.wiley.com/doi/10.1111/desc.13325.

Varnhagen, Connie K. 2000. "Shoot the Messenger and Disregard the Message? Children's Attitudes Toward Spelling." *Reading Psychology* 21 (2): 115–28.

Wallace, Ronald. 1983. "Grandmother Grace." In *Tunes for Bears to Dance To.* Pittsburg, PA: University of Pittsburg.

Weaver, Constance. 1996. *Teaching Grammar in Context.* Portsmouth, NH: Heinemann.

———. 2002. *Reading Process and Practice.* 3d ed. Portsmouth, NH: Heinemann.

Weaver, Constance, Lorraine Gillmeister-Krause, and Grace Vento-Zogby. 1996. *Creating Support for Effective Literacy Education: Workshop Materials and Handouts.* Portsmouth, NH: Heinemann.

Williams, Paige. 2022. "The Right-Wing Mothers Fueling the School-Board Wars." *The New Yorker,* November 7. https://www.newyorker.com/magazine/2022/11/07/the-right-wing-mothers-fuelling-the-school-board-wars.

Wilson, J. Ormond, and Edith A. Winship. 1917. *The Merrill Speller* Book 1. New York: Charles E. Merrill Company.

Winn, Beth, Christopher H. Skinner, Renee Oliver, Andrea D. Hale, and Mary Ziegler. 2006. "The Effects of Listening While Reading and Repeated Reading on the Reading Fluency of Adult Learners." *Journal of Adolescent and Adult Literacy* 50 (3): 196–205. https://eric.ed.gov/?id=EJ750751.

Wolf, Maryanne. 2007. *Proust and the Squid: The Story and Science of the Reading Brain*. New York: HarperCollins.

———. 2018. *Reader, Come Home: The Reading Brain in a Digital World*. New York: HarperCollins.

Wright, Tanya S., and Gina N. Cervetti. 2017. "A Systematic Review of Research on Vocabulary Instruction That Impacts Text Comprehension." *Reading Research Quarterly* 52 (2): 203–26.

Wolf, Maryanne. 2008. *Proust and the Squid: The Story and Science of the Reading Brain*. New York: Harper Perennial.

———. 2016. *Tales of Literacy for the 21st Century: The Literary Agenda*. Oxford: Oxford University Press.

———. 2018. *Reader, Come Home: The Reading Brain in a Digital World*. New York: Harper.

Wood, Karen D. 1984. "Probable Passages: A Writing Strategy." *The Reading Teacher* 37 (6): 496–99.

Wright and Cevetti. 2016.

Wylie, Richard E., and Donald D. Durrell. 1970. "Teaching Vowels Through Phonograms." *Elementary Education* 47 (6): 787–91.

Zeman, Anne, and Kate Kelly. *Everything You Need to Know About American History Homework: A Desk Reference for Students and Parents*. New York: Scholastic.

Trade Books

The following trade books are listed by title and author because hardback and paperback editions often have different publishers.

A Day No Pigs Would Die (Robert Newton Peck, 1972)

A Tale of Two Cities (Charles Dickens, 1859)

Ain't I a Woman (bell hooks, 1981/2015)

Alan Cole Is Not a Coward (Eric Bell, 2017)

All American Boys (Jason Reynolds and Brendan Kiely, 2015)

"All Summer in a Day" (Ray Bradbury, 1954)

American Dirt (Jeanine Cummins, 2020)

Angel of Greenwood (Randi Pink, 2021)

Angels and Demons (Dan Brown, 2009)

Animal Farm (George Orwell, 1996)

Aristotle and Dante Discover the Secrets of the Universe (Benjamin Alire Sáenz, 2012)

At Her Majesty's Request (Walter Dean Meyers, 1999)

Basher Five-Two (Scott O'Grady and Michael French, 1998)

Between the World and Me (Ta-Nehisi Coates, 2015)

Black Hands, White Sails (Patricia C. McKissack and Frederick L. McKissack, 1999)

Black Ink (Stephanie Stokes Oliver, ed., 2018)

Bridge to Terabithia (Katherine Paterson, 1977)

Brown Bear, Brown Bear, What Do You See? (Bill Martin Jr., 1967/2007)

Caste (Isabel Wilkerson, 2020)

Coaching for Equity (Elena Aguilar, 2020)

Cultivating Genius (Gholdy Muhammad, 2020)

Everything You Need to Know About American History Homework (Anne Zemen and Kate Kelly, 2005)

Fahrenheit 451 (Ray Bradbury, 1953)

Frog and Toad (Arnold Lobel, 1985)

Gender Queer (Maia Kobabe, 2019)

George (Alex Gino, 2017)

Go Tell It on the Mountain (James Baldwin, 1963)

Heart of Aztlán (Rudolfo Anaya, 1976)

How to Be an Antiracist (Ibram X. Kendi, 2019)

I Am Malala (Malala Yousafzai, 2015)

I Know Why the Caged Bird Sings (Maya Angelou, 1969)

If You Give a Mouse a Cookie (Laura Numeroff, 1985/2010)

Inferno (Dan Brown, 2016)

Just Mercy (Bryan Stevenson, 2014)

Landed (Milly Lee, 2006)

Leaving Home (David Celani, 2021)

Letters to My Daughters (Judith Minty, 1980)

Light in the Darkness (Lesa Cline-Ransome, 2013)

Literature as Exploration (Louise Rosenblatt, 1938/1983)

Living Up the Street (Gary Soto, 1985)

Maggie's American Dream (James Comer, 1989)

Maus (Art Spiegelman, 1991)

"Mother to Son" (Langston Hughes, 1922)

Moving to Higher Ground (Wynton Marsalis with Geoffrey Ward, 2008)

Nevada (Clint McCullough, 2012)

New Kid (Jerry Craft, 2019)

Number the Stars (Lois Lowry, 1989)

Open Windows, Open Minds (Afrika Afeni Mills, 2023)

Other People's Children (Lisa Delpit, 1995/2006)

Out of My Heart (Sharon M. Draper, 2021)

Out of My Mind (Sharon M. Draper, 2012)

Outliers (Malcolm Gladwell, 2008)

Parable of the Sower (Octavia E. Butler, 1993)

Pushout (Monique Morris, 2016)

Reader, Come Home (Maryanne Wolf, 2018)

Reading Lolita in Tehran (Azar Nafisi, 2008)

"Rogue Wave" (Theodore Taylor, 1996)

Roll of Thunder, Hear My Cry (Mildred D. Taylor, 1976)

Rosie Revere, Engineer (Andrea Beaty, 2010)

Separate Is Never Equal (Duncan Tonatiuh, 2014)

Sing, Unburied, Sing (Jesmyn Ward, 2017)

"Sonrisas" (Pat Mora, 1966)

Stamped (Jason Reynolds and Ibram X. Kendi, 2020)

Stamped from the Beginning (Ibram X. Kendi, 2016)

Starfish (Lisa Fipps, 2021)

"Thank You, M'am" (Langston Hughes, 1958)

The Bluford series (Ben Alirez, D. M. Blackwell, Karyn Folan, Peggy Kern, John Langan, Paul Langan, and Anne Schraff, 2002–21)

The Color Purple (Alice Walker, 1985)

The Crossover (Kwame Alexander, 2014)

The Da Vinci Code (Dan Brown, 2006)

The Diary of Anne Frank (Anne Frank, 1947)

The Fire Next Time (James Baldwin, 1963/2013)

The Giver (Lois Lowry, 1993)

The Hate U Give (Angie Thomas, 2015)

The House on Mango Street (Sandra Cisneros, 1984)

The Little Engine That Could (Watty Piper, 1930)

The New Jim Crow (Michelle Alexander, 2010/2012)

The Piñata That the Farm Maiden Hung (Samantha R. Vamos, 2019)

The Tattooist of Auschwitz (Heather Morris, 2018)

"The Tell-Tale Heart" (Edgar Allan Poe, 1843)

The Warmth of Other Suns (Isabel Wilkerson, 2010)

The Word (Marita Golden, ed., 2011)

Thomas and Beulah (Rita Dove, 1986)

Truth Decay (Jennifer Kavanagh and Michael D. Rich, 2018)

Warriors Don't Cry (Melba Pattillo Beals, 2003/2007)

We Are Still Here! (Traci Sorell, 2021)

We Want to Do More Than Survive (Bettina L. Love, 2019)

White Fragility (Robin DiAngelo, 2018)

Why Are All the Black Kids Sitting Together in the School Cafeteria? (Beverly Daniel Tatum, 1997/2017)

INDEX

Continued from page ii.

The author and publisher wish to thank those who have generously given permission to reprint borrowed material:

Front cover; p. i; p. 18, Figure 2.1; p. 30, Figure 3.3; p. 57–58, Figure 6.1; p. 83, Figure 7.1; p. 108, Figure 8.1; p. 136, Figure 9.1; p. 168, Figure 10.1; p. 169, Figure 10.2; p. 206, Figure 13.1; p. 211, Figure 13.2; p. 228, Figure 14.2, p. 233, Figure 14.5; p. 246, Figure 15.1; p. 248, Figure 15.2, p. 249, Figure 15.3; p. 250, Figure 15.4; p. 251, Figure 15.5; p. 253, Figure 15.6; p. 257, Figure 15.7, p. 258, Figure 15.8; p. 271, Figure 16.2; p. 272, Figure 16.3; p. 281, Figure 16.6; p. 289–290, Figure 17.1; p. 294, Figure 17.3; p. 300, Figure 18.1: © aqua-tarkus/Getty Images. P. xiv: © Witthaya Prasongsin/Getty Images. P. 12, 161: © Henrik Sorensen/DigitalVision/Getty Images. P. 15: Beers, Kylene. "Editor's Message: Boundaries" Voices from the Middle 13.3, March 2006, pp. 4–5. Copyright © 2006 by the National Council of Teachers of English. Reprinted with permission. P. 18, Figure 2.1 and inside back cover: © mimacz - stock.adobe.com. P. 32: © Marc Romanelli/Getty Images. P. 45–48: "She Unnames Them" by Ursula K. Le Guin. Copyright © 1985 by Ursula K. Le Guin. First appeared in *The New Yorker*, published in 1985 in Buffalo Gals, published by Capra Press in 1987. Reprinted by permission of Ginger Clark Literary, LLC. P. 53: © kmls / Shutterstock. P. 65: Excerpts from "Thank You, M'am" from SHORT STORIES by Langston Hughes. Copyright © 1996 by Ramona Bass and Arnold Rampersad. Reprinted by permission of Hill and Wang, a division of Farrar, Straus and Giroux. All Rights Reserved. Reprinted by permission of Harold Ober Associates. Copyright 1958 by the Langston Hughes Estate. P. 72: "Your great-grand-father dreamed that his son" from *Letters to My Daughters* by Judith Minty. Copyright © 1980 by Judith Minty. Published by Mayapple Press. Reprinted by permission of the publisher. P. 94, Figure 7.6: Photo © Heinemann. P. 97, Figure 7.8: © Houghton Mifflin Harcourt/HIP. P. 97, 345: "Grandmother Grace" from *Tunes for Bears to Dance To* by Ron Wallace, © 1983. Reprinted by permission of the University of Pittsburgh Press. P. 113: "Sonrisas" from *Borders* by Pat Mora is being reprinted with permission from the publisher of Borders by Pat Mora (© Arte Público Press - University of Houston). P. 125 and p. 127, Figure 8.10; p. 129, Figure 8.12a; and p. 130, Figure 8.14: Cover and excerpts from *Notice & Note: Strategies for Close Reading* by Kylene Beers and Robert E. Probst. Copyright

© 2013 by Kylene Beers and Robert E. Probst. Published by Heinemann, Portsmouth, NH. Reprinted by permission of the publisher. All Rights Reserved. P. 125 and p. 128, Figure 8.11; p. 129, Figure 8.12b; and p. 130, Figure 8.13: Cover and excerpts from *Reading Nonfiction: Notice & Note Stances, Signposts, and Strategies* by Kylene Beers and Robert E. Probst. Copyright © 2016 by Kylene Beers and Robert E. Probst. Published by Heinemann, Portsmouth, NH. Reprinted by permission of the publisher. P. 143–44: From EVERYTHING YOU WANTED TO KNOW ABOUT AMERICAN HISTORY HOMEWORK by Anne Zeman and Kate Kelly. Copyright © 1994, 2006 by Scholastic Inc. Reprinted by permission of Scholastic Inc. P. 146, Figures 9.7 and 9.8: "Retellings Rubric" and "Retellings Progress Chart" from *Reading Strategies Handbook for High School: A Guide to Teaching Reading in the Literature Classroom* by Kylene Beers. Copyright © 2000 by Holt, Rinehart and Winston. Reprinted by permission of Houghton Mifflin Harcourt. P. 150, Figure 9.9 and p. 161, Figure 9.17: From DISRUPTING THINKING by Kylene Beers and Robert Probst. Copyright © 2017 by Kylene Beers and Robert Probst. Reprinted by permission of Scholastic Inc. P. 152, Figure 9.12: Photo by Lindsey Ellis. P. 153, Figure 9.13: Photo by Linda Rief. P. 162, Figure 9.18: Photo by Buffy Hamilton. P. 164: © Image Source/Getty Images. P. 174, Figure 10.4: From Holt California *SOCIAL STUDIES, UNITED STATES HISTORY: INDEPENDENCE TO 1914,* Student Edition. Copyright © by Houghton Mifflin Harcourt Publishing Company. All rights reserved. Used by permission of the publisher. P. 177, 178: Excerpt from "Can Dung Beetles Battle Global Warming?" by Jennifer S. Holland from *National Geographic*, September 6, 2013. Copyright © 2013 by Jennifer S. Holland. Reprinted by permission of the author. P. 179, Figure 10.5: Photo by Cheryl Bair. P. 264: © Terry Vine/Getty Images. P. 277, Figure 16.4: Photo by Kylene Beers. P. 293, Figure 17.2: Photo by Kylene Beers. P. 317, Figure 19.1: Photo by Kylene Beers. P. 318, Figure 19.2: Photo by Robert Probst. P. 327, Figure 20.2: Photo by Anita Gildea. P. 338: Photo by Kylene Beers. P. 339: Photo by Baker Beers. P. 340: © David Madison/Getty Images. P. 391–94, Appendix CC: Used with permission from John Wiley & Sons, adapted from "The Utility of Phonics Generalizations in the Primary Grades" by Theodore Clymer and R.G.S. from *The Reading Teacher,* by the International Reading Association, Vol. 16, No. 4, 1957; permission conveyed through Copyright Clearance Center, Inc. Back cover: Photo by Lester Laminack